# Celluloid Couches,
# Cinematic Clients

SUNY series in Psychoanalysis and Culture

Henry Sussman, editor

# Celluloid Couches, Cinematic Clients

## Psychoanalysis and Psychotherapy in the Movies

❦

*Edited by*

## Jerrold R. Brandell

STATE UNIVERSITY OF NEW YORK PRESS

Published by
State University of New York Press, Albany

© 2004  State University of New York

All rights reserved

Printed in the United States of America

For information, address State University of New York Press,
90 State Street, Suite 700, Albany, NY 12207

Production by Marilyn P. Semerad
Marketing by Fran Keneston

**Library of Congress Cataloging-in-Publication Data**

Celluloid couches, cinematic clients : psychoanalysis and psychotherapy in the movies / edited by Jerrold R. Brandell.
   p.  cm. — (SUNY series in psychoanalysis and culture)
Includes bibliographical references and index.
ISBN 0-7914-6081-9 (alk. paper) — ISBN 0-7914-6082-7 (pbk. : alk. paper)
   1. Psychoanalysis in motion pictures. 2. Psychoanalysis and motion pictures. I.
Brandell, Jerrold R. II. Series.

PN1995.9.P783C47 2004
791.43'653—dc22

                                                                    2003059573

10  9  8  7  6  5  4  3  2  1

# CONTENTS

# ILLUSTRATIONS

# ACKNOWLEDGMENTS

A number of individuals provided much-appreciated assistance and support during the preparation of this book. I am grateful to James Peltz, Editor-in-Chief at SUNY Press, for his early interest in this project and continuing encouragement throughout its duration, and to the SUNY Press production staff, particularly Ms. Marilyn Semerad, for their consummate professionalism and meticulous attention to detail. I am indebted to Dean Phyllis Vroom of the Wayne State University School of Social Work, for her willingness to support my research—which is at least two standard deviations from anything that might be considered customary and usual for a social work academic. I also thank my father-in-law, documentary filmmaker Victor Teich, for his enthusiasm as well as his very helpful advice at several critical points in the life of this project. I wish to acknowledge the valuable assistance of Ms. Terry Geesken and Ms. Mary Corliss of the Museum of Modem Art, Film Stills Archive; Joshua Hirsch, Research Coordinator at the UCLA Film and Television Archive; and the staff at Harpo Productions, through whose generosity I was able to obtain a screening copy of the 1998 production of *David and Lisa*. Last, but most assuredly not least, I thank my wife, Esther, and my three children, Andrea, Joey, and Stevie, for putting up with my trips to California and New York, as well as the other distractions this research endeavor has created for our family. Their patience, acceptance, and interest have been vital to this project's success.

Three chapters in this anthology are revised and/or expanded versions of earlier published works. Jerrold Brandell's chapter, "Kids on the Couch: Hollywood's Vision of Child and Adolescent Treatment," is a significantly revised and expanded version of "Listening at the Movies," which first appeared in *Readings 15:* 1, pages 6-11 [March 2000]. Andrea Slane's chapter, "The Interracial Treatment Relationship in the Cold War Period: *Pressure Point* in Analysis," originally appeared as chapter 5 in her book, *A Not So Foreign Affair: Fascism, Sexuality, and Cultural Rhetoric of American Democracy,* Duke University Press, 2001; and as "Pressure Points: Political Psychology, Screen

Adaptation, and the Management of Racism in the Case History Genre," *Camera Obscura 45*, 15.3, pages 70-113 [2000]). Janet Walker's chapter was originally published as "The Institutional Edifice" in Janet Walker, *Couching Resistance: Women, Film, and Psychoanalytic Psychiatry* (University of Minnesota Press, 1993).

# INTRODUCTION

---

## JERROLD R. BRANDELL

Freud's eyes fall on the doll which is propped up on the couch.
After a pause:

FREUD

Cecily, how did your father come to
give you the doll?

Cecily has a prolonged nervous coughing spell.

FREUD
(Gently suggesting)

Perhaps you should lie down on the
couch.

—From the screenplay to *Freud,* 1962

Psychoanalysis, with more visibility now than at any other time in its hundred-year history, continues to capture the public imagination and to excite controversy. Despite the implementation of draconian measures by health maintenance organizations that limit mental health treatment, and the promulgation of such aberrations as single-session psychotherapy, psychoanalysis and psychodynamic psychotherapy are, by recent estimates, practiced by greater numbers of clinicians than at any point in the past.[1] Increasingly, psychologists, clinical social workers, psychiatric nurses, and others, once barred from psychoanalytic institutes, have sought such training. Psychoanalytic ideas, now more or less adrift from mainstream American psychiatry, which

1

has become increasingly biological, have also found fertile ground in such academic disciplines as literature, anthropology, linguistics, and film studies. Indeed, Hollywood has never been more interested in the treatment process and relationship in psychotherapy and psychoanalysis, to which a spate of recent films—*Girl, Interrupted* (Mangold, 1999), *Instinct* (Turteltaub, 1999), *Good Will Hunting* (Van Sant, 1997), *The Sixth Sense* (Shyamalan, 1999), and the popular HBO series, *The Sopranos* (Chase, 1998)—attests. This cultural fascination with the unique intimacy of the treatment situation is also reflected in the popularity of literary narratives about the therapeutic process. Two very recent examples are Emily Fox Gordon's *Mockingbird Years,* and Daphne Merkin's *Quitting the Nairobi Trio.*

In this transdisciplinary anthology, which consists of contributions from psychoanalysts and psychotherapists representing three clinical disciplines and academics from such fields as literature and cinema studies, important themes and controversies in the cinematic depiction of psychoanalysis and psychotherapy over the last seventy-five years of moviemaking are highlighted. More specifically, each of the contributors was asked to examine how the therapeutic process is represented on the screen. Oftentimes, cinematic efforts to portray the treatment process in psychoanalysis or psychotherapy are idiosyncratic, misleading, distorted, or even pathological; boundary violations, magical cures, and negative portrayals are so common as to constitute a cinematic cliché. Yet, for the most part, we are not nearly as interested in denouncing such portrayals here, the existence of which has been rather well documented (Greenberg, 1993; Gabbard & Gabbard, 1999). Rather, our collective effort has been to examine those films—granted, fewer in number—that offer us the opportunity to explore important psychoanalytic themes and issues from a vantage point outside our usual reference frame. We must ask ourselves what we learn from the movies about our professional selves and the nature of the therapeutic endeavor rather than simply what the screenwriters and directors got wrong. How have movie portrayals of the therapeutic process changed as our conceptions of treatment have changed? Aside from their obvious dramatic appeal, what may account for the popularity of certain themes or clinical dilemmas (for example, treatment of psychopathic patients, institutional oppression, erotic countertransference reactions and enactments)? How can psychic structuralization, largely a silent and incremental process, be captured convincingly? In what discrete ways have cinematic characterizations of psychoanalysts and psychotherapists been shaped by cultural forces? These and other questions are interpolated into the nine chapters that comprise this collection.

All of the contributors to this book either subscribe to particular psychoanalytic theories or in any event, selectively deploy them as a framework for their scholarly analysis of "celluloid" therapy. At least five different psychoanalytic traditions, in fact, are represented among these nine chapters: classical Freudian, object-relational, intersubjective-relationalist, self psychological, and Lacanian. Lacanian ideas have, in particular, proven especially popular among film scholars, with their emphasis on semiotics, signification, and the viewer's experience of the film. Such an approach, it has been observed, represents a shift away from the psychoanalysis of characters or even of the filmmakers themselves, a point of view represented in earlier film scholarship (Gabbard & Gabbard, 1999). However, we note that in the present collection, there is no dominant framework, perhaps because this anthology by its very nature does not represent film scholarship in the more restrictive sense of that term. Lacanian-inspired analysis (for example, Socor and Cohen), intersubjective-relational ideas (Ringel), and self psychological analysis (Brandell), among other viewpoints, contribute to what might be termed the anthology's "creative tension."

Inasmuch as this anthology is intended for a general audience, it may be useful to define several key psychoanalytic concepts used throughout this work. *Transference*, an idea that has been central to psychoanalytic thinking since the publication of Freud and Breuer's *Studies on Hysteria* (1893–95/1973), is one such concept. Broadly defined, transference is the reflexive, unconscious repetition or revivification of varying combinations and patterns of ideas, fantasies, affects, attitudes, or behavior, originally experienced in relation to a significant figure from one's childhood past, that have been displaced onto a contemporary interpersonal relationship. Such displacements always evince a certain degree of distortion, and may occur in virtually any ongoing relationship. Psychoanalysts and psychotherapists, however, tend to be far more interested in this phenomenon when it occurs within the context of treatment—which it invariably does. *Countertransference* is another important concept, often though not always linked to the patient's transference to the analyst. Countertransference may be defined as the broad range of subjective reactions, whether conscious or unconscious, educed from the therapist in the context of ongoing therapeutic interaction with a patient. These reactions may include fantasies, thoughts, attitudes, affects, and behavior. Although specific countertransference reactions may involve displacements of affects, fantasies, ideas, and so forth from historically important relationships of the therapist, this is neither a universal feature nor a requirement. Psychoanalysts in the time of Freud tended to view countertransference as a hindrance or obstacle to effective therapy, although many contemporary analysts have adopted a perspective at considerable variance with Freud's ideas. Today, countertransference is increasingly characterized in *intersubjective* or *relational* terms. Exponents of these positions emphasize the mutuality and reciprocal shaping, even coconstruction of the matrix of transference and countertransference by analyst and patient. Some even believe transference and countertransference to be inextricable elements in a dual unity created by the analyst and patient, and find value in introducing countertransference elements into the therapeutic dialogue.

◎✛◎

The lead chapter, "Kids on the Couch: Hollywood's Vision of Child and Adolescent Treatment," examines how the process of therapy with children and adolescents is captured on film, with particular attention to three movies: *I Never Promised You a Rose Garden* (Page, 1977), *Ordinary People* (Redford, 1980), and *The Sixth Sense*. It might be argued that the difficulty in portraying a realistic therapeutic process with child patients is every bit as daunting as the depiction of adults in treatment. Sometimes, as in *Good Will Hunting*, therapy comes to be redefined as something nontraditional; treatment parameters are permitted if not welcomed, countertransferences are enacted with positive therapeutic effect, and the therapist's personal revelations become a vehicle for therapeutic cure. In other films, such as *Harold and Maude* (Ashby, 1971), therapy is sterile and the analyst doctrinaire; resistance in such an instance is an affirmation of psychological health. In still others, treatment is curative, but at such cost to creativity and individuality that we feel something of great importance has been lost even as more enduring and healthier adaptations are forged (for example, *Equus* [Lumet, 1977]).

*I Never Promised You A Rose Garden* is, of course, based on a true story, that of the writer Joanne Greenberg, whose treatment was conducted in the 1950s at Chestnut Lodge Sanitarium in Rockville, Maryland, by the legendary psychoanalyst Frieda Fromm-Reichmann. *Rose Garden* is, in certain respects, an unusual film inasmuch as it is based on a book that was originally marketed as a work of fiction, but that was later revealed to be the essentially faithful account of its author's journey into and out of psychosis. The cinematic portrayal of Deborah's treatment by Dr. Fried in *Rose Garden* represents a therapeutic process that seems to balance meaningful interpretive work, clinical intuition, and a gradually evolving working alliance. It has, however, been criticized for its "complete erasure" of the principal characters' Jewish identitites (Hornstein, 2000), and the intimation, via Dr. Fried's revelation to Deborah that she is childless and divorced, that a competent and dedicated female analyst could not also enjoy a satisfying personal life (Gabbard & Gabbard, 1999).

If *Rose Garden* highlights the importance of the role of intuition and the need for sustaining a strong working alliance in the treatment of a psychotic adolescent, *Ordinary People* appears to emphasize specific qualities of the transference relationship between Conrad, the trauma survivor, and his therapist, Dr. Berger. Conrad appears to seek out in Berger not only the therapist's capacity to contain his grief, despair, and rage, but also his strength and stead-fastness, qualities that may be aptly described as elements of an idealizing transference. *The Sixth Sense,* unlike either of these other films, seems to embrace a different, fundamentally intersubjective view of the treatment process. Its unlikely paranormal suspense genre seems to reinforce the inter-changeability of the patient's and doctor's roles, the vector at which transfer-ence meets countertransference, and the ineffability of internal experience, making for a radically different vision of the healing process.

The popularization of psychoanalytic ideas has sometimes led to unusual cinematic products, experiments that can be considered provocative if not completely successful. One such example, detailed in Andrea Slane's chap-ter, "The Interracial Treatment Relationship in the Cold War Period: *Pressure Point* in Analysis," examines Stanley Kramer's 1962 production of *Pressure Point* (Cornfield, 1962), a movie about a black prison psychiatrist forced to treat a disturbed prisoner who is also an ideologue of American Nazism. The movie, which featured the unlikely combination of Sidney Poitier as the prison psychiatrist and Bobby Darin as his patient, is actually based on a case study originally published in 1954 by psychoanalyst-author Harold Lindner. There is, however, a critical difference between the literary and movie versions of this story, which is the central theme of Slane's detailed analysis. In the original case study, Lindner furnishes a veridical account of his treatment of Anton, a prisoner serving time at a federal penitentiary in which Lindner was then employed as chief of the Psychiatric-Psychological Division. Anton, like his counterpart in the cinematic version of the case, was a racist and anti-Semite. However, Lindner is Caucasian and Jewish, a fact that, in Slane's esti-mation, complicates the transposition to black doctor-white patient in the film version and which for several important reasons cannot be its equivalent nor possess the narrative integrity of the original story.

In Lindner's treatment of Anton, who, like the character portrayed by Bobby Darin in the film, is originally referred because of blackout spells, Lindner's Jewishness is equated with conspiratorial institutional authority in a way that Poitier's blackness cannot be. Accordingly, Lindner's counteraggres-sive enactment, culminating in his challenge to the unceasing provocations of his real-life patient to fight him "man-to-man," and made as he removes his insignia tabs and thus symbolically disidentifies with the authority of the institution, has a very different meaning in the movie version. In the film, when Poitier makes the same offer to his racist patient, Slane suggests that he is "no less a black man than he was with his jacket on" owing to the fact that there is no equivalent alignment of black men with institutional authority. Indeed, the movie psychiatrist's removal of his coat may, paradoxically, make him even an even greater threat, Slane argues, owing to the racial stereotype of black male brutality.

Slane's depiction of this cinematic treatment relationship contextualizes the film as a cold war-era narrative, establishing a link between the concept of totalitarianism and social prescriptions for the resolution or management of internal political disputes and conflicts, racial prejudice being chief amongst them. Her analysis is, therefore, informed by detailed considerations not only of the film's prominent psychoanalytic themes (for example, the transference-countertransference dimension of the relationship between doctor and patient), but also of the sociohistorical milieu in which the film was made. In her discussion of the popularization and Americanization of psychoanalysis, Slane also mentions that Freud's theories were often shaped so as to bring them into conformity with "conventional American moral and religious values as well as normative sexual practices." Complex theoretical ideas were often misrepresented, subjected to reductionism, or simply not incorporated into popular depictions of psychoanalysis and dynamic psychotherapy. Slane makes special mention of Freud's theory of bisexuality in this regard, which he regarded as a universal human disposition. In consequence of the small child's identification with both parents at different points in development, Freud believed all persons to be capable of investing sexual drive energy (or libido) in both genders. In the usual course of development, however, one component was relegated to an unconscious existence, making possible a more or less exclusive preference for either homosexual or heterosexual relationships. Moreover, Freud believed that manifestly homosexual behavior, or *inversion*, the term he preferred, neither signaled degeneracy nor was it necessarily associated with other psychological problems or symptoms (Freud, 1905). This perspective was not, of course, synchronous with prevailing American stereotypes of gender normality, and led to significant distortions not only in the popular media (for example, Lindner, 1966), but also in the professional literature (see, for example, Rado, 1940; Socarides, 1968; and Ovesey, 1969).

In "Women in Psychotherapy on Film: Shades of Scarlett Conquering," Marilyn Charles argues that cinematic representations of women have relied historically on the patriarchal assumptions of writers and directors, thus leading to portrayals in which women are less subjects creating their own narratives than they are "others," or object repositories of the meanings attributed to them. However, even when efforts are made to represent a woman's story authentically, from her own viewpoint, seemingly insoluble problems may arise. For the *voix féminine*, it turns out, cannot be acknowledged or recognized, which we may attribute to the fact that such narratives are dyssynchronous with the dominant male discourse of Western society. This leads to a conundrum. The alternative to the objectification of the female voice appears to be the establishment of woman as subject, the narrator of her own story; and yet, such narratives must be juxtaposed against a baseline social context in which the woman's discourse cannot attain coherence, owing to its construction on societal truths from which she has been historically excluded. Inasmuch as filmic representations of women are unlikely to be of a recognizable self, unambivalent identifications with such images, Charles continues, are inherently problematic for the female viewer.

Using such examples as Campion's *An Angel at My Table* (Campion, 1990) and *Frances* (Clifford, 1982), Charles explores the theme of involuntary commitment and its concomitant, a dehumanizing and destructive psychiatric establishment. In these two films, each based on veridical events, electroconvulsive therapy, drugs, leucotomies, and lobotomies become the instruments through which the systematic institutional subjugation of women is attempted, if not achieved. Such extreme measures, the author suggests, seem bound to a viewpoint in which the woman subject's attempts at self-definition, liberation, and assertion are judged to be dangerous.

In other portions of Charles's chapter, several films—*We Don't Live Under Normal Conditions* (Collins 2000); *Girl, Interrupted;* and *Dialogues with Madwomen* (Light, 1993)—are used to highlight the impact of a feminine voice on the portrayal of women in treatment. These films, which include both documentaries and commercial productions, are directed, written, or produced by women. Collectively, they convey a different understanding of the oppressive power of a mental health system that demonstrates little or no respect for the perspective of women patients, a system that can be both dehumanizing and retaliative. Such films, Charles asserts, are moreover no longer tied to a vision of women as a problem to be fixed or rehabilitated by males, but have gradually advanced to a differing view, one in which women's problems are expressed, defined, understood, and ultimately resolved by women protagonists themselves.

The dual themes of psychiatric authority and the subjugation of women are revisited in Janet Walker's chapter, "Psychotherapy as Oppression? The Institutional Edifice," though with greater attention to both the role of mental asylums themselves and the historical context within which these cinematic portrayals are made. Walker points out that despite the humanitarian critique of repressive institutional care that, at first blush, seems to characterize many Hollywood depictions, such criticism upon closer examination may prove disingenuous. Particularly where women are concerned, social adjustment and gender role conformity become prescriptive for emotional well-being, and fulfillment comes with acceptance of the role of mother and spouse.

*The Snake Pit* (Litvak, 1948), the first of several films Walker offers detailed analyses of in this chapter, seems uniquely suited to Hollywood's tendency to offer a social critique of repressive and inhumane practices in the asylum while simultaneously upholding the very practices it decries. The sadism of electroconvulsive therapy is counterbalanced insofar as it becomes a vehicle for promoting the patient's availability for the insight work that follows; psychiatric cure becomes coterminous with the capacity of protagonist Virginia to recognize her husband and accept her gender role assignment in the marriage. Awareness of the psychogenesis of her illness is much less Virginia's narration of her own story than it is a formulaic account closely based on classical psychoanalytic theories of development that she has been taught by her (male) physician, Dr. Kik. *The Snake Pit*, however, is not reducible to a simple defense of adjustment psychiatry and the gender-normative practices associated with the postwar era. Indeed, Walker observes, it offers an indictment of the social conditions that contribute to mental illness, and moreover, allows the "delusional" Virginia the feminist-inspired parapraxis of substituting her maiden name for her married name, as well her critique of the "regimentation" of the asylum.

In *The Snake Pit*, Dr. Kik, we are told, has no real family, no life aside from his professional role at Juniper Hill, a convenient state of affairs that seems to insure his dedication without the distraction of extramural relationships that might compete with the needs of his patients. Nothing, however, could be further from the interpersonal conflicts of Dr. McIver in *The Cobweb* (Minnelli, 1955), a story where the "misalignment between marriage and authoritative psychiatry," Walker informs us, becomes central. In fact, it is through the fallibility of the central character and his relational conflicts that the critical shortcomings of psychiatric authority are highlighted in this film. Walker's contention is that the effectiveness of *The Cobweb*, which she deems more progressive than *The Snake Pit*, is in good measure a result of its successful juxtaposition of these parallel plot lines: Dr. McIver's unfulfilling and conflict-laden relationship with his wife and family, and his work at the mental institution. The thematic ubiquity of enacted countertransference in more recent films is arguably foreshadowed in Dr. McIver's complex character, his extramarital affair, and so forth, but it also underscores the fact that *The Cobweb* achieves what many of these later films seem unable to accomplish without sensationalizing the doctor-patient relationship. In effect, it isn't necessary for therapists to abandon their professional judgment or compete with their sickest patients in order to portray their own internal conflicts.

Walker also discusses *Titicut Follies* (Wiseman, 1987) and *One Flew Over the Cuckoo's Nest* (Forman, 1975). Like *The Snake Pit*, she warrants, *One Flew Over the Cuckoo's Nest* appears to be an indictment of institutional psychiatry, but that impression, not unlike the latent meaning obscured by the manifest content of the dream, may be misleading. Walker submits that "it is not psychiatric or psychotherapeutic practices" that are inculpated, but rather the fatal error of ceding power to nonpsychiatric professionals and to females in particular. The institutional evils seem more proximally connected to Nurse Ratched though far more distally with Dr. Spivey and the psychiatric staff, much as the frustrated and dangerously punitive Nurse Davis of *The Snake Pit* was counterposed against an essentially benign Dr. Kik. Finally, *Titicut Follies*, a Frederick Wiseman documentary so controversial in its stark depiction of the pernicious nature of institutional life that legal challenges prevented unabridged screenings of the film for twenty-two years, is offered as an essentially unambiguous social critique of the mental institution.

The limitations of anthologies notwithstanding, no anthology on the depiction of psychoanalysis in film could be considered complete without some reference to the work of the American filmmaker, Woody Allen. In "Woody Allen and Freud," Alain J.-J. Cohen observes that Allen has maintained a "lifelong dialogue . . . with the world of psychoanalysis," and perhaps more so than any other filmmaker, prominently interpolates therapy scenes and discussion about psychoanalysis into virtually every picture he has made since the early 1970s. Allen's treatment of the psychoanalytic theme is, however, both idiosyncratic and complex and, Cohen warns, continuously "transforms itself as a polymorphous signifier." It may be invoked as a verbal reference, presented imagistically, in tropical form, as a process, or per narrative, inter alia.

Before proceeding with his analysis of Allen's *Annie Hall* (Allen, 1977) and *Deconstructing Harry* (Allen, 1997), Cohen discusses the several ways in which psychoanalytic interpretations may be applied to literary and cinematic domains. He notes that, inasmuch as Woody Allen is often both protagonist and film director, and the continuity between his life and his art intentional yet also inescapable (for example, the parallel between Allen's own well-known "interminable" psychoanalysis, the references made by such characters as Alvy in *Annie Hall* to his "fifteen years in analysis," and indeed, the repetition of the psychoanalytic theme in so many of his films), the psychoanalytic exploration of his work becomes exponentially more complex an undertaking.

In a juxtaposition of Allen with Freud and Freud with Hitchcock, Cohen uses Hitchcock's *Spellbound* (Hitchcock, 1945) to illustrate how the psychoanalytic case, fictive or historically factual, in its presentation of both proleptic and analeptic positions, "moves forward and backwards, downstream and back upstream."[2] He then discusses *Annie Hall*, with particular attention to Allen's use of split-screen technique, a cinematic convention that in this film highlights the dramatic contrast between Alvy's New York Jewish family background and Annie's midwestern WASP origins, and later reveals the intimate details of "his" and "her" psychotherapies. In *Deconstructing Harry*, the protagonist, once again, seems destined to remain in analysis into perpetuity, having had at least six "shrinks" in addition to three wives. Thematically, boundary transgressions abound, almost reflexively linked with the mantra of countertransference. Cohen also discusses this film, as he does *Annie Hall* and later *Stardust Memories* (Allen, 1980), in terms of a *spectatorial principle* wherein particular, often inherently conflictive reactions are evoked in the viewer in consequence of the director's manipulation of various elements—

script, camera angles, the mise-en-scène. Finally, Cohen comments on *Manhattan* (Allen, 1979), in which the free associations of Woody-Ike furnish a vehicle for mourning and creativity, though here sans analyst.

Cohen also reminds us that the concept of transference has a very special meaning when applied to cinematic art and technique. He suggests that the use of flashbacks, for example, effects a displacement from the "there-and-then" to the "here-and-now." Film itself is akin to the unconscious: the rules of chronology often do not apply, and there is a blending of veridical and narrative truths so that the one may become indistinguishable from the other. Indeed, in the cinema, we may also effortlessly exchange what Freud referred to as secondary process, the language of adulthood, with the language of primary process, the "forgotten" language of childhood, a language of symbols, dreams, Freudian slips, and artistic creativity—whose domain is the timeless unconscious.

Sanford Gifford's detailed historical analysis of the early G. W. Pabst film, *Secrets of a Soul* (Pabst, 1926), also provides us with an account of the only two films Freud was known to have seen. Extrapolating from sources such as Freud's correspondence with his family and Ernest Jones (whose reportage may have been tainted by a competitive relationship with Sandor Ferenczi), Gifford offers us an intriguing if partly conjectural glimpse of Freud's earliest known experiences with the cinema. These encounters, both of which occurred prior to 1910, may likely have also contributed subtly to Freud's long-held mistrust of the popularization of psychoanalytic ideas, which led to his rejection of a potentially lucrative offer to serve as a consultant to Goldwyn Studios. In the remainder of his chapter, Gifford furnishes us with a fascinating account of *Secrets of a Soul*, the dramatic tensions it caused within the psychoanalytic movement, and how it evolved from its original proposal as an essentially educational movie or *Lehrfilm* to its production as a commercial film. The film itself, the original script for which was evidently based on a psychoanalytic case known to Sachs and Abraham, possesses what Gifford refers to as "an innocent charm." It is, interestingly, not the exploitative, sensationalistic, or dangerously distorted picture of psychoanalysis that Freud, Jones and others within the psychoanalytic movement had feared. In fact, Gifford suggests that this film, which was a modest commercial success when first released in 1926, was a reasonably "convincing picture of psychoanalysis, with all due allowances for its didactic content and its aim for a general public."[3] He observes that the film, via "childhood scenes, early memories of the patient's marriage, fantasies," and analytic interpretations, attempts to represent the analytic process. *Secrets of a Soul* also contains what may have been the first cinematic dream sequence, in this instance, one that relies on the Expressionism of which Pabst had been an early exponent but that also adumbrates a later cinematic movement—*Die Neve Sachlichkeit*.

In "Talk Therapy: The Representation of Insight in the Cinema," Shoshana Ringel begins with an examination of the impact that changing sociocultural and scientific standards have exerted on the psychoanalytic concept of insight. In turn-of-the-century Vienna, psychoanalytic interpretations were themselves presumed to be curative, sequentially linked via a closed system to the analysand's insights, and culminating in enduring structural change. However, this classical viewpoint, if not completely supplanted by an increasingly relational view of therapeutic action, certainly no longer seems modal. The relational and intersubjective positions are far more likely to locate therapeutic change along a transference-countertransference axis, where the emotional relationship between analyst and analysand serves as a crucible in which structural change is forged. The classical approach to dream interpretation, a procedure long regarded as critical to the promotion of insight, has undergone a comparable transformation, according to Ringel. In classical psychoanalysis, the whole analytic effort involved the circumnavigation of the forces of censorship and repression, with the ultimate objective being the uncovering of latent meaning, a view that contrasts sharply with more contemporary relational and self psychological perspectives on the function of dreams and their interpretation.

Ringel proceeds to discuss two films, *The Dark Past* (Mate, 1948) and *Silence of the Lambs* (Demme, 1990), and the HBO television series *The Sopranos* (Chase, 1998–). In *The Dark Past*, the therapeutic relationship is structured according to the prevailing one-person psychology of the 1940s, and the treatment itself, somewhat transparently id psychological. The effort is quite simply to uncover the unconscious determinants of the gangster protagonist's homicidal rage and conversion reaction, a unilateral effort into which the analyst professor's analysis of a recurring traumatic dream figures rather prominently. Although the treatment "relationship" of *The Silence of the Lambs* is arguably more metaphoric than anything else, Ringel contends that it does portray a very different process through which insight is acquired. Agent Starling and Dr. Lecter, she observes, engage in a variant of Ferenczi's "mutual analysis," each seeking from the other the answers to important questions. Unlike the sagely and contemplative, abstinent classical analyst of *The Dark Past*, Dr. Lecter is a deliberate analytic presence, shaping if not subverting the mutuality of this analytic process. The treatment relationship between Dr. Jennifer Melfi and her patient, Tony Soprano *(The Sopranos)*, while far more conventional than that of Clarice Starling and Dr. Lecter, exemplifies the two-person psychology of contemporary psychoanalytic theory and clinical practice. The interplay of transference and countertransference themes, often colored by erotic desire on the part of both doctor and patient, is prominent. Unlike earlier portrayals, such as that of Dr. Collins in *The Dark Past*, Dr. Melfi makes errors, is capable of strong emotional reactions, and even appears, at times, to transgress professional and ethical boundaries; she is essentially human. Tony's insights, perhaps in part owing to the fact that *The Sopranos* is a series rather than a two-hour movie, accrue incrementally and also seem inextricably tied to the transference dimension of the treatment relationship. The analysis of Tony's dreams, too, suggests a more realistic and convincing clinical interaction, the value of which may reside less in analytic brilliance or omniscience than in a careful reading of the dreamer's self-state.

Psychoanalysis and film, Barbara J. Socor advises, may be considered analogous projects in that both strive to construct narrative coherence and establish subjective meaning, with the ultimate aim of the creation of a satisfying story rather than revealing incontrovertible, historical truths. The subject matter of her chapter, "Imagining Desire and Imaging the Real: A Love Story," is the cinematic depiction of transference love and the reactions, fantasies, and enactments which it educes in the analyst, collectively referred to as the countertransference. Drawing on the work of Lacan, and more specifically, his theory of the three psychic Orders (the *Real,* the *Symbolic,* and the *Imaginary*) in respect of the phenomenon of transference, Socor furnishes us with a detailed analysis of two films, *The Prince of Tides* (Streisand, 1991) and *Final Analysis* (Joanou, 1992). Lacan, in his insistence that the unconscious is structured by language, asserts that the transference actually functions as an adversary of the unconscious, serving instead to suppress it. In the Lacanian vision of psychoanalysis, Socor avers, the analysand's recognition of the unconscious is promoted through a penetration of the transference that attempts to obscure it. Tracing the subject's original alienation of self to what has been termed the *stade du miroir* or "mirror stage"—the infant's identification with his image in the mirror—Lacan conceives of transference, in part, as an effort to maintain the fictive, undivided self. Should the analyst unconsciously collude with the analysand, so that complementary reactions or countertransference enactments are elicited, the illusion of completeness might be upheld.

*The Prince of Tides,* with its erotic enactment in the transference-countertransference between Tom Wingo and Dr. Lowenstein, seems ideally suited to Socor's Lacanian analysis. Focusing less on the psychiatrist's strident breaches in professional ethics and boundary transgressions, Socor explores the shared illusion of patient and therapist that their love for each other, once enacted, will be curative. This, of course, is not to be, and Tom Wingo's journey, Socor tells us, must finally include the recognition that he is incomplete, and that this incompleteness cannot be assuaged through his relationship with Dr. Lowenstein or, for that matter, anyone else. This critical insight signifies Tom's mastery of the Imaginary and a corresponding capacity for experiencing the Symbolic, which represents the completion of his emotional odyssey.

*Final Analysis* is a story about a dedicated, apparently highly competent though unhappy psychiatrist, Dr. Isaac Barr, who has surrendered his personal life to his professional activities. Paradoxically, however, his work is no longer fulfilling, and he yearns to be "surprised" by something or someone he doesn't understand. Perhaps Dr. Barr, like Dr. Lowenstein in *The Prince of Tides*, evinces a sort of "countertransference readiness." Although Dr. Barr's enactment is with his patient's sister—and therefore perhaps not as egregious a lapse in his professional ethics—the consequences appear just as profound. Once again, the failure within the transference-countertransference to acknowledge the Symbolic—and with it, unconscious knowledge of the self as incomplete—must finally be resolved through internal recognition of the original wound of incompleteness. Although Dr. Barr is able to do this, his lover-patient, Heather, is unable to enter this psychic space, lost, Socor tells us, in "the immediacy of the Real."

The translation of psychotherapy narratives from literature into film, a challenging project under the best of circumstances, is often less than completely successful. The author's original vision of the treatment process may become subverted as story becomes screenplay, undergoing revision after revision; or as characters' identities are altered beyond recognition; or because critical details are simply omitted in order to keep the film's length commercially viable. The ninth and concluding chapter, "Translating Psychotherapy Narratives from Literature onto Film: An Interview with Theodore Isaac Rubin," examines the process by which one psychotherapy narrative became a commercially produced film.

Originally published in 1961, Theodore Isaac Rubin's book, *David and Lisa*, may be considered unique in several respects. Though fictive, it is written with the insights of a seasoned clinician, a psychiatrist with many years' experience working with disturbed children and adolescents. The film version of *David and Lisa*, which represented Frank Perry's directorial debut, was produced in 1962 and starred Keir Dullea as David, Janet Margolin as Lisa, and Howard da Silva as the sympathetic Dr. Swinford. *David and Lisa* may have also have represented a breakthrough film of sorts. Independently produced for less than $200,000—a small budget even by 1962 standards—*David and Lisa* offered a fresh, even daring alternative to the usual Hollywood treatment of cultural mythologies involving relationships between parents and children (Gabbard & Gabbard, 1999). Moreover, it offered viewers a psychotherapist whose clinical effectiveness seemed more closely tied to his genuineness and compassionate acceptance of his patient than to charismatic healing or brilliant interpretations magically intuited from meager data. Even now, forty years later, *David and Lisa* is often described as one of the most realistic movie portrayals of the psychotherapy process.

In 1998 *David and Lisa* (Kramer, 1998) was remade, becoming perhaps the only feature-length movie in which psychotherapy is accorded genuine thematic prominence to hold this distinction. The second version of the film, an ABC television movie produced by Oprah Winfrey and directed by Lloyd Kramer, featured Sidney Poitier as Dr. White, Lukas Haas as David, and Brittany Murphy as Lisa. As in the first film version, Dr. Rubin was also coauthor of this screenplay.

꧁꧂

We have made the deliberate decision not to survey the vast number of films, probably now exceeding 500, in which some mention of psychotherapy or psychotherapists is made, a project that others have already undertaken (Gabbard & Gabbard, 1999). Instead, we have assembled a scholarly anthology. Few such anthologies, it may be argued, can presume to be comprehensive in scope or treatment of a particular theme or domain. This collection, though admittedly modest in respect to its length, offers a compensatory richness that is born of its transdisciplinary nature. As the reader will likely discover, apart from the important commonalities that each of these chapters offers—similarities that seem to transcend disciplinary differences—they also seem to be written from distinctively different vantage points. The clinician (and of course, there are three different clinical professions represented within this volume), the film historian, the literary scholar—all bring unique traditions and insights to their analyses of the filmic works presented here, contributing to what we hope you will agree constitutes the volume's ultimate success.

## NOTES

1. The combined membership of the five largest American psychoanalytic membership organizations (the American Psychoanalytic Association, Division 39 [Division of Psychoanalysis] of the American Psychological Association, the National Association for the Advancement of Psychoanalysis, the National Membership Committee on Psychoanalysis in Clinical Social Work, and the American Academy of Psychoanalysis) now exceeds 11,000. Although this figure represents a nearly three-fold increase in the number of affiliated psychoanalysts over the last 25 years, it is a conservative estimate that probably accounts for less than 25% of all those who practice psychoanalysis, according to Dr. Murray Meisels, former President of Division 39 (Murray Meisels, Ph.D., personal communication).

2. Interestingly, Hitchcock's oeuvre has been the subject of nearly endless fascination for film scholars, particularly those who favor psychoanalytically informed film criticism; *Spellbound* was only the first in a series of films about which there has been considerable psychoanalytic commentary. Others have included *The Wrong Man* (Hitchcock, 1956), *Vertigo* (Hitchcock, 1958), and *Psycho* (Hitchcock, 1960). Perhaps such commentary was, in part, occasioned by Hitchcock's exploration of morbid themes and the macabre, everything ranging from murder to fetishism; or his techni-

cal and artistic gifts for generating suspense or for educing voyeuristic involvement from film audiences; or perhaps his interest in portraying human psychopathology as monstrous (for example, the character of Norman Bates in *Psycho*) but ultimately comprehensible (Scotty in *Vertigo*), and even treatable *(Spellbound)*.

3. The participation of "scientific directors" Hans Sachs and Karl Abraham in this production was apparently not merely perfunctory. Gifford mentions that Sachs wrote a thirty-two-page essay, "Psychoanalysis: Riddles of the Unconscious," that was handed out to opening-night audiences at the movie's Berlin premiere.

## REFERENCES

Allen, W. (Director), & Gallo, F. (Producer). (1977). *Annie Hall* [Motion picture]. United States: United Artists.

Allen, W. (Director), & Rollins, J., Joffe, C. (Producers). (1979). *Manhattan* [Motion picture]. United States: United Artists.

Allen, W. (Director), & Greenhut, R. (Producer). (1980). *Stardust memories* [Motion picture]. United States: United Artists.

Allen, W. (Director), & Doumanian, J. (Producer). (1997). *Deconstructing Harry* [Motion picture]. United States: Fine Line Cinema.

Ashby, H. (Director), & Lewis, M., Higgins, C. (Producers). (1971). *Harold and Maude* [Motion picture]. United States: Paramount.

Breuer, J., and Freud, S. (1973). Studies on hysteria. In J. Strachey (Trans.), *The Standard Edition of the Complete Psychological Works of Sigmund Freud* (Vol. 2, pp. 1–335). London: Hogarth Press. (Original work published 1893–95)

Campion, J. (Director), & lkin, B. (Producer). (1990). *An angel at my table* [Motion picture]. New Zealand: Hibiscus Films/N.Z. Film Commission/TV New Zealand/ABC.

Chase, D. (Director/Creator). (1998–). *The Sopranos* [Television series]. United States: HBO.

Clifford, G. (Director), & Sanger, J. (producer). (1982). *Frances* [Motion picture] United States: EMI/Brooksfilm.

Collins, R. (Director/Producer). (2000). *We don't live under normal conditions* [Video]. United States: Fanlight Productions.

Cornfield, H. (Director), & Kramer, S. (Producer). (1962). *Pressure point* [Motion picture]. United States: Larcas Productions.

Demme, J. (Director), & Saxon, E., Utt, K., Bozman, R. (Producers). (1990). *Silence of the lambs* [Motion picture]. United States: Orion Pictures.

Forman, M. (Director), & Zaentz, S., Douglas, M. (Producers). (1975). *One flew over the cuckoo's nest* [Motion picture]. United States: UA/Fantasy Films.

Freud, S. (1905). *Three essays on sexuality.* In J. Strachey (Ed. and Trans.), *Standard edition of the complete pyschological works of Sigmund Freud* (Vol. 7, pp. 123–245). London: Hogarth Press. (Original work published 1905)

Gabbard, G., and Gabbard, K. (1999). *Psychiatry and the cinema.* Washington, DC: American Psychiatric Press.

Greenberg, H. (1993). *Screen memories: Hollywood cinema on the psychoanalytic couch.* New York: Columbia University Press.

Hitchcock, A. (Director), & Selznick, D. (Producer). (1945). *Spellbound* [Motion picture]. United States: Selznick Studios.

Hitchcock, A. (Director), & Coleman, H. (Producer). (1957). *The wrong man* [Motion picture]. United States: Warner Bros.

Hitchcock, A. (Director/Producer). (1958). *Vertigo* [Motion picture]. United States: Paramount.

Hitchcock, A. (Director/Producer). (1960). *Psycho* [Motion picture]. United States: Shamley.

Hornstein, G. (2000). *To redeem one person is to redeem the world.* New York: Basic Books.

Joanou, P. (Director), & Roven, C., Junger Witt, P., Thomas, A. (Producers). (1992). *Final analysis* [Motion picture]. United States: Warner/Roven-Cavallo.

Kramer, L. (Director), & Winfrey, O. (Producer). (1998). *David and Lisa* [Motion picture]. United States: Oprah/ABC.

Light, A. (Director/Producer). (1993). *Dialogues with madwomen* [Motion picture]. United States: Light-Saraf Films.

Lindner, H. (1966). *The fifty-minute hour: A collection of psychoanalytic tales* (20th ed.). New York: Bantam Books.

Litvak, A. (Director/Co-producer), & Bassler, R. (Co-producer). (1948). *The snake pit* [Motion picture]. United States: TCF.

Lumet, S. (Director), & Holt, D. (Producer). (1977). *Equus* [Motion picture]. United States: United Artists/Winkast.

Mangold, J. (Director), & Wick, D., Konrad, C. (Producers). (1999). *Girl, interrupted* [Motion picture]. United States: Columbia/Red Wagon/Global.

Mate, R. (Director), & Adler, B. (Producer). (1948). *The dark past* [Motion picture]. United States: Columbia.

Minnelli, V. (Director), & Houseman, J. (Producer). (1955). *The cobweb* [Motion picture]. United States: MGM.

Ovesey, L. (1969). *Homosexuality and pseudohomosexuality.* New York: Science House.

Pabst, G.W. (Director), & Neumann, H. (Producer). (1926). *Secrets of a soul* [Motion picture]. Germany: UFA.

Page, A. (Director), & Corman, R. (Producer). (1977). *I never promised you a rose garden* [Motion picture]. United States: New World.

Perry, F. (Director), & Heller, P. (Producer). (1962). *David and Lisa* [Motion picture]. United States: Continental.

Rado, S. (1940). A critical examination of the concept of bisexuality. *Psychosomatic Medicine, 2*, 459–467.

Redford, R. (Director), & Schwary, R. (Producer). (1980). *Ordinary people* [Motion picture]. United States: Paramount/Wildwood.

Shyamalan, M. (Director), & Marshall, F., Kennedy, K., Mendel, B. (Producers). (1999). *The sixth sense* [Motion picture]. United States: Buena Vista/Hollywood/ Spyglass.

Socarides, C. (1968). *The overt homosexual*. New York: Grune & Stratton.

Streisand, B. (Director/Co-producer), & Karsch, A. (Co-producer). (1991). *Prince of tides* [Motion picture]. United States: Columbia/Barwood/Longfellow.

Turteltaub, J. (Director), & Taylor, M., Boyle, B. (Producers). (1999). *Instinct* [Motion picture]. United States: Miramax.

Van Sant, G. (Director), & Bender, L. (Producer). (1997). *Good Will Hunting* [Motion picture]. United States: Miramax.

Wiseman, F. (Director/Producer). 1987. *Titicut follies* [Motion picture]. United States: Zipporah.

# 1

# Kids on the Couch

*Hollywood's Vision of Child and Adolescent Treatment*

JERROLD R. BRANDELL

## INTRODUCTION

The psychotherapeutic process is a theme that Hollywood has explored from time to time in a series of films dating back to the 1930s, though with but a few notable exceptions, the results have been rather disappointing. More often than not, psychotherapy has been lampooned and psychotherapists caricatured. In Hitchcock's classic *Spellbound* (Hitchcock, 1946), even enlisting the artistic genius of Salvadore Dali to create patient Gregory Peck's posttraumatic dream could not hide Hitchcock's fundamental ambivalence about psychoanalysis, which in this film is uncomfortably situated at the midpoint along a continuum whose polar extremes are legitimate science and intellectual charlatanism.[1]

Therapists are often portrayed in the cinema as being the least well equipped to provide help to their suffering patients. In fact, their biases, vulnerabilities, and tragic character flaws have been exposed in a long list of films that cover several different genres. In *Lilith* (Rossen, 1964), Warren Beatty succumbs to an erotized countertransference when he falls in love with his patient, a theme that is reprised in *Mr. Jones* (Figgis, 1993). In the suspense thriller *Final Analysis* (Joanou, 1992), psychiatrist Isaac Barr (Richard Gere) shows poor judgment when he becomes romantically involved with his patient's sister, though by the time the film reaches its dénouement, Dr. Barr's breaches of professional ethics have become ever more flagrant. The most disturbing of these occurs when he places another troubled patient, a young man named Pepe who has several times been convicted of petty theft, in harm's way in order to intercept a parcel with evidence that falsely incriminates the good doctor in a murder scheme. The therapist in *An Unmarried Woman* (Mazursky, 1978) is herself struggling in the aftermath of a divorce as she attempts to help Jill Clayburgh recover from her own failed marriage. Although she has exhorted her patient to seek out male companionship, a chance social encounter between the two suggests the therapist has experienced difficulty in following her own advice.

In the more recent film *Instinct* (Turteltaub, 1999), psychiatrist Theo Caulder (Cuba Gooding, Jr.) nearly begs for permission to perform a psychiatric assessment of Ethan Powell, a violently psychotic anthropologist (portrayed by Anthony Hopkins). Shamelessly self-serving, Dr. Caulder is seemingly motivated by his desire to write a book about this homicidal academic's life among the mountain gorillas. Even more troubling, his countertransference fantasy is shared by Dr. Caulder's mentor and supervisor, Dr. Ben Hillard (played by Donald Sutherland). Dr. Hillard then goes to considerable lengths to install his young protégé at Harmony Bay, the rigidly administered forensic psychiatry unit that houses the notorious anthropologist and a number of other severely disturbed felons. Aside from a formulaic plot and notably unimaginative characters (the disaffected and inept resident psychiatrist, the sadistic guard, the "good ol' boy" prison director whose main job evidently is to speak in a southern drawl and discourage young upstart shrinks from deviating from the status quo), there are other problems. To no one's surprise, a relationship begins to develop between Dr. Caulder and his patient, and then Dr. Caulder has an epiphany. He abandons his ambition of topping the New York Times bestseller list with the definitive popular psychology case study (which might be titled "The Anthropologist Who Mistook a Band of Mountain Gorillas for His Family") and with it, what remains of his professional role, to become his patient's advocate, coach, and friend. What seems evident as the story reaches its conclusion is that the inmate-residents, however disturbed, may actually be less confused than the psychiatrists treating them.

Often, therapists are portrayed humorously, dispensing useless advice or making glaring errors. In the comedy classic *A Day at the Races* (Wood, 1937), veterinarian Groucho Marx takes over as chief of psychiatry at an institution for the mentally ill amidst the usual Marx Brothers antics and mayhem. In *Deconstructing Harry* (Allen, 1997), Woody Allen's middle-aged spouse, a psychoanalyst, confronts him after learning that he has been having an affair with her female patient. It becomes both horrifying and comical as she excuses herself repeatedly from the consulting room (where her very neurotic patient, Mr.

Farber, has assumed the recumbent position) to scream obscenities at her husband for his infidelity, all of which poor Mr. Farber cannot help but overhear.

Children and adolescents have not typically fared any better at the hands of celluloid therapists. In *Equus* (Lumet, 1977), the therapist bemoans the fact that treatment, despite its being curative, has been at great cost to his adolescent patient Alan's creativity and passion, and that some irreplaceable essence has been sacrificed in exchange for healthier adaptations. A series of vignettes in the movie *Harold and Maude* (Ashby, 1972) reveals a wooden, doctrinaire, and unintentionally comedic therapist, seemingly an agent of Harold's manipulative mother, who is intent on delivering the nineteen- or twenty-year-old Harold from his pathology. Harold is wisely resistant to these efforts, and his relationship with Maude in the end proves far more therapeutic than anything his therapist is able to offer. In *Good Will Hunting* (Van Sant, 1997), therapist Sean McGuire (Robin Williams) is portrayed somewhat more three-dimensionally. Dr. McGuire is obviously far more "real" and clinically more astute than his rather inept and otherwise unattuned predecessors, who are clearly not up to the task of working with so brilliant yet disturbed an adolescent as Will Hunting. At the same time, his work with Will soon reveals Dr. McGuire's own conflicts and struggles over the loss of his wife, problems that are fundamentally countertransference driven and that lead to rather frightening enactments with this late adolescent patient. Dr. McGuire sacrifices not only orthodox technique but also clinical wisdom in creating a boundaryless domain that threatens to disrupt the process of treatment far more than it seems to enhance it.

It is not, of course, surprising that Hollywood views the psychotherapy profession with ambivalence and perhaps disillusionment if not outright disdain; some of its most famous, among them Judy Garland, Frances Farmer, and Marilyn Monroe, have not been especially well served by it. Nevertheless, there are notable exceptions to the problematic portrayals of psychotherapy and psychotherapists described above. In these films, the psychotherapeutic process is not only central to the story, but is portrayed with greater balance and authenticity rather than consisting of a handful of consulting room clichés. Three movies, *I Never Promised You a Rose Garden* (Page, 1976), *Ordinary People* (Redford, 1980), and *The Sixth Sense* (Shyamalan, 1999), all of which explore the treatment process and relationship with young patients, are arguably among the best examples of this. The first is based on a true story, that of writer Joanne Greenberg, whose treatment with Frieda Fromm-Reichmann at Chestnut Lodge Sanitarium is neatly paralleled in the fictional relationship between the young schizophrenic Deborah and her therapist Dr. Fried. *Ordinary People,* a film that is surprisingly faithful to the novel by Judith Guest, poignantly reveals the intricacies and challenges of treating a traumatized adolescent. A more recent example of how the process of psychotherapy may be depicted artfully in the cinema, *The Sixth Sense,* comes from an entirely unexpected genre, that of psychological horror. This movie, with both depth and exquisite sensitivity, convincingly captures aspects of the clinical process with a deeply troubled nine-year-old boy.

## I *NEVER PROMISED YOU A ROSE GARDEN*

Joanne Greenberg immortalized her four and a half years of psychoanalytic treatment with Frieda Fromm-Reichmann when, in 1964, she published *I Never Promised You A Rose Garden* under the pseudonym Hannah Green. Although the author has described her work as fictional, it bears an uncanny resemblance to her experiences as a profoundly disturbed sixteen-year-old patient at Chestnut Lodge Sanitarium. In fact, some years prior to the publication of her novel, Greenberg and Fromm-Reichmann had decided to collaborate on a detailed study of their work together. The plan was for Greenberg to prepare a history of her illness and a detailed discussion of her treatment at Chestnut Lodge; Fromm-Reichmann would, in turn, prepare a complementary discussion of the psychoanalytic work from her own perspective. Though Greenberg completed her portion in 1956, two years after her discharge from Chestnut Lodge, Fromm-Reichmann died before she was able to complete her part. Fortunately, a tape recording preserved comments she made on the case in one of her last public lectures (given in 1956), a transcript of which was published some years later (Fromm-Reichmann, 1982). In addition to her book, Greenberg has been interviewed several times regarding this treatment experience.

In a relatively recent interview (McAfee, 1989) Joanne Greenberg has suggested that her recovery may have been aided by phenothiazines or other antipsychotic medications not yet available fifty years ago, when she first became ill. At the same time, she has steadfastly maintained that her psychotherapy with Fromm-Reichmann was a critical and transformative experience that ultimately led to her recovery. But what, more specifically, may have contributed to Fromm-Reichmann's now celebrated success with this psychotic adolescent whose prognosis would otherwise have been so bleak, whose chances for full recovery so unlikely? In fact, the odds against a successful course of therapy may have been even greater. Fromm-Reichmann, whose work was almost exclusively with adults, had so little experience in the treatment of adolescents that she sought out consultation from Hilde Bruch at the time she began to treat her new patient (Bruch, 1982).

When she first arrived at Chestnut Lodge, Joanne Greenberg was floridly psychotic: "She saw blood pouring from faucets, gates that locked behind her eyes; always there was the sound of voices, whispering and screaming inside her mind" (Hornstein, 2000, p. 229). Indeed, hers appeared to be a classical picture of adolescent-onset schizophrenia, complete with paranoia, somatic delusions, self-mutilation, and vivid auditory as well as visual hallucinations. She was also at high risk for suicide. For a couple of years preceding her admission to Chestnut Lodge, where she held the distinction of being the youngest patient in residence, Joanne had been in outpatient treatment with Richard Frank, a psychiatrist and psychoanalyst. However, her deteriorating condition finally made this impossible, and, at the urging of Dr. Frank, her parents brought her to Chestnut Lodge.

Joanne's distrust of adults and of authority, which is so powerfully portrayed in the movie, may have had its origins in a traumatic experience that occurred when she was five years old. For some time, Joanne had wet herself—a painful symptom for which she suffered "all kinds of punishments and depreciation," until the organic basis of her enuresis had been established (Fromm-Reichmann, 1982, pp. 128–129). Ultimately, she had a series of operations, which her cinematic self, Deborah Blake, angrily describes in a damning revelation to Dr. Fried early in their treatment relationship (see Figure 1.1). Assuming that Dr. Fried's response to her young patient in this early scene is a reasonably close parallel to Joanne's real-life encounter with Fromm-Reichmann, one might make several observations. We are immediately struck by the genuineness of the therapist's response. She shares the indignation, hurt, and anger of her patient, passionately decrying the dishonesty and subterfuge of the doctors and the presumed collusion of Deborah's parents. For a brief moment, patient and therapist become allies in a common effort, and we sense the potential for the development of a real treatment alliance. Deborah reveals that she never really "lost" the tumor; that it has remained inside of her. Dr. Fried then observes that this has served to punish Deborah rather than the true objects of her rage, and Deborah, momentarily unguarded, responds "*Upuru* punishes us all." However, this revelation from the inner world of *Yria* is dangerously premature, and Deborah flees, returning to the safety of her private gods and their secret world. Nevertheless, a window has been opened and contact made, however brief.

One of Fromm-Reichmann's greatest gifts may have been the way in which she positioned herself long before any real treatment alliance had cohered as a passionate though benevolent presence in Joanne's efforts to move out of psychosis. On the one hand, she had told Joanne from their very first meeting that she expected her only to get well, and had emphasized Joanne's complete autonomy in respect to giving up her symptoms. When Joanne reported that she was forbidden by *Anterrabae*, god of *Yria*, to speak with her, Fromm-Reichmann recalls having said the following: "I'll tell you something. As far as I am concerned, he doesn't exist and your whole *Yria* doesn't exist other than in your mind. But since right now it does exist in your

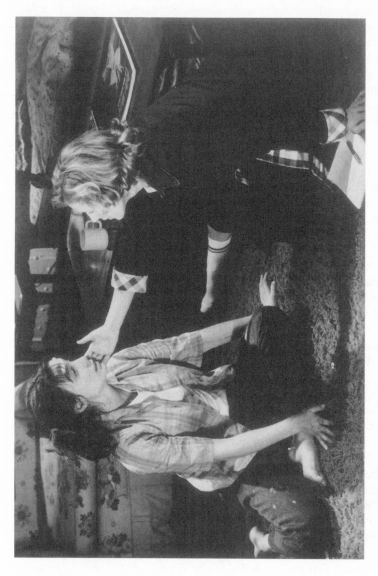

FIGURE 1.1. Dr. Fried (Bibi Andersson) working with deeply troubled adolescent patient, Deborah Blake (Kathleen Quinlan) in *I Never Promised You a Rose Garden* (New World Pictures, 1977). Courtesy of the Museum of Modern Art/Film Stills Archive.

mind, I'm willing for the time being to communicate with you on those terms, and we'll see what will happen" (Fromm-Reichmann, 1982, p. 131). After a respectable period during which Joanne's "gods" failed to demonstrate that they had Joanne's best interests and well being in mind, Fromm-Reichmann felt free to express herself without equivocation. In fact, she made no apologies for being angry with Joanne's gods. "She hated them," Joanne has said. "She didn't want anything to do with them. She said, 'I don't like them, tell them I don't believe in them, tell them I think they're keeping you from everything that's good and valuable, tell them we are at war. Make no apology for that. I'm not on their side. I'm on your side.'" Not only did this serve as the basis for strengthening the evolving treatment alliance; it also set the stage for Fromm-Reichmann to introduce a critically important idea that gradually attained the status of a therapeutic leitmotiv in their analytic work. She was finally able to say to Joanne, "These gods of yours, whatever good they wanted to do you, have certainly not succeeded in making you happy, so now you and I have to work and try" (Fromm-Reichmann, p. 132).

Interestingly, Greenberg has observed that although Fromm-Reichmann consciously espoused a view of the doctor-patient relationship as a "vertical" one, essentially consonant with the prevailing medical model of American psychoanalysis, her approach to the therapeutic relationship was always "horizontal." Though the terms "working alliance" (Zetzel, 1956) and "treatment alliance" (Greenson, 1965) were not yet in use, it seems clear that in practice, Fromm-Reichmann regarded the development of this aspect of the relationship to be an essential component in the ultimate success of the therapy. This was particularly true in her work with schizophrenic patients. Greenberg recalls,

> Frieda kept saying, "Take me along. If you don't take me along, how can I know where you are going? Where are you now?" It happened a lot. Frieda would say, "I don't know what it's like to be mentally ill. I don't have a clue. That's your job to tell me. It's your job to share with me. Do your job! How can I know where you are unless you take me and do your job? You're the expert." (McAfee, 1989, pp. 515–516)

Fromm-Reichmann practiced psychoanalysis and psychotherapy at a time when few believed that successful psychotherapeutic treatment of schizophrenia was possible.[2] Partly in consequence of her close affiliation with Harry Stack Sullivan, but also undoubtedly due to formative experiences in her own childhood and during her medical training in pre–World War I Germany, Fromm-Reichmann approached the psychotherapy of schizophrenia with genuineness, empathy, and emotional honesty. This is revealed both in her writings and in the legacy she has left behind as a therapist and supervisor. In fact, her emphasis on intuition and the therapist's empathic process has been regarded by some as an important forerunner of more contemporary ideas associated with the psychology of the self (Bruch, 1982).

Fromm-Reichmann's genuineness and her gift for using empathy to feel herself into those parts of the patient's experience that were beyond her immediate comprehension were complementary to a technical mastery of the interpretive process. She could experience deep affective resonance with the most primitive material one moment, and then, in the next moment, move almost effortlessly to articulate and interpret the essence of such primary process communications in an accessible, coherent secondary process mode. Moreover, she was able to accomplish this without sacrificing the fundamentally "horizontal" relational alliance of which Joanne Greenberg has spoken. Put in slightly different language, Fromm-Reichmann's clinical sensitivity and wisdom not only equipped her to employ the treatment relationship effectively as a vehicle for analytic interventions; it also prevented her from placing that relationship in jeopardy. According to Josephine Hilgard, who worked for many years with Fromm-Reichmann,

> Frieda would do a great deal to get into communication with a patient; if necessary, climbing on the furniture or sitting on the floor next to a patient who refused to talk sitting in a chair. She was not always able to explain why she acted in a particular way, but when pressed she was apt to reply, "It just occurred to me that it was the right thing to do." (Hilgard, 1989, p. 226)

In another, later vignette from the movie, Deborah has made substantial progress in her work with Dr. Fried. She continues to move in and out of psychosis and the secret world of *Yria*, although now with a greater capacity to recompensate following decompensations. Furthermore, these episodes have become less frequent and less extreme, and her ego functioning is, in general, significantly better than it had been at admission. Although this scene from the movie (described below) may or may not have occurred in the manner depicted in the veritable, real-life clinical encounter between Fromm-Reichmann and her patient, it is quite consistent with what we know about her therapeutic style. Deborah has revealed to Dr. Fried that her father once accused her of behaving seductively, thereby nearly causing an older man to sexually molest her. Her father had slapped her, an abusive act that she has been unable to forgive. As Deborah elaborates on her unwillingness to permit her father to visit, Dr. Fried, at a propitious moment, makes an interpretation that offers Deborah clarity regarding the motives that underlie her father's unceasing admonitions to her about "the men." Perhaps, Dr. Fried gently suggests, her father was afraid of impulses and fantasies that he saw in himself, but which were projected outwards. The success of this interpretation, which may be regarded as a mutative one, becomes apparent as Deborah permits herself to experience her father's pain and conflict. As she cries, Dr. Fried observes that she has "just touched the pain of another." Both therapist and patient realize the importance of this reaction, for it signals Deborah's return to a world of sentient experience, where passionate feelings may be felt, even revealed. Deborah smiles through her tears, tears that she describes as "feeling like wine." Indeed, they are intoxicating and a cause for celebration because they herald the end of a numbing and lonely existence in a private world of abject fear and pain. She also says that Dr. Fried has "made her cry." This is indisputably true, but perhaps not only in the way Deborah intends it.

In the scene that immediately precedes this one, Deborah has learned that a very troubled former ward attendant named Hobbes, recently fired due to professional misconduct, has committed suicide. Since she had a significant role in bringing Hobbes's sadistic behavior toward the patients to light, Deborah views herself at the beginning of this vignette as "poisonous," as though she were directly responsible for Hobbes's demise. However, she has begun to demonstrate an emerging capacity to view her father, like Hobbes, as a person who not only causes suffering, but also suffers himself. Struggling with the moral ambiguities in her relationship with Hobbes, Deborah has now become emotionally available for Dr. Fried's interpretations about her father's motives.[3] Her capacity to empathize with her father's pain is directly linked via identification to Dr. Fried's own empathic generosity. But perhaps there is even more to it than that. Dr. Fried's tolerance and acceptance, her compassionate understanding, have become internally available to Deborah through a process of incremental accretion, in consequence of what Heinz Kohut (1971) would have termed *transmuting internalization*. The journey from the nonexistence of *Yria* cannot commence in earnest until Deborah can both feel and feel for.

At the time of her death, Fromm-Reichmann was deeply involved in a research project to study the contribution that nonverbal communications make to the therapist's clinical intuitions. She hoped to demonstrate that such psychiatric judgments were both quantifiable and teachable, and that effective treatment was based upon objective criteria, and therefore replicable (Leeds-Hurwitz, 1989). Fromm-Reichmann, according to Greenberg, held an incontrovertible belief that psychiatry was a science rather than an art:

> She believed that the gifts she had—humor, empathy, indignation, intuition, a first-rate intellect, linguistic sensitivity, and the endearing quality of not exploiting her patients to prove herself or her theories—she believed that these things could be taught and learned, and that anyone who was reasonably intelligent could cultivate them to a degree equal to or exceeding her own. (Rubin, 1972, p. 206)

It was quite possibly this conviction that may have contributed to what Joanne has described as a significant therapeutic breach in Fromm-Reichmann's work with her. Fromm-Reichmann had always emphasized the metaphorical meaning of her patient's symptoms, being careful never to confuse the underlying illness with its various metaphoric expressions. However, when Fromm-Reichmann left for vacation one summer during Joanne's treatment, she assigned her care to other staff at Chestnut Lodge, believing them as capable of continuing the work of therapy as she herself was. Joanne, however, found these doctors to be "literalists," possessing neither Fromm-Reichmann's genuineness nor her clinical astuteness and skill in reaching beyond the elaborate metaphors Joanne had erected to obscure her pain and terror. The disappointment, frustration, and anger she experiences are revealed in Deborah's first interview with Dr. Roysen, whose stiff, intellectual manner contrasts so starkly with the emotional acessibility and warmth of her absent therapist.

Joanne acted out a great deal in Fromm-Reichmann's absence, burning and cutting herself. Devastated and enraged, she withdrew once again into the private sanctuary of *Yria,* suffering a major setback in direct consequence of the therapeutic breach. However, not even this chasm proved so vast that it was impossible to bridge. Fromm-Reichmann's patient persistence, her unwavering commitment to Joanne's treatment, and finally, her acknowledgment and acceptance of her own limitations as a healer were certainly factors in this. It is also a matter of no small importance that Joanne sensed that Fromm-Reichmann liked her:

> When I threatened to kill myself, Frieda would say, "Well, I think that that would be a hell of a waste after being together all these years, a hell of a waste." But it came across that while she might feel sad, she was telling me, "You do what you have to do, Joanne, and I will, too." But something in Frieda looked beyond my illness into where I was and she liked me, and that meant a lot because nobody did at all. The big thing is that she liked me for the health that was in me, not the sickness in me . . . the part of me that could joke and the part that rope danced . . . (and) she liked my writing. (McAfee, 1989, p. 526)

The cinematic portrayal of Deborah's psychotherapy with Dr. Fried, while representing a therapeutic process bearing the stamp of authenticity in its depiction of interpretive work, clinical intuitions, and the gradually evolving therapeutic alliance, has also been criticized for its complete erasure of the principal characters' Jewish identities (Hornstein, 2000). Another disturbing feature of the film is the intimation established through Dr. Fried's personal revelation to Deborah that she is childless and divorced, suggesting that a female analyst must sacrifice personal satisfaction in order to be a dedicated and skilled professional.[4]

Greenberg's recovery was not uncomplicated, and there were relapses before she and Fromm-Reichmann finally concluded their work in 1954. It is of some historical interest that the psychiatric response to the publication of Joanne Greenberg's book was an admixture of disbelief and hostility. Critical reviews of the book appeared soon after its original publication (for example, Kubie, 1966) and even years afterward (North & Cadoret, 1981), disputing Greenberg's account of recovery, indeed insisting that no such recovery would be possible without drugs or shock treatment (Hornstein, 2000).[5]

## ORDINARY PEOPLE

A few years ago, the writer was at a social gathering with a group of analysts and therapists when the topic turned to adolescent psychotherapy. Someone mentioned the movie *Ordinary People,* which elicited comments from several of those present. One comment, made by an experienced analyst and therapist with a reputation as a sensitive and skilled clinician, was particularly evocative. He remarked, "You know, that movie made my professional life difficult. I remember patients talking about it when it first came out, wanting me to be Judd Hirsch. And I mean, who could possibly compete with the therapist in that film?" A few others at the table nodded their heads in agreement, and then the discussion turned to other topics. The comment, however, was an intriguing one: precisely what was it about Dr. Berger, and his relationship with his young patient, Conrad Jarret, that might elicit such a reaction?

Perhaps a brief summary of the plot would be helpful. Conrad Jarret is a trauma survivor. One fateful July afternoon, he and his older brother, Buck, take the family sailboat out onto Lake Michigan. The weather changes and the two find themselves in the middle of a storm. Their boat capsizes. Although Conrad is able to hold onto the boat until he's rescued, Buck isn't and he drowns, a catastrophic event that marks the beginning of a long nightmare for Conrad. We learn that he has attempted suicide, that he spent the better part of his junior year in high school in a psychiatric hospital, and now, some fifteen months after the accident, he is back home again. We also learn about his parents. His mother, Beth, attractive, highly social, a perfectionist, appears both narcissistic and distant. Losing Buck has been devastating for her, though in one sense, she may be the last to discover this. Conrad's father, Calvin, a successful tax attorney, is devoted to Beth and Conrad, although his life, overshadowed by a numbing loss, has become one of Thoreauvian "quiet desperation." He is warm, genuine, concerned, perhaps a bit naïve, but unconflicted in his love for Conrad. Beth's feelings toward her surviving son, however, are highly conflicted: she feels thinly disguised rage if not contempt for Conrad, but very little compassion. Buck's loss has created an inner emptiness that she is unable to assuage. This loss is so great, her pain so unremitting, that neither her family, nor European vacations, nor her frantic efforts to fill up her social calendar can provide surcease. It gradually becomes apparent that from Beth's perspective, the wrong child has survived this family tragedy.

It is against this backdrop that we are introduced to Dr. Berger. Berger is the outpatient therapist recommended to Conrad at the time of his discharge from the psychiatric hospital in the event that he should require ongoing treatment. Although initially resistant to the idea, Conrad finally decides to consult with this adolescent therapist (see Figure 1.2). In their first interaction, Berger appears to us to be a rather casual, "straight-from-the-hip" kind of guy. We also notice that his office is the negative image of Conrad's house: here things are in hopeless disarray: papers clutter all the surfaces; the door to the bathroom hangs wide open; the lighting is muted if not dim; and an unimaginative décor accentuates well-worn and rather mismatched furniture. There is no perfectionism here. Interestingly, the recording that we hear as Conrad enters Berger's office, apparently having interrupted the doctor's efforts to repair his stereo receiver, is the final theme from the "Autumn" movement of Vivaldi's *Four Seasons,* played fortissimo. Aside from the comic relief this lends to the scene, it may well be our first indication that Conrad's therapy will be intensive, challenging. The "four seasons" may signify the distinctive emotional climates associated with different aspects of the family tragedy and Conrad's posttraumatic adaptation to it. In another sense, one might understand the seasons to represent the phases of Conrad's treatment, the continuities and discontinuities in the change process itself that culminate in emotional growth and new adaptations. In Conrad's case, these might include a gradual acceptance of the feelings he has about his brother's death, his mother's limitations, and his own survivorship.

There is a kind of dance here, as well, an odd combination of honesty and artlessness. Conrad's adolescent awkwardness is mirrored in Berger's false starts and his fumbling. In fact, Berger himself at times seems adolescent. Paradoxically, this may be reassuring to Conrad, establishing both the proximal quality of this relationship and of Berger's authenticity as a healer. When Conrad consents to twice-weekly treatment, we are left with the distinct impression that an important connection has already occurred. But what is the nature of this connection?

Whereas Dr. Fried's greatest challenge in her work with Deborah may well have been sustaining a strong therapeutic alliance despite her patient's retreats into psychosis, Berger's challenge is seemingly of a different nature. It is of course true that Berger is also quite adept at shaping the alliance, an observation easily made of their interaction in the very first hour. As the treatment relationship deepens, we see that Berger's approach to psychotherapy, though stylized, is also fundamentally psychoanalytic. Both dynamic and

FIGURE 1.2. Trauma survivor Conrad Jarret (Timothy Hutton) and his rather unconventional psychiatrist, Dr. Berger (Judd Hirsch) in *Ordinary People* (Paramount Pictures, 1980). Courtesy of the Museum of Modern Art/Film Stills Archive.

genetic interpretations are made, and, in general, his pace is synchronous with that of his patient. At the same time, Berger is always very real; his is an active therapeutic modus operandi. He challenges and confronts his patient and at times seems almost angry, telling Conrad to "leave 'I don't know'" out in the waiting room with the rest of the magazines. All of these elements are essential to the success of Conrad's therapy, and gradually lead to the emergence of a coherent narrative. However, there is one additional ingredient we have yet to consider: the nature of Conrad's transference attachment to his therapist, and Berger's handling of it.

Conrad's transference to Berger might be viewed through several different lenses. Those who are classically inclined will perhaps see elements of phallic competitiveness and oedipal anxiety. Though I do not share this perspective, it may have a certain explanatory power. Hasn't Conrad always wanted to capture his mother's affection and admiration, yet been thwarted in doing so by Buck, while he was alive? Such sibling rivalry for many possesses an undeniably oedipal quality. We might also consider the affectively charged climate in which the therapy occurs, an atmosphere that at times is nearly redolent of adolescent aggression and sexuality, and of their counterpart, powerful feelings of guilt. We even have Conrad's revelatory fantasy about Berger's sex life: "I think you're married to a fat woman and you go home every night and fuck the living daylights out of her," he tells Berger in one heightened affective exchange midway through the treatment.

Others may frame the transference more with respect to its preoedipal or maternal elements. According to such an object-relational model, Berger becomes a transference screen for Conrad's thwarted dependency needs. In such a transference configuration, the unavailability of the maternal supplies that his rejecting and unloving mother has withheld are underscored; that is, the basis of this transference is his hunger for contact with an early primordial mother, the mother of infancy. Once again, there is more than a modicum of truth here. In the very first family scene, Beth disposes of Conrad's uneaten breakfast with such dispatch that her husband, anxiously concerned over Conrad's poor appetite, appears shocked. Much later, Conrad's abject depression is revealed as his posttraumatic symptoms begin to remit and he understands, for the first time, that his mother is incapable of loving him uncritically and unconditionally, and furthermore, that she probably always has been. This, one may argue, seems consistent with a model of early, anaclitic depression. Perhaps it even represents the recrudescence of an infantile depression that has existed as an unthought known, a preternatural, ineffable yet felt experience that, while never fully unconscious, remains incompletely accessible to consciousness and to the realm of secondary process.

Neither of the two ways in which I have depicted the transference is incorrect, although one might propose yet a third model, one that addresses the question I raised originally regarding my colleague's comments about Judd Hirsch. The single most salient quality in Conrad's transference attachment to Berger is that of idealization. Conrad of course requires many different things from this relationship. Berger's acceptance of his patient, his attunement, the high value he places on emotional expression, even his willingness to adopt an adversarial posture, all serve to enhance Conrad's experience of therapy. The healing that ultimately occurs in this therapeutic encounter, however, is intimately linked to Berger's acceptance of an important selfobject dimension revealed through Conrad's transference attachment: the need for merger and resonance with Berger's strength, self-confidence, resiliency, mastery, and wisdom. Berger, for his part, is also comfortable as an object of idealization, and equally, with the requirement that the therapeutic ambience provide uplifting care, figuratively speaking. It is, in fact, Berger's tolerant acceptance of such selfobject needs, inter alia, that assures the success of this therapy.

In a later sequence, which represents the film's dénouement, Conrad has just learned of the suicide of his friend Karen. This scene, with its power and poignancy, virtually assured the four Academy Awards this picture and its director, Robert Redford, received in 1980. What is it, however, that makes the scene so moving? We are certainly affected by Conrad's reenactment of the trauma, a painful though necessary step in the process of remembering and working through. We empathize with his agonizing guilt, a burden that few adults and even fewer adolescents will ever carry, and the tragedy of yet another loss. But finally, it is the relationship between Berger and Conrad, and Berger's capacity to contain his patient's grief, despair, and rage, and yet still offer him the strength and steadfastness Conrad has sought without success from his mother and his father, that makes this scene so profoundly affecting. Thus, when Conrad asks Berger how he knows that having and expressing such feelings and being a survivor is a good thing, Berger answers in the only way he can: "Because I'm your friend." Does this mean that he has forsaken his therapeutic role, or that the psychotherapy, as some have suggested (Gabbard, 1996) is a "love cure"? Perhaps. Indeed, Berger might have said, "Because I care about you," or suggested that it was too early to abandon hope, or found some other way to convey his concern. But, in a sense, this critique obscures the scene's most critical dimension: that of the transference relationship. My understanding of this scene's raw, transformative power is in its depiction of the selfobject transference, which has evolved incrementally and silently, and is here revealed in its purest and most elemental distillation. Indeed, it is the physical merger between Conrad and his therapist that calls forth such a deep emotional response in the viewer. It is also this scene that I strongly suspect my colleague and his patients had in mind.

Interestingly, Berger does make mistakes. At times, he pushes too hard, seemingly imposing his own agenda on Conrad's therapy. Even in this scene, Berger errs in interpreting prematurely when he refers to Conrad's guilt over his friend's suicide. This gives rise to a minor empathic breach, and he is compelled at that point to pursue a different path. In other words, Berger isn't perfect, so it is not that everything he says or does represents pure wisdom. It is rather, that he doesn't attempt to diminish the power of Conrad's selfobject transference at its zenith. This makes him a trustworthy friend as well as a very good therapist. Perhaps Berger is also a therapeutic ideal.


## THE SIXTH SENSE


As this story begins, Dr. Malcolm Crowe (Bruce Willis), a fortyish child psychologist, has just returned home from a romantic evening of celebration with his adoring wife, Anna. Unbeknownst to them, a patient whom Dr. Crowe had treated as a child some twelve years earlier has broken into their home, and waits silently in an upstairs bathroom clad only in his undershorts. Vincent Grey, the former patient, is barely coherent and enraged when he confronts Dr. Crowe. He bitterly accuses his former therapist of the profoundest insensitivity and emotional betrayal, but before Dr. Crowe is able to respond, Vincent shoots him and then suicides by turning the gun on himself. Eight or nine months pass, during which Dr. Crowe becomes obsessed with this case and its tragic outcome. Despite the fact that his mantelpiece is adorned with thank-you notes from grateful young patients and his high professional competence and dedication are formally acknowledged in a special award given to him by the City of Philadelphia, he feels little pride. This dramatic treatment failure and the endless ruminations to which it gives rise have nullified all his prior accomplishments. In the aftermath of the trauma, his work and his marriage are both affected. Dr. Crowe pores over his notes from Vincent's treatment, searching for answers that continue to elude him.

Still not fully recovered, he takes on a new patient (see Figure 1.3). Cole Sear (Haley Joel Osment), like Vincent at the time he began therapy, is also in midlatency and unusually compassionate; in other respects, too, he is uncannily reminiscent of Dr. Crowe's earlier patient. In the remainder of the film, Dr. Crowe and his young patient confront their respective demons, and a poignant therapeutic encounter between a traumatized boy and his traumatized therapist is gradually revealed.

Cole is a bright, sensitive boy who lives in a small apartment with his mother. His father evidently has abandoned the family several years earlier, and Cole and his mother struggle to survive on whatever income she is able to generate from working long hours at two jobs. Cole has two cherished possessions

FIGURE 1.3. Cole Sear (Haley Joel Osment) and therapist, Dr. Malcolm Crowe (Bruce Willis) both have demons to confront in *The Sixth Sense* (Hollywood Pictures/Spyglass Entertainment, 1999). Courtesy of the Museum of Modern Art/Film Stills Archive.

that once belonged to his father: a pair of eyeglasses (which he wears in the beginning of the film sans lenses because the lenses hurt his eyes), and a wristwatch that no longer works that he discovered in his father's drawer. Cole's relationship with his dad, like the empty frames and the stopped wristwatch, seems as ghostly as the apparitions he sees. Chronological time has ceased to have meaning in Cole's life, for his own pain and disappointments have become gradually commingled with the tragedies that extrude, hauntingly, into his consciousness. Cole is metaphorically suspended in the twilight intersection of past and present, neither capable of reflecting on the meaning of what has been nor able to imagine what may come.

Several important messages can be found in this film. Therapists and their patients are, of course, well accustomed to the intrusive and occasionally persistent reappearance of "ghosts" from the patient's past, figurative apparitions for which periodic therapeutic exorcisms must be performed, metaphorically speaking. However, in this movie, the ghosts have their own stories to narrate; and because these "ghost stories" are so well crafted, shock and fright compel the viewer to listen even more carefully. Furthermore, as we gradually discover, the matter of what leads to such a spectral existence—indeed, who becomes a ghost and what is signified in such a transmogrification—assumes central importance for both Cole and his therapist as their relationship deepens.

Although the film's title refers to Cole's ability to visualize dead people, it also refers to the "sixth sense" that good therapists are able to develop and use in their work. Much of what makes therapy therapeutic is not readily definable, nor can its most salient ingredients always be quantified. The therapist's sixth sense, the capacity to intuit and apprehend essential dynamic themes, issues, symbols, transference communications and other clinical information through processes that lie outside of the usual pathways of consciousness has, of course, been referred to by other names. Theodore Reik termed this phenomenon "listening with the third ear," though it may also be described as "empathic attunement." Since I believe the movie's title actually refers to the sixth sense of both client and therapist, it may be somewhat more enlightening to approach Dr. Crowe's relationship with Cole from the perspective of intersubjectivity theory.

The precursor to the contemporary concept of intersubjectivity appears to have originated with the work of the late French psychoanalyst Jacques Lacan, whose recondite theories and enigmatic personality spawned a cultlike following and a legion of interpreters rivaling that of Hegel. Lacan, a hermeneuticist, began in the early fifties to view psychoanalysis as a kind of *intersubjective dialogue* which "runs its course entirely in a relationship of subject to subject, signifying in effect that it retains a dimension which is irreducible to any psychology considered as an objectification of certain properties of the individual" (Lacan, as translated by Wilden, 1968, p. xi).

Nowadays, intersubjectivity is most often used to refer to the idea of reciprocal mutual influence in the therapeutic relationship, and includes the notion of a continuous interplay between the patient's transference and the therapist's countertransference. An important corollary is that patient and therapist are each subject to the other's influence at all times, a perspective that is at striking variance with traditional psychoanalytic prescriptions for how the treatment relationship is intended to work. The American psychoanalysts Robert Stolorow and George Atwood and their followers have attempted to expand this concept into a unifying framework that views all psychological phenomena as occurring contextually, as part of a greater relational field, or at the intersection of mutually interacting experiential domains. Such a framework, moreover, reflects a significant shift from the objectivism of classical psychoanalytic theory to an epistemology of perspectivalism, a viewpoint that is fundamentally appreciative of the importance of the personal psychic realities of both therapist and patient (Stolorow, Atwood, & Brandchaft, 1994).

But how may such an idea be applied meaningfully to the relationship that develops between Cole and his therapist? In the first encounter between Dr. Crowe and his youthful patient, which takes place in a Catholic church, Cole's posttraumatic play provides Dr. Crowe with a glimpse of the madness that this small boy carries within. What the viewer witnesses is a joyless, driven play scenario, more on the order of a compulsive reenactment rather than the healthy creativity of the primary process, the language of fantasy play, that one might ordinarily expect to see in a child of Cole's age. One of the small icons Cole plays with in a dimly lit pew is a tortured soldier who utters the Latin phrase "De profundus clamo ad Te Domine" or "Out of the depths, I cry to you, Oh Lord." Dr. Crowe is immediately fascinated by this case, deeply motivated by his wish to understand and help this child find a pathway leading out of his profound despair and pain. But Cole has a secret that he is not at first prepared to share, not even with this dedicated and compassionate therapist. Cole has little reason to believe that Dr. Crowe has anything to offer that is substantively different from the other adults in his life. Like so many children, Cole has concluded that the truth is dangerous and off-putting for adults; perhaps more significantly, that most adults are far less interested in listening to children than they may at first claim. Rather, their interests are in having children conform to the rules, in directing their play and work, offering advice and guidance, or perhaps simply in hearing themselves speak. Cole no longer draws pictures of the ghastly images he sees, since it proved far too disturbing for the staff at his school. "I draw pictures of rainbows and dogs running," he says. "They don't have meetings about rainbows." It is, of course, no surprise that Cole begins to feel freakish, for his distrust includes peers, as well: no one, it seems, can be entrusted with his awesome secret.

It is only after Dr. Crowe has convincingly demonstrated his commitment to Cole that Cole can begin to describe the ineffable. From his hospital bed, at a critical juncture in the beginning of a real therapeutic alliance between patient and therapist, Cole whispers to Dr. Crowe, "I see dead people." It is significant that Dr. Crowe, though moved by Cole's painful struggle, is not at first able to believe Cole's story. With great resignation, he views Cole as more disturbed than he had originally thought, a paranoid child subject to powerful visual hallucinations who appears to be suffering from some sort of "school-age schizophrenia." He begins to consider the possibility that drugs or hospitalization may be required, all the while sounding more and more distant. As he focuses increasingly on Cole's symptomatology, the objectification of his young patient seems to be leading Dr. Crowe to the inevitability of repeating his earlier error with Vincent.

Soon Dr. Crowe realizes the dilemma with which he is confronted. Though he wants desperately to help Cole, he feels powerless in the face of this boy's terrifying psychotic-like symptoms. He cannot accept Cole's description of his paranormal experiences, and yet without being able to take this step, to believe what Cole tells him, Dr. Crowe is unable to join his patient as an ally in this nightmare world. Helpless and frightened, Dr. Crowe tells Cole that he isn't able to meet with him any longer, that he will be transferring his case. Cole, facing yet another abandonment, feels more alone than ever. He beseeches Dr. Crowe to reconsider this decision, arguing tearfully that Dr. Crowe is the only one who can help him, the only person who does believe him. Sensing a widening emotional chasm, Cole then poses a critically important question: "How can you help me if you don't believe me?"[6]

It is at this moment in *The Sixth Sense*, however, that the unremitting pain both therapist and child feel becomes almost palpable. Dr. Crowe's tragic treatment failure with Vincent looms so large that it has gradually overshadowed his successes with so many others, leaving him wounded and filled with self-doubt, no longer able to believe in himself or his skills as a therapist nor even capable of finding solace in his marriage. Cole's abandonment by his father and social ostracism by peers have created a painful inner emptiness that amplifies the sense of freakishness he feels due to his paranormal abilities. He is overcome by an abiding sense of powerlessness and hopelessness. He is haunted, however, not only by his own past but also by the unfathomable pain and bitterness of the spectral beings that seek him out, souls whose human lives have ended unfairly, starkly, and in tragedy.

In an important sense, both Cole and Dr. Crowe are caught in the timelessness of their pasts; each requires the other in order to establish a new telos, and to plot the trajectory that will lead to a final resolution. "Therapist" and "patient," therefore, become rather ambiguous roles as this treatment alliance begins to cohere. Dr. Crowe learns about a spectral order from a boy who sees and hears things that he cannot; ironically, he is able to show his young friend a new way of listening and communing with the very souls whose existence the therapist was initially unable to accept. In this fundamentally intersubjective and evolutionary process, Dr. Crowe, the wounded healer, also acquires the strength and insight to confront painful truths that he himself has disavowed for many months, if not longer. (And, in fact, it is through this personal journey of the therapist that the movie offers up its final, shocking plot twist.)

Dr. Crowe's personal struggle to help Cole is always obvious to both patient and doctor. At one point, Dr. Crowe, speaking to Cole *per metaphor,* describes his earlier work with Vincent, making an allusion to its poor outcome; the possibility that he may be helpful to Cole, Dr. Crowe continues, represents a second chance, an opportunity to wrest meaning from tragedy and professional defeat. Several times, Dr. Crowe tries somewhat half-heartedly to evade Cole's questions to him about his personal life, but Cole's feelings and insights about his therapist are unerringly accurate; Dr. Crowe is compelled to speak of his troubled marriage, perhaps even with a sense of relief. That such spontaneous self-disclosure is born of countertransference seems to be an incontrovertible truth. Does it bode poorly for the treatment process? Apparently it does not. In *Good Will Hunting,* the therapist's feelings and conflict-laden issues threaten a fragile alliance almost continuously, sometimes erupting into the most deplorable and countertherapeutic countertransference enactments. Although Dr. Crowe has a powerful personal agenda from his very first encounter with Cole, his professional concern and an abiding love for his patient appear finally to guide his clinical decisions. Not all of these decisions are correct, however, and one, in particular, represents a glaring error.

That error is Dr. Crowe's resistance to accepting the importance of his patient's narrative, which follows Cole's hospital-bed revelation, "I see dead people." As previously suggested, when Dr. Crowe begins to think of Cole as a very disturbed child, or perhaps more accurately, as a collection of disturbing, psychotic-like symptoms, he removes himself from the intersubjective field, which both therapist and child experience as alienating. This is not a problem confined to the movies, however, nor is it even an exceptional one in child treatment. As a matter of fact, it is a nearly ubiquitous issue, and one that many contemporary child clinicians are curiously unconcerned about.

This is an age in which identifying, targeting, and treating children's symptoms and disorders through the most efficient treatments available has become a desideratum. Descriptive clinical diagnoses derived from an ever-increasing list (currently numbering 340) of psychological disorders appearing in the American Psychiatric Association's *Diagnostic and Statistical Manual of Mental Disorders* (DSM-IV) have become the shorthand by which children's psychological problems are understood and clinical interventions launched. Very specific diagnostic criteria inform the therapist, for example, that Johnny suffers from *attention deficit hyperactivity disorder,* or Jane from *oppositional-defiant disorder.* Such a system of classification, unfortunately, prompts us to think of Johnny and Jane principally with respect to the nature and severity of their symptomatology. We may become much less inclined to focus on complex dynamic issues or to extract the humanizing personal narratives that allow us to become immersed in their experience of the world, a sine qua non for any child treatment worthy of the name.

Many dynamically trained clinicians are increasingly uncomfortable with the widespread use of this psychiatric taxonomy since at best, it is somewhat less than compatible with psychoanalytic thinking. Indeed, within this framework, there is little room for such ideas as the therapeutic relationship, transference, or dynamic meaning in general. It appears to represent a return to the medical model par excellence, a model that, not for want of effort on the part of its proponents, has never enjoyed the same goodness of fit with psychological problems that it has with physical diseases and conditions. Symptoms within such a philosophical system are regarded as things to be controlled, alleviated, excised, or otherwise eliminated though not necessarily understood. After all, one doesn't need to understand a migraine in order to treat it successfully with analgesics or anti-inflammatory agents (though even on this question, there may not be complete consensus). In fact, when psychotropic drugs can achieve the desired effect, that is, if they are ameliorative (and often they are not), psychotherapy may actually be thought of as superfluous. Were Cole to be seen by a staff therapist at the local community mental health clinic, it might be determined that what he really needs is a brief in-patient hospitalization to stabilize him and get him started on antipsychotic medications. Then, after he's been discharged, perhaps ten or twelve sessions of solution-focused therapy and an occasional quarter-hour consultation with the child psychiatrist to monitor his Risperdal®. And so on.

The most serious problem with such a treatment model is that in its narrowed focus on an expedient "cure" it all too agreeably exchanges understanding for relief, though one may legitimately question *whose* relief. Clearly, it's much easier for everyone else if Cole draws happy pictures with rainbows, children playing, and dogs running. If one no longer has symptoms, so this argument goes, then perhaps there no longer is a problem.[7] So rather than an interweaving of therapist's and child's texts in the creation of a coherent narrative, the interventions arising from such a model become scripted; they are carefully plotted on some "treatment planner" where heart and soul and spontaneity are all too willingly sacrificed. What, we may inquire, has become of the child therapist's traditional defining role, that of a careful listener? And finally, if the willingness to suspend one's disbelief in order to become fully immersed in the psychic world of a child patient is no longer necessary or desirable, what has taken its place?

Dr. Crowe, too, has begun the perilous trek down this path as he leaves Cole's hospital room. However, just as Dr. Crowe is beginning to question his small patient's sense of reality, Cole's apparitions become visible for us, the audience. Perhaps this is intended to signify the new meaning these ghostly images acquire through Cole's profound admission to his therapist. They have become more real, acquiring visual form because Cole has described them and made them a part of his treatment. It now becomes Dr. Crowe's task to accept as a verisimilitude what Cole has revealed to him without dismissing such paranormal experiences as the hallucinations of a psychotic child. This is not, of course, easily accomplished either in real life or in good movies. In this instance, Dr. Crowe can only permit himself to be convinced of what Cole tells him after returning to an audiotape of an interview with Vincent made a dozen years earlier. Because Cole has taught him how to listen and what to listen for, he hears things that have always been there but that had previously eluded him. Suddenly, Cole's fantastic claims are no longer as frightening, and a significant therapeutic breach has been repaired. Enlightened, Dr. Crowe is able to reenter Cole's world, and a real therapeutic process begins.

A good child and adolescent therapist has to do more, of course, than simply listen. Sometimes action is required, or advocacy, or interventions with other systems. Twice during what must, in fairness, be described as a somewhat unconventional course of therapy, Dr. Crowe attends Cole's class plays, which may be criticized by some psychoanalytic clinicians as constituting a "parameter" in the treatment.[8] Perhaps this sort of direct participation in Cole's life wasn't necessary; on the other hand, the success of Cole's treatment may have depended in some measure on Dr. Crowe's willingness to modify or even suspend certain clinical precepts when close adherence to them might have proven countertherapeutic.

It is surprising to consider the possibility that a ghost story (granted, a well-made one) about a child with paranormal gifts might actually capture something of importance about the process of child psychotherapy. In this instance, little-discussed aspects of the therapeutic relationship in child treatment are explored with a candor and sensitivity rarely approached in the clinical literature, where detailed studies of clinical process have given way to concise case summaries that are efficiently presented but lifeless, and without dimension. I suppose I am making the argument that this is a very good movie, but not only for the usual reasons. *The Sixth Sense* is a story about an extraordinary encounter between a therapist and a child. In part because this story, like those of Deborah Blake and Conrad Jarrett, is so well told, but also because it permits us entrée to the intersubjective field of child therapist and patient, it offers us valuable lessons about the nature of healing that the clinical journals, textbooks, and modern-day practice too often neglect.

## CONCLUSION

In each of these three films, those elements and qualities that make the relationship in child and adolescent psychotherapy therapeutic occupy center stage. In each instance, particular challenges to the relationship must be overcome to assure therapeutic success. Using different conceptual frameworks and various principles of psychoanalytic treatment, I have attempted to understand more completely the nature of the therapeutic action in each case. For example, in *Rose Garden*, the focus is on the importance of the role of intuition and the need to maintain a strong therapeutic alliance; in *Ordinary People*, on the significance of the selfobject transference; and in *The Sixth Sense*, on the role of intersubjectivity as an organizing motif. As to whether the depiction of psychotherapy in these films possesses authenticity, we leave this perplexing question to others to debate. Indeed, while none of these three films can be thought of as a model for treatment, each reveals elements of its process with a certain sagaciousness that is strangely resonant with clinical reality.

## NOTES

This chapter is a significantly expanded version of an essay originally published in *Readings, 15*, 6–11 (March 2000).

1. Nevertheless, as one may extrapolate from Cohen's discussion of *Spellbound* in chapter 5, it would be rather unfair to judge the significance of this film solely by virtue of Hitchcock's ambivalence toward psychoanalysis. Indeed, this movie appears to have been a special case inasmuch as David O. Selznick, who produced *Spellbound* as well as three other Hitchcock films (*Rebecca, Notorious,* and *The Paradine Case*) was instrumental in engaging the services of his psychiatrist, May E. Romm, as a technical advisor on the film.

2. With but few exceptions (Karon, 1995; Benedetti, 1987), this is equally true of contemporary treatment approaches to schizophrenia, a disorder which, even in the absence of compelling scientific data, is considered to be heritable and neurogenic, and most effectively approached pharmacotherapeutically.

3. I am grateful to Erika Schmidt, MSW, for her comments made in response to an earlier draft of this piece that links Deborah's conflicted feelings toward Hobbes with conflicts experienced toward her father in this scene.

4. Some (e.g., Gabbard & Gabbard, 1999) have argued that such cinematic portrayals are part of a greater, nearly archetypal, pattern in which female analysts and therapists are shown to suffer dissatisfaction in their personal lives, often leading to role reversals with patients, erotic countertransference enactments, and so forth.

5. Although there are some "experts" on schizophrenia who would deny Greenberg the triumph of her recovery from this disabling psychosis through psychotherapy (e.g., North & Cadoret, 1981), she herself is not in doubt. Shortly after leaving Chestnut Lodge, Greenberg married, then graduated with a degree in anthropology from American University, and by the early 1960s had two children, both of whom are now in middle adulthood. She has led a productive and rewarding life in a semirural suburb of Denver, having taught cultural anthropology at a nearby college, tutored severely disabled children, and even volunteered as a firefighter and emergency medical technician in her mountaintop community. And, of course, she is a writer, having published some seventeen novels after penning *Rose Garden*.

6. In a sense, Cole's question recapitulates a dilemma faced by Joanne Greenberg and her therapist in *Rose Garden*. Dr. Fried (Fromm-Reichmann), in that instance, had been relentlessly critical of Joanne's "gods," although she fully accepted the realness of Joanne's delusional world. Furthermore, she was very careful to preserve Joanne's autonomy in the matter: Joanne was completely free to continue to believe in her punishing gods, the existence of which was never a subject of debate. Dr. Fried, however, was far more interested in allying with the healthy parts of her patient, and conveyed this consistently throughout their work together. In a sense, she was able to suspend her disbelief so that she could become more fully immersed in Joanne's delusional world, simultaneously retaining her conviction that Joanne's symptoms represented a retreat from the world of felt experience, and therefore represented sickness rather than health.

7. One is tempted to add that such a philosophy of treatment appears to be linked to the highly questionable practice of prescribing stimulants, antidepressants, and other psychiatric drugs to even very young children, a shocking finding originally reported with great fanfare by the New York Times in early 2000 (Goode).

8. Actually, Cole's part in the second play *(The Sword in the Stone),* which occurs at the conclusion of their work together, is that of the stable boy who is able to wrest the sword from the stone. It is a moment of triumph for both Dr. Crowe and for Cole, who has learned how to use his paranormal gifts in much the same way Arthur makes use of his sword, from a position of strength and mastery.

## REFERENCES

Allen, W. (Director), & Doumanian, I (Producer). (1997). *Deconstructing Harry* [Motion picture]. United States: Fine Line Cinema.

American Psychiatric Association. (1994). *Diagnostic and statistical manual of mental disorders* (4th ed.). Washington, DC: Author.

Ashby, H. (Director), & Lewis, M., Higgins, C. (Producers). (1971). *Harold and Maude* [Motion picture]. United States: Paramount.

Benedetti, G. (1987). *Psychotherapy of schizophrenia.* New York: New York University Press.

Bruch, H. (1982). Personal reminiscences of Frieda Fromm-Reichmann. *Psychiatry, 45,* 98–104.

Figgis, M. (Director), & Greisman, A., Greenfield, D. (Producers). (1993). *Mr. Jones* [Motion picture]. United States: Columbia TriStar.

Fromm-Reichmann, F. (1982). Frieda Fromm-Reichmann discusses the "Rose Garden" case. *Psychiatry, 45,* 128–136.

Gabbard, G. (1996). *Love and hate in the analytic setting.* Northvale, NJ: Jason Aronson.

Gabbard, G., & Gabbard K. (1999). *Psychiatry and the cinema.* Washington, D.C.: American Psychiatric Press.

Goode, E. (2000). Sharp rise in psychiatric drugs for the very young. *The New York Times,* February 23, Late Edition Final, Section A, Page 1, Column 6.

Green, Hannah. (1964). *I never promised you a rose garden.* New York: Holt, Rinehart, and Winston.

Greenson, R. (1965). The working alliance and the transference neurosis. *Psychoanalytic Quarterly, 34,* 155–181.

Guest, J. (1976). *Ordinary people.* New York: Viking Penguin Books.

Hilgard, J. (1989). The anniversary syndrome as related to late-appearing mental illnesses in hospitalized patients. In A. Silver (Ed.), *Psychoanalysis and psychosis* (pp. 221–247). Madison, CT: International Universities Press.

Hitchcock, A. (Director), & Selznick, D. (Producer). (1945). *Spellbound* [Motion picture]. United States: Selznick Studios.

Hornstein, G. (2000). *To redeem one person is to redeem the world: The life of Frieda Fromm-Reichmann.* New York: Free Press/Simon & Schuster.

Joanou, P. (Director), & Roven, C., Junger Witt, P., Thomas, A. (Producers). (1992). *Final analysis* [Motion picture]. United States: Warner/Roven-Cavallo.

Karon, B. (1995). Psychotherapy for schizophrenia. In J. Barber & P. Crits-Cristoph (Eds.), *Dynamic therapies for psychiatric disorders* (pp. 84–130). New York: Basic Books.

Kohut, H. (1971). *Analysis of the self.* New York: International Universities Press.

Kubie, L. (1966). Review of "I never promised you a rose garden." *Journal of Nervous and Mental Disease, 142,* 190–195.

Leeds-Hurwitz, W. (1989). Frieda Fromm-Reichmann and the natural history of an interview. In A. Silver (Ed.), *Psychoanalysis and Psychosis* (pp. 95–127). Madison, CT: International Universities Press.

Lumet, S. (Director), & Holt, D. (Producer). (1977). *Equus* [Motion picture]. United States: United Artists/Winkast.

Mazursky, P. (Director/Co-producer), & Ray, T. (Co-producer). (1978). *An unmarried woman* [Motion picture]. United States: TCF.

McAfee, L. (1989). Interview with Joanne Greenberg: with three poems by Joanne Greenberg. In A. Silver (Ed.), *Psychoanalysis and Psychosis* (pp. 513–533). Madison, CT: International Universities Press.

North, C., & Cadoret, R. (1981). Diagnostic discrepancy in personal accounts of patients with 'schizophrenia.' *Archives of General Psychiatry, 38,* 133–137.

Page, A. (Director), & Corman, R. (Producer). (1977). *I never promised you a rose garden* [Motion picture]. United States: New World.

Redford, R. (Director), & Schwary, R. (Producer). (1980). *Ordinary people* [Motion picture]. United States: Paramount/Wildwood.

Reik, T. (1948). *Listening with the third ear: The inner experience of an analyst.* New York: Farrar Strauss.

Rossen, R. (Director/Producer). (1964). *Lilith* [Motion picture]. United States: Columbias/Centaur.

Rubin, S. (1972). Conversations with the author of "I never promised you a rose garden." *Psychoanalytic Review, 59,* 201–215.

Shyamalan, M. (Director), & Marshall, F., Kennedy, K., Mendel, B. (Producers). (1999). *The sixth sense* [Motion picture]. United States: Buena Vista/Hollywood/Spyglass.

Stolorow, R., Atwood, R., & Brandchaft, B. (1994). *The intersubjective perspective.* Northvale, NJ: Jason Aronson.

Turteltaub, J. (Director), & Taylor, M., Boyle, B. (Producers). (1999). *Instinct* [Motion picture]. United States: Buena Vista/Touchstone/Spyglass.

Van Sant, G. (Director), & Bender, L. (Producer). (1997). *Good Will Hunting* [Motion picture]. United States: Miramax.

Wilden, A. (1968). *The language of the self.* (Translation with notes and commentary on J. Lacan's *The function of language in psychoanalysis*). Baltimore: Johns Hopkins University Press.

Wood, S. (Director), & Weingarten, L. (Producer). (1937). *A day at the races* [Motion picture]. United States: MGM.

Zetzel, E. (1956). The concept of transference. In *The capacity for emotional growth* (pp. 168–181). New York: International Universities Press.

# 2

## The Interracial Treatment Relationship in the Cold War Period

### Pressure Point *in Analysis*

ANDREA SLANE

Sidney Poitier and Bobby Darin played a prison psychiatrist and his American Nazi patient in *Pressure Point* (Cornfield, 1962), a not particularly successful "social problem film." Stanley Kramer, the film's producer, was a major player in the social problem genre, part of the cinematic variant of the studies of social and political problems that had gained unprecedented influence in the World War II and Cold War periods. Taken together with one of his first films, *Home of the Brave* (Robson, 1949), *Pressure Point* represents Kramer's second effort as a producer to depict psychoanalytic explanations for racial prejudice.

The film *Pressure Point* is the last version of a story that, like many Cold War narratives, finds its genesis in World War II, when psychoanalyst Robert Lindner, who wrote the case history on which the film is based, worked at a federal penitentiary and treated an American fascist incarcerated there. Psychological theories of political behavior picked up momentum in the postwar period, and expanded by two interrelated developments with the defeat of fascism: the ascendancy of the concept of totalitarianism, which combined Communism with fascism and so extended wartime theories into the Cold War, and the turn to questions of domestic politics and the social management of conflicts internal to the nation, especially racial prejudice.[1] *Pressure Point*'s narrative dramatizes the latter effort to cure racial prejudice, but also reveals the ideological tensions embedded in a project that depends so centrally on normative gender and sexual behavior. Further, in the process of converting Lindner's 1942 case history to the 1962 film script, producer Kramer cast Poitier in the doctor's role, thereby changing the analyst's ethnicity from Jewish to African American. Because of this change, the film's script is exceptionally revealing of tensions between race-specific versions of these gender and sexual norms as they manifest in the treatment relationship.

## POPULAR PSYCHOANALYSIS

The case history that comprises the narrative of *Pressure Point* went through a series of media in its journey from couch to screen. The case itself appeared in popular print form as "Destiny's Tot" in Lindner's collection of "psychoanalytic tales" called *The Fifty Minute Hour,* which became a national bestseller in 1954 (Lindner, 1966). Its next version was a one-hour *Public Affairs* presentation that was aired on a Sunday afternoon in January of 1960 by NBC News.[2] And finally it became the feature-length film directed by Cornfield. Kramer produced both the television and film versions. This case history's journey through various media thus spans the twenty-year heyday of psychoanalysis in American culture—both on the level of influence on social policy and of popular familiarity and support.

Robert Lindner was chief of the Psychiatric-Psychological Division at the federal penitentiary at Lewisburg, Pennsylvania, and then professor of psychology at Lehigh University. He treated "Anton," whose case history *Pressure Point* dramatizes, at Lewisberg. Lindner is best known for his popular books, especially *The Fifty Minute Hour* and *Must You Conform?* (Lindner, 1956).[3] Most of the publicity materials for *Pressure Point* include references to Lindner, sometimes even if Cornfield, the director, is unnamed. Some of the advertising for the film employs the line "Some men and some motion pictures just won't conform" and Kramer is referred to as a "nonconformist" in the press releases: all of which points to the assumed familiarity of the public with Lindner and his writings.

The road to the popularization of psychoanalytic theories was such that even by 1940, most of the audience would have been familiar with a number of psychoanalytic concepts, all of them rather simplified, including the idea of the unconscious (its expression in dreams and psychosomatic behavior), the importance of early childhood and of sexuality, the power of repression, and a basic continuum between normal and abnormal behaviors. In a survey of popular magazine articles on psychoanalysis, historian Nathan Hale (1995, pp.

76–77, 276) found that psychoanalysis was treated seriously, typically portraying analysts as both highly trained experts and ordinary Americans, while patients were people with whom readers could identify. These articles tended to downplay Freud's emphasis on sexuality and exaggerate the curative potential of analysis.[4]

In their narrative conventions, the five case histories in *The Fifty Minute Hour* resemble other popular depictions of psychoanalytic therapy. In their print and movie forms, therapeutic practices are inevitably successful, illustrating simplified Freudian concepts like the effectiveness of catharsis, and the interpretation of psychosomatic symptoms as caused by traumatic experiences. They illustrate the importance of dreams, which invariably reveal repressed oedipal guilt. They often feature psychodrama, the literal acting out of scenes from the patient's past between the doctor and the patient.[5] Popular psychoanalytic cases de-emphasize the complexities of the sexual and instead endorse rigidified male and female gender roles, jettisoning Freud's theory of bisexuality for a conviction that heterosexual object choice is the innate norm. In general, they reflect that as Freud's theories became more widespread in both popular and professional forms, they were increasingly reconciled with both conventional American moral and religious values and normative sexual practices.[6]

Anton comes into Lindner's care involuntarily, as he seeks help with blackout spells while imprisoned for sedition in the course of the war. As with the Communist who is the subject of another of the psychoanalytic "tales" in the same book, Lindner sees his patient as politically ill and will not consider him cured, despite the alleviation of symptoms, until he changes his beliefs. In keeping with the large-scale ambitions of the case history genre, Anton's case dramatizes in print and television form how an American suffering from anti-Semitism might be brought back into line with appropriate democratic male subjectivity, and in the filmed version, Kramer modifies the case to extend its pedagogical function to address white/black racism.

The significance of social problem films seeking a cure for racism, despite their simplicity, should not be underestimated. Anti-Semitism was not generally considered an undemocratic belief in American mainstream political culture at the time. Indeed, some of the rhetoric of the moral crusaders who sought to clean up the content of Hollywood films in the 1920s and 1930s routinely invoked anti-Semitism to claim that what they saw as the moral depravity of Hollywood films (and indeed Hollywood culture) could be blamed on the disproportionate number of Jews employed by the industry and in charge of studios.[7] With the rise of fascism in Europe and the escalation of the Nazi pogrom against Jews, wartime rhetoric enforcing sharp oppositions between fascism and democracy still did not routinely include a denunciation of anti-Semitism as fundamental to democracy. Wartime films tended not to focus on Nazi anti-Semitism, opting instead for general references to Nazi prejudice, or to ways in which the Nazi regime oppressed all citizens. This lack of attention to Nazi anti-Semitism could be a result of the censorship campaigns and the resulting efforts of the industry not to appear self-interested by focusing too much on Jews.

But at the end of the war, when the massive magnitude of Nazi atrocities became widely known, the notion that anti-Semitism is incompatible with democratic society did gain a greater foothold, as did liberal humanist antiprejudice rhetoric in general. Indeed the movement for the greater civil rights of African Americans also benefited from the mainstreaming of liberal antiprejudice rhetoric wrought in the opposition of fascism and democracy. The struggle against enduring American racism towards blacks indeed overshadowed discussions of American anti-Semitism, as the more pressing issue in American culture. Evidence of this newfound central rhetoric can be found in the first films in the social problem film cycle that emerged after World War II, which addressed American anti-Semitism: *Crossfire* (Dmytryk, 1947), and *Gentleman's Agreement* (Kazan, 1947). Shortly thereafter the social problem genre, like American political and social psychology and policy, turned to white racism against blacks, with *Home of the Brave, Lost Boundaries* (Werker, 1949), *Pinky* (Kazan, 1949), *Intruder in the Dust* (Brown, 1949), and *No Way Out* (Mankiewicz, 1950).[8]

Two of these films, *Home of the Brave* and *No Way Out*, are important precursors to the project that finally became *Pressure Point*—the former being the first Kramer production to deal with the psychology of racism, and the latter the breakthrough film for Poitier, which began the lifelong series of roles, including *Pressure Point*, in which he played restrained black men who endure the injustices of racism with patience and dignity. These roles represented the type of Hollywood liberal vision that held sway throughout the 1950s and into the early 1960s, even as they lagged behind the actual events of the Civil Rights movement.

*Home of the Brave,* like *Pressure Point,* is a case history, except that it deals with the cure of a black patient's racism-induced psychological problems. In the film, a vaguely Jewish psychiatrist treats a black soldier named Moss for the symptoms of partial amnesia and hysterical paralysis, from which he is, as was the norm for the popular genre, miraculously cured through the analysis.[9] The origin point of the patient's paralysis lies with the death of his friend and his feelings of guilt associated with it. His guilt derives from the fact that, because his friend nearly called him a "nigger" right before he was shot, he feels in some measure glad that his former friend and platoon mate is dead. The cure lies in Moss realizing that his gladness instead issues from the quite universal feeling of relief that it was not he who was killed. The issue of Moss's sense of betrayal at his friend's utterance is thus never adequately addressed. Instead, the conclusion holds out the liberal hope that, in fact, underneath it all, there are really no differences between men. As with other psychological theories of social problems, the progressive intentions of the antiracist sentiment are somewhat tempered by a deflection of attention away from an analysis of systematic racism both in the army and in white society at large by focusing instead on personal or universal solutions.

Much like the casting choice which would later alter the course of Lindner's case history, *Home of the Brave* is an adaptation of Arthur Laurents's (1946) play by the same name about anti-Semitism: here it is the patient whose identity is changed from Jewish to black. The perceived ease with which a black patient was substituted for a Jewish one reflects the focus of postwar studies on racism which either left "prejudice" unspecified, implying a generalizable phenomenon, or which were primarily concerned with black-white relations, but extrapolated them from studies of Nazi anti-Semitism.[10]

Psychoanalyst Franz Fanon (1967), working in colonial and postcolonial France contemporaneously with the upsurge of psychoanalytic work on the effects of racism in the United States, has addressed the specificity of white racism against blacks and how this differs from anti-Semitism. He has argued that to the prejudiced white man, the black man's threat is not intellectual, as the Jewish man's is, but rather sexual: "When a white man hates black men, is he not yielding to a feeling of impotence or of sexual inferiority? . . . In the case of the Jew, one thinks of money and its cognates. In that of the Negro, one thinks of sex" (pp. 159–160). A bit later, Fanon puts it most directly: "The Negro symbolizes the biological danger; the Jew the intellectual danger" (p. 165). Studies of prejudice in the United States, however, by and large did not make distinctions between different forms of racism, even as the categories "Jewish" and "black" were culturally rather rigidly separated at the time.

As part of the effort to generalize rather than to specify forms of prejudice, antiracists in the 1940s and 1950s endeavored to make race a more central issue by claiming that racism was not only something which detrimentally affected blacks, as in *Home of the Brave*, but was also something prejudiced white people "suffered from." As historian Ruth Feldstein puts it, "This dual focus helped to redefine racism as undemocratic and un-American. In particular, focusing on how prejudice hurt whites helped to make race relations a national problem, and issues of race more central to liberal discourse generally" (1998, p. 145). Lindner's case reflects this sort of strategy in that Anton's symptoms—his nightmares, blackout spells, and insomnia—are all painful manifestations caused by the same psychic factors as his political bigotry. When Kramer had his scriptwriters adapt this case in order to accommodate his casting of Poitier in the doctor's role, this focus on the suffering of the racist white man was retained, but was also significantly augmented by more overt efforts to claim equal levels of psychic damage done to black and white men in a racist society, in part by addressing black hatred of whites as a parallel to white hatred of blacks. Exaggerating tendencies already present in Lindner's case and echoing Kramer's strategy from *Home of the Brave*, *Pressure Point* makes masculinity the primary ground over which this drama unfolds. But it is ultimately a narrative logic that has difficulty reconciling the material and theoretical differences between black and white male subjectivity in its efforts to equalize the causes and experiences of racism.

In my analysis of the two most significant versions of this case history, Lindner's print version and Kramer's screen version, the alterations required to accommodate the change in the doctor's ethnicity (from Jewish to black) are the most revealing of the normative agendas embedded in the psychoanalytic case history genre and the textual failure of the liberal project of generalizing prejudice as a problem experienced similarly by everyone. The changes made to the script after Poitier was cast significantly modify the logic of the patient's analysis, mainly because the new script has difficulty fitting black masculinity into the same template into which Jewish masculinity was inserted in Lindner's original version.[11]

## Anti-Semitism, Racism, and Transference

The interpretive strategies of psychoanalysis scrutinize both the patient's past and the dynamics of the present dialogue between the analyst and analysand.[12] It is clearly the second narrative which is most affected by the casting choice of Poitier in the doctor's role. In Lindner's published version of the case, the Jewish doctor's and the anti-Semitic patient's mutual struggles over transference lay the groundwork for Lindner's theory of the relationship between sexuality and racism. Lindner discusses his own understandable disgust, as a Jew, for his patient and the patient's views, while the patient in turn wields his anti-Semitism at his Jewish doctor, merging it with his hatred for his own father. This connection is then exacerbated by the patient's sense of the doctor's disgust, making it parallel to his sense of rejection from his own father, and thereby preventing—for a time—the successful enabling of the process that will allow him to see the root of his actions: his identification with his father's brutality, covering over his homosexual desire for his father's affections.

Understanding the ambivalence of his hatred for his father is thus akin to Anton's reckoning with his racialist hatred for the Jewish doctor. By Lindner's account, the process for achieving this (and the crucial incident through which it is achieved) has everything to do with the correlation of paternal authority with the authority of the prison hierarchy, the doctor's profession, and ultimately the perception of Jewish alignment with science and knowledge. This latter component is clearly not available to the doctor as played by

Poitier, because science and knowledge are generally not associated with blackness. Racist conceptions of blackness instead associate it with irrationality, primitivism, and brute strength.

To keep the two versions of the story straight, as I go on to compare them further, I will use the name "Lindner" to designate the doctor in the print version, and "the Doctor" to designate him in the film, where he is unnamed. Likewise, I shall use "Anton" to designate the patient in the book, and "the Patient" for the film. This is in fact how they appear in the final version of the film's script, underscoring the ways in which the film aspires to present a general template for political psychobiography, with the patient serving as an all-purpose bigot rather than as any one particular case.

First I will discuss Lindner's formulation of the role of Jewishness in Anton's therapy. As noted above, Lindner's theory appears to coincide with Fanon's as to the source of anti-Semitism, an "intellectual" fear. But, as cultural historian Sander Gilman (1991, 1993) observes, this theory might as well mask a deeper cultural logic wherein sexual fears, akin to though not the same as those associated with blacks, are more primary than the theory allows. Gilman notes that Freud's own Jewishness is curiously absent from his theoretical formulations, racial difference being deflected instead onto sexual difference. Thus race, commonly thought of as neglected in Freud's work, actually resides at its core.[13] Gilman postulates that Freud's deflection represents his own efforts to negate the anti-Semitic alignment of Jewish men not with "money and its cognates," but with femininity and sexual deviance. By elevating sexual difference to premiere importance, Freud projected qualities formerly projected onto Jewish men onto the category of woman, while constructing men as figures of authority, as fathers or as the sons who want to become them.[14] Gilman argues that Freud was reacting against the nineteenth-century racialization of Jews and the development of a medical discourse of race in general—by reorienting explanations for human behavior toward a sexual system which affirmed the patriarchal order of things.

Lindner, trained in the psychoanalytic tradition, retains Freud's focus on sexual difference and sexuality, but reintroduces the question of the analyst's Jewishness—a move in keeping with the tenor of political psychology and its postwar focus on racial prejudice described above. Like Freud, however, Lindner does not acknowledge the anti-Semitic association of Jewish men with femininity, and instead overtly names the role of his Jewish maleness in the therapy as dependent on its alliance with scientific, governmental, and ultimately paternal authority. Some of this is conveyed by way of Lindner's description of the patient's brand of anti-Semitism, which identifies a powerful Jewish conspiracy as justification for his views. In the first meeting with the patient (before he actually enters analysis) Anton scoffs at the Jewish doctor for thinking his opinions are pathological, by way of the following exchange:

ANTON: A Jew psychologist! What the hell else can I expect from you!

LINDNER: You can go anytime you like. But I'd like to know why you think a Jew psychologist can't give a valid opinion on whether or not you're crazy.

ANTON: Because you Jews are all the same. You've wanted to get me for a long time. You put that crippled bastard into the White House and now you think you're in the saddle! Well, all right, so you got me in this joint and there's nothing I can do about it now. You can call me crazy and lock me up. That's just what a Jew psychologist would do—But . . . you can't keep me here forever![15]

This exchange of course reflects the patient's clichéd opinions about Jewish conspiracy, which Lindner subsequently tries to use as bait by saying that maybe he could conspire to have Anton committed on the basis of his connections to other "Jew psychologists." But while this sort of pervasive belief in the conspiracy of Jews typically hinges on a "parasitic" vision of Jewish power (achieved via manipulation and other such indirect "feminine" methods), Lindner ultimately elides this persistent subtext by instead insisting that the patient perceives Jewish power as paternal power. What Lindner's insistence misses then is the way that the "feminization" of Jewish power in anti-Semitic thought is actually a means of defending paternal power for whiteness, by associating Jewishness with the insidious corrosive feminine which undermines paternal authority through proximity or intimacy therewith.

Instead, the association of Jews with scientific and governmental authority and thus with paternal or patriarchal power is central to the logic of both Lindner's theory of the patient's transference and his own countertransference. The patient is meant to identify with the doctor as an authority figure and so to work out his neurosis with regard to his father. Lindner, meanwhile, is charged with seeing himself as a father figure in relation to this hostile wayward son, and indeed to see himself in him as well. The analysis then bears this out: an analytic breakthrough follows Anton's discovery that his blackout spells are precipitated by seeing a shadowy figure—identified first as his father, then as himself. He is subsequently able to understand the oedipal nature of his symptoms. In typical popular style, the revelation of the patient's never-verbalized hatred for his father (and the buried guilt expressed by his substitution of himself for the murdered body) miraculously alleviates the symptoms. Anton therefore believes himself cured, and stops coming to therapy. Lindner, however, does not think his patient is cured, and indeed he can neither comfortably occupy the father's role nor identify with him, because Anton still holds the same political beliefs. When asked to comment on his eligibility for parole, the doctor says he will not recommend Anton on these grounds. Thus ensues the conflict between analyst and analysand that occasions the larger connection that the book, and then the film, hopes to make between racism and the oedipal drama.

After some time, Lindner has occasion to encounter Anton again, when he fills in for a medical officer charged with screening prisoners requesting medical attention. Anton refuses to tell Lindner why he is there, then yells out in front of other inmates, "You know damn well what's wrong, you Jew bastard!" and storms out. Lindner recognizes that he has to do something about the breach of discipline by confronting Anton man to man—shedding his "Jewishness" and authority in the process. As Lindner confronts Anton in his cell, the patient initially doesn't respond, saying the doctor wouldn't be so brave if he weren't wearing a uniform. Lindner takes his insignia tabs off and says "I don't have any uniform on. There's just the two of us here and I won't call the guards. Will you apologize or do I have to make you?" (Lindner, 1966, pp. 147–148). After some hesitation, Anton backs down and apologizes—and says he wants to come and start therapy again.

Lindner's analysis of this confrontation stresses his role as a paternal symbol in that his refusal to recommend parole reminds Anton of rejections he suffered at the hands of his father. Lindner extrapolates from this to the patient's anti-Semitism:

> He wanted to strike back and I, as the living immediate representational figure of the childhood drama, was the aptest subject for his hostility. Further, through me, he could get at larger groups: the Jews, whom I represented, and the authoritarian world that restricted him, of which I was a symbol. My response to his challenge had impressed him not only because it indicated something personal about me, but because by it I had destroyed the illusory links and synapses by which he could connect the paternal image with the wide world: my individualization of the conflict had forced him to face the way he so mechanically ascribed his problems and frustrations to external groups or forces. (1966, p. 149)

In other words, by stripping himself of institutional authority, Lindner breaks the theorized link between father, Jews, and authority, so that the patient's fury can once again be directed where it belongs—at his father. This is also a breakthrough moment for Lindner, then, for he is only here able to assert direct masculine authority—in other words, truly to assume the father role.

The longer history of anti-Semitism—and in particular the variant which imagines a Jewish conspiracy—is not typically one which obtains from Jews embodying an "immediate representational figure" of paternal authority, however. Instead, the male Jewish conspirators and authority figures of anti-Semitic lore are, as Michael Rogin describes it, of a "feline, spidery, parasitic, sexually ambiguous character": in a word, feminine. Thus the diagnosis of anti-Semitism as an extension of oedipal desires for parricide are, as Rogin goes on to say, "partly a male Jewish wish for rational authority, a flight from the identification, by assimilating Jews as well as gentile anti-Semites, of the

'infected and infecting' Jewish man with the *ostjudisch,* black and female body"
(1996, p. 69). Lindner, after Freud, thus plays up his show of threatening masculinity as central to the drama of transference, even as he confesses to being
ill equipped for physical confrontation. Lindner's efforts to fortify Jewish masculinity with patriarchal authority thus sublimate the feminine. Tellingly,
then, when the doctor's racial identity is changed to that of an African American, some of this sublimation leaks through.

In the film, the black psychiatrist does not have the same recourse to
institutional power, and so the film script alters the initial exchange to reflect
instead Jewish advocacy for black advancement. The Patient says, "Now that
the Jews put that cripple in the White House you people think you've got it
made." When the Patient says he can't be kept there forever, the Doctor then
replies "Oh I don't know about that—I could team up with some Jew Psychiatrists and have you committed." Black male authority is thus highly medi-
ated—"parasitic" in a way that Jewish authority is not in both Lindner's and
the film's formulation. The Patient's originally scripted transference of hostility from his father to Jews is thereby uncomfortably extended to blacks. This
move not only leaves unexamined the specifics of white racism against blacks,
the "intellectual" versus "biological" danger in Fanon's terms, but ultimately
projects the textually sublimated "femininity" of anti-Semitism's images of
Jewish men onto black men instead.[16]

In the film, the Patient comes to the Doctor's office in order to solicit
his support for his parole hearing. The confrontation between the Doctor and
Patient takes place immediately, in the office, with no one else around. The
Patient demonstrates his unchanged political views, claiming that when the
Nazis take over the United States, "they won't have to make Negroes wear
armbands," clearly threatening that blacks, like Jews in Nazi Germany, will be
targeted for persecution and extermination. The Doctor demands an apology
for the Patient's aggression, and when he doesn't get it, he takes off his jacket
to encourage the Patient to fight him man-to-man. As in Lindner's version of
the confrontation, it is only at this point that the Patient backs down and
apologizes. As in Lindner's version, the Doctor offers an analysis, asserting
that when he denied the Patient his parole recommendation, the Patient felt
rejected, and hence the Doctor reminded him of his father. Again, because he
is a doctor and thus an authority figure, the patient is said to be unable to
strike out directly, and so attacked him "as a Negro."

This is the point where the parallel comes apart: the Doctor says that
when he took his jacket off he was "no longer a figure of authority, nor even a
Negro—just a man. And to one man it is easy to apologize." In Lindner's case,
as in the subsequent script versions prior to Poitier's casting, the act of taking
off the insignia is seen as disaligning the Jewish doctor from the conspiratorial stereotype he came in that moment to represent: taking off the insignia

thus individualizes the doctor, making it possible to get beyond the racial association. But when Poitier takes off his jacket, he is no less a black man than he was with his jacket on, since no similar stereotypical association of black men with institutional authority exists. If anything, taking off his jacket makes the black doctor even more of a threat, closer to the bodily danger that Fanon describes above. The black man's threat to the white man might echo the physically threatening father, but the echo is not dispelled by his taking off the doctor's coat (see Figure 2.1). Nor would the doctor's problem with countertransference be alleviated in such a convenient visible gesture.[17]

The relevance of this slip is symptomatically revealed in the press materials used to promote the film. Trying to build on Kramer's success with *The Defiant Ones* (Kramer, 1958), the posters for *Pressure Point* all feature virtually the same graphic scheme as those for the successful film: a white and black man facing off as if about to grapple in a physical fight. In *The Defiant Ones*,

FIGURE 2.1. In the first film depiction of a transracial treatment relationship, black prison psychiatrist-analyst Sidney Poitier angrily confronts racist patient Bobby Darin at the conclusion of their work together in this scene from *Pressure Point* (United Artists, 1962), produced by Stanley Kramer. Courtesy of the Wisconsin Center for Film and Theater Research.

Poitier plays against Tony Curtis, and the two are fugitive convicts, literally chained together and therefore dependent on each other for their escape. Physical conflict does occur in the course of the film, although the final message, like that of many liberal social problem films, is that conflict can be assuaged by kindness and generosity on the part of the oppressed minority. The conflict sells the film, while its dispersal in the course of the narrative assuages the genre's liberal message. In *Pressure Point*, the Doctor of course still exhibits exceptional patience and magnanimity (in keeping with Poitier's star persona) although this attitude seems more narratively warranted than in *The Defiant Ones* since it is part of his role as a doctor.

The ad campaign, however, by exploiting the saleability of racial conflict, in fact robs Poitier's character of his status. While viewers could already have come to expect Poitier's character to rise above this sort of brute facing off of black and white masculinity, it is precisely because of the excessive brutality accorded to black men that he must be portrayed as so exceptionally in control. The racist expectation of black male brutality in the ad campaign is exacerbated by promotional slogans like "This is what happens when White-hot Rage and Black Fury reach the Pressure Point!" which further equalizes the men's hostility toward one another, balancing white racism and black racism, transference and countertransference. The ad materials thus inadvertently reveal the unconscious of the scene that actually does appear in the film: a scene in which the Doctor's taking off his jacket if anything increases his signification as a potentially brutal, dangerous black man. No longer a doctor, he is what the racist image imagines, that is, a physical menace. The only reference in these promotional materials to the fact that Darin's character is a Nazi is that their bodies have been arranged in such a way as to suggest a swastika; that it is both of their bodies that comprise this emblem further underscores the parallelism for which liberal rhetoric and popular psychology in particular strive.

It is more likely the sexual nature of the unconscious menace that the brutal black man inspires, however, rather than anything as complex as trouble with countertransference, that the publicity materials bank on. This is further supported through the graphic placement of a white woman with a tic-tactoe board on her back, sometimes between the men, sometimes to the side. On some lobby cards, her image is accompanied by the sensational cry-out quote, "There are Some Men Worse Than Killers . . . Some Things Worse Than Murder!" The figure references a scene where the Patient recounts his sexual assault on a woman, one of the plot points where his failed heterosexuality helps to characterize the psychopathology of his politics. The publicity materials, however, leave the question as to who committed these "things worse than murder" unanswered. Given the long history of projecting the rape of white women onto black men, the ideological work done by this image again completely obscures the actual gender dynamics of the story. The white woman indeed plays a role as a marker of the Patient's (political) illness, but on the lobby card, she instead appears potentially as a figure to be fought over by the men, or else perhaps to be protected by the white man from the black man's sexual predation.[18] The publicity materials therefore make visible what is actually but a momentary leak in the logic of the film which otherwise allows Poitier the quiet dignity that his liberal role requires, revealing how the Doctor's blackness cannot be fully reconciled with the already somewhat phantasmatic paternal part originally written by and for a Jewish doctor.

The second consequence of this substitution builds in a seemingly contradictory fashion on the black man's perceived sexual menace: Poitier's position as a black man not only reflects a repressed image of black male brutality, but it is also feminized. Gilman (1985) is again useful here, in that he documents the ways in which, in the course of the nineteenth century, menacing black male hypersexuality became conceptually aligned with female hypersexuality.[19] Nineteenth-century scientific racism linked "inferior races" to women and children, who were thought to be closer to nature or their "animal" origins, even as women were being divided into hypersexual and largely asexual categories, based on both race and class. While surely submerged in most racist imagery of the sexually ominous black man, this connection by way of mental "primitivism" persists in the deep structure of racism and sexism as they are combined. It is also legible by a contrary logic in the liberal convolutions of *Pressure Point* as it attempts to extend Poitier's exceptional gentility to a strictly gendered psychoanalytic schema.

The genteel, feminized black man is a staple of the literary tradition of antiracism and abolitionism—the most celebrated example being Harriet Beecher Stowe's maternal Uncle Tom, who sacrifices himself for the lost child Little Eva in *Uncle Tom's Cabin* (1852). This image attempts to counteract the image of the hypersexualized (and thus hypermasculinized) black man, by aligning him with the nobler view of feminine nature. The same strategy might be read in several of Kramer's social problem films where black men (Moss in *Home of the Brave*, Poitier's character in *The Defiant Ones*) are portrayed as caring for their white companions: both films even similarly contain scenes where the black man cradles the dying white man in his arms. But this combination of tendencies—the unconscious conceptual association of black masculine hypersexuality with feminine hypersexuality, and the attempt to counter the image of black hypermasculinity with an image of the maternal black man—results in two converging iconographic codes that associate the black man with femininity and femininity with long-suffering selflessness and weakness.

The first instance of feminization in *Pressure Point* occurs after a scene in which the patient has recounted a scenario where his often drunk father brings home an equally drunk woman and torments his mother with his infidelity. The boy is imaged as struggling not to succumb to his mother's seduction, but he ultimately gives in to caring for her, stoically receiving her cloying embraces after the father has left. The Patient describes these moments as ones when he did not feel sorry for his mother, even as he appeared to soothe her. The Doctor consequently intervenes to ask why not, to which the Patient responds that he doesn't know. The Doctor presses forward, asking, "Don't you feel sorry for people who are weak?" which affords a topical segue to a discussion not of the Patient's feelings towards his mother, but rather of his racism toward blacks.

The Patient responds that he admires a weak man who competes. He says he thinks "Negroes are inferior" but admits, on the Doctor's prompting, that he admires them on the basis of their efforts to compete regardless of their inferiority. The Doctor then asks about Jews, whom the Patient says are more dangerous than blacks because they can pass for white and are smart. Jews are thus again aligned with authority, while African Americans are instead aligned with maternal weakness. As African American women are undertheorized in both psychoanalysis generally and in the film's version thereof, what this logical convolution reflects is the film's efforts to offer Poitier's persona as a substitution for the racist image of the brutal black man—but it does so by aligning him with the patient's mother. In the narrative logic of the case history genre, this move reflects the interrelation of two somewhat contradictory aims: while modeling the psychoanalytic cure as the production of a proper democratic subject, the film's makers reveal their own anxieties about race, gender, and sexuality.

Attempts to portray the Doctor's subjectivity thus also emphasize his feminine identification. Ironically, the female assault victim so ambiguously featured in the publicity materials plays a crucial role. The scene, which does not appear in the original book version nor in the television version, but rather was added in the course of rewriting the script for the cinema, portrays a past event in which the Patient and his rowdy buddies wreak havoc on a bar owner and his wife when they are told they can't have any more to drink. The scene is part of the larger effort to link the patient's sexual dysfunction (here, his cruelty toward women) with his political psychology, but inexplicably the doctor says in his omniscient voice-over, "That was the point at which I became frightened—I wasn't sure exactly what I was frightened of." This uncertainty seems odd—certainly there would be something frightening about sitting across from a rapist—but the doctor claims to feel an indescribable fright, clearly larger than his empathy for the woman who has been victimized and humiliated and indeed marked by her assailants, like the walls of the bar, with tictactoe boards all over her body and face. A more hopeful reading would be that he feels a sense of mutual devaluation in the political world. But in a film that, like psychoanalysis itself at the time, insists so much on gender as a defining characteristic, this progressive read is instead revealed to reflect the kind of feminization of black men that is typical of liberal approaches to racism. For it is mainly in this indescribable fear that Poitier reveals his trouble with countertransference—not in direct hostility, as Lindner does in the case history.

The cause of the Doctor's inchoate fright is explained in the film after the Patient has gone through his entire account of how he came to join the American Nazi Party. At the end of this account, the Doctor says that the Nazis have no hope of succeeding because everything they're driving for is a lie (meaning white superiority), to which the Patient responds that the United States is based on an even bigger lie: "All Men are Created Equal." The Patient says that as a black man, the Doctor should know how deep that lie runs. In another omniscient voice-over, the Doctor then states, "Right then and there I knew what I was frightened of"—meaning that the patient has a point: there is in fact a gap between the rhetoric and the reality of equality in the United States, which might prove the ground for his heinous party's success. Going back, however, to the point at which the Doctor's fright originally emerged, it is significant that he would begin to get an inkling of this problem after hearing of the Patient's cruelty toward women, and not be able to name what bothers him until later. While largely unexplored as a sentiment, the implication is that the Doctor not only empathizes with the woman but in the end unconsciously identifies with her as a sacrificial victim to the disturbed white male psyche. The tictactoe boards written on her body literalize their mutual belonging to marked identity categories, against which the white man defines himself. No such parallel identification occurs in any of the previous versions of the script, teleplay, or book, in which the doctor is Jewish, since the counterracist effort in those texts was to assure that Jewish men had direct access to paternal power.

Indeed the film's script complicates the black man's access to psychoanalytically understood power further, by excising references to the homosexual desire the boy Patient is theorized to feel towards his brutal and emotionally distant father in the book and teleplay. The film's final script instead makes the Patient's relationship to women more prominent in the profile, wherein he either idealizes or denigrates them.[20] Hence while in all versions of the case it is the mother who most influences the young man's capacity for psychosis and Nazism, further suppressing the psychic role of the father in the film results in the black man being more sexually ambiguous than the Jewish man was originally scripted to be.

*Pressure Point*'s variant of American popular psychoanalysis thus features a treatment relationship which foregrounds the reinforcement of patriarchal relations between men, doctor and patient, as a solution to racial prejudice. But the underlying anxieties that racial difference presents when doctor and patient are of different ethnic origin keep undermining the underlying liberal mantra of "We're all men here." What *Pressure Point* reveals then, upon analysis, is that the interracial treatment relationship is fraught with conflicting gender and sexual associations, and that the category "men" is not as representationally uniform as the popular theory of the treatment requires.

## NOTES

Earlier versions of this chapter appeared as "Pressure points: Political psychology, screen adaptation, and the management of racism in the case history genre" in *Camera Obscura, 45,* 71–113 and as chapter 5 of my book, *A Not So Foreign Affair: Fascism, Sexuality and the Cultural Rhetoric of American Democracy,* published in 2001 by Duke University Press.

1. Relevant studies include Bettelheim & Janowitz 1950; Erikson 1950; Adorno, Frenkel-Brunswik, Levinson, & Sanford 1950; Smith 1949; and Allport 1954.

2. In the television version, the patient is played by Robert Duvall, the analyst by Alexander Scourby.

3. See also Lindner 1944, 1946, and 1952. Lindner was trained by one of Freud's students, Theodor Reik.

4. Benjamin Spock, whose 1946 book *Baby and Child Care* virtually raised a generation of children, selling 19 million copies in 1965, was also a popularizing force: Spock attended a psychoanalytic institute in the 1930s (Spock 1968).

5. See Hale's chapter on popular psychoanalytic accounts (1995, especially p. 280).

6. This conservatism is indeed mirrored in the negative responses of American psychoanalytic professional organizations to the findings of the Kinsey reports (1948 and 1953) which asserted how highly varied American sexual practices statistically were, and their opposition to the depathologization of homosexuality, even as late as 1973, when it was removed from the APA list of mental disorders.

7. The industry established the Production Code Administration to appease these crusaders and quell the movement towards the establishment of a national censorship board. See Couvares 1996 and Black 1994 (p. 159).

8. Race relations and racial imagery have been central to the American film industry for the entire length of its history. See Rogin 1996; Cripps 1977; Bogle 1991; and Guerrero 1993.

9. For a fuller discussion of this film, see Wallace 1993.

10. Postwar examples include Warner et al. 1947; Sutherland 1952; and Karon 1958. The strong history of Jewish and black alliance in the fight against racism also forms a part of the historical milieu.

11. In a script marked "final draft" and dated September 13, 1961, the doctor is still Jewish. With the announcement in *Variety* two months later that Poitier had been cast in the role, the new series of significant revisions began, with a script close to the shooting script finally completed by March 3, 1962 (the film was released in September). The first version of the film script was written by S. Lee Pogostin, who also adapted Lindner's case for television. Hubert Cornfield, the director of the film, took over revisions after this first version. *Pressure Point* file, University of California, Los Angeles, Department of Special Collections-University Research Library.

12. For an extended discussion of the narrative nature of psychoanalysis, see Schafer 1981.

13. See also Boyarin 1996.

14. Included in this shift is that woman comes to signify castration and lack. As Ann Pellegrini notes in her discussion of this phenomenon in Freud's thinking, Jewish women are left out of the equation (1979, p. 4).

15. This is how the exchange appears in the first film script by S. Lee Pogostin, which is an accurate but more compact transcription of the exchange in Lindner (1966, p. 122). *Pressure Point* file, University of California, Los Angeles, Department of Special Collections-University Research Library.

16. The relevance of racial differences between patient and analyst is explored by later clinical work examining the particular dynamics of analytic situations like the one dramatized in *Pressure Point*. See Schachter & Butts 1971. For discussion and criticism of this article, see Altman 1995, p. 91.

17. To Kramer and Cornfield's credit, a new dimension is added to the patient/doctor conflict around the parole hearing confrontation, in that two new scenes, not present in any of the earlier versions, portray the Doctor in conflict with his professional peers who do not heed his judgment. The black doctor is thus not comfortably aligned with the professional establishment.

18. As Rogin writes,

Racial subordination formed the American nation, giving racist stereotypes an intractable material base resistant to the liberal wish for equality. Thus white predation was inverted and assigned to colored nature, most famously in the attributions to Indians of violence and lack of respect for the property of others, and in the assignment to black men of laziness and sexual desire for white women. (1996, p. 25)

19. Gilman delineates the connection especially between black hypersexuality and "deviant" female sexuality (lesbians, lower-class prostitutes) and cites the fixation of doctors and anthropologists on the supposedly "overdeveloped" genitalia of African women, lesbians, and prostitutes.

20. As in virtually all of psychoanalysis, homosexuality is seen in studies like *The Authoritarian Personality*, for instance, as part of a panoply of perversions of the "healthy" heterosexual norm—most of the others being heterosexual in nature (Adorno et al., 1950, p. 318).

REFERENCES

Adorno, T. W., Frenkel-Brunswik, E., Levinson, D. J., & Sanford, R. N. (1950). *The authoritarian personality.* New York: Harper and Brothers.

Allport, G. (1954). *The nature of prejudice.* Cambridge, MA: Addison-Wesley.

Altman, N. (1995). *The analyst in the inner city: Race, class, and culture through a psychoanalytic lens.* Hillsdale, NJ and London: Analytic Press.

Bettelheim, B., & Janowitz, M. (1950). *Dynamics of prejudice: A psychological and sociological study of veterans.* New York: Harper.

Black, G. D. (1994). *Hollywood censored: Morality codes, Catholics, and the movies.* Cambridge and New York: Cambridge University Press.

Bogle, D. (1991). *Toms, coons, mammies, mulattoes and bucks: An interpretative history of blacks in American films.* New York: Continuum.

Boyarin, D. (1996). *Unheroic conduct: The rise of heterosexuality and the invention of the Jewish man.* Berkeley: University of California Press.

Brown, C. (Director, Producer). (1949). *Intruder in the dust* [Motion picture]. United States. Metro- Goldwyn-Mayer (MGM).

Cornfield, H. (Director) & Kramer, S. (Producer). (1962). *Pressure point* [Motion picture]. United States. Larcas Productions.

Couvares, F. G. (1996). *Movie censorship and American culture.* Washington: Smithsonian Institution Press.

Cripps, T. (1977). *Slow fade to black: The Negro in American film.* Oxford: Oxford University Press.

Dmytryk, E. (Director) & Scott, A. (Producer). (1947). *Crossfire* [Motion picture]. United States. RKO Radio Pictures Inc.

Erikson, E. (1950). *Childhood and society.* New York: Norton.

Fanon, F. (1952/1967). *Black skins, white masks* (C. L. Markmann, Trans.). New York: Grove Press.

Feldstein, R. (1998). Antiracism and maternal failure in the 1940s and 1950s. In M. Ladd-Taylor & L. Umansky (Eds.), *"Bad" mothers: The politics of blame in twentieth-century America.* New York and London: New York University Press.

Gilman, S. L. (1985). *Difference and Pathology: Stereotypes of Sexuality, Race and Madness.* Ithaca, NY: Cornell University Press.

Gilman, S. L. (1991). *The Jew's body.* New York: Routledge.

Gilman, S. L. (1993). *Freud, race, and gender.* New York: Routledge.

Guerrero, E. (1993). *Framing blackness: The African American image in film.* Philadelphia: Temple University Press.

Hale, N., Jr. (1995). *The rise and crisis of psychoanalysis in the US: Freud and the Americans, 1917–1985.* New York and Oxford: Oxford University Press.

Karon, B. (1958). *The Negro personality: A rigorous investigation of the effects of culture.* New York: Springer.

Kazan, E. (Director) & Zanuck, D. (Producer). (1947). *Gentleman's agreement* [Motion picture]. United States. 20th Century Fox.

Kazan, E. (Director) & Zanuck, D. (Producer). (1949). *Pinky* [Motion picture]. United States. 20th Century Fox.

Kramer, S. (Director, Producer). (1958). *The defiant ones* [Motion picture]. United-States. Curtleigh Productions Inc.

Laurents, A. (1946). *Home of the Brave.* New York: Random House.

Lindner, R. (1944) *Rebel without a cause . . . the hypnoanalysis of a criminal psychopath.* New York: Grune and Stratton.

Lindner, R. (1946). *Stone walls and men.* New York: Odyssey Press.

Lindner, R. (1952). *Prescription for rebellion.* New York: Rinehart.

Lindner, R. (1956). *Must you conform?* New York: Rinehart.

Lindner, R. (1966). *The fifty-minute hour: A collection of true psychoanalytic tales.* (20th ed.) New York, Toronto, and London: Bantam Books.

Mankeiwicz, J. (Director) & Zanuck, D. (Producer). (1950). *No way out* [Motion picture]. United States. 20th Century Fox.

Pellegrini, A. (1997). *Performance anxieties: Staging psychoanalysis, staging race.* New York: Routledge.

Robson, M. (Director) & Kramer, S. (Producer). (1949). *Home of the brave* [Motion picture]. United States. Screen Plays Corp.

Rogin, M. (1996). *Blackface, white noise.* Berkeley: University of California Press.

Schachter, J., & Butts, H. (1971) Transference and countertransference in inter-racial analyses. *Journal of the American Psychoanalytic Association, 16,* 792–808.

Schafer, R. (1981). Narration in the psychoanalytic dialogue. In W. J. T. Mitchell (Ed.), *On narrative.* Chicago: University of Chicago Press, 1981.

Slane, A. (2001) *A not so foreign affair: Fascism, sexuality and the cultural rhetoric of American democracy.* Durham, NC: Duke University Press.

Slane, A. (2001). Pressure points: Political psychology, screen adaptation, and the management of racism in the case history genre. *Camera Obscura, 45,* 71–113.

Smith, L. (1949). *Killers of the Dream.* New York: Norton.

Spock, B. (1968). *Baby and child care.* New York: Hawthorn Books.

Stowe, H. (1852). *Uncle Tom's cabin.* Boston: J. P. Jewett.

Sutherland, R. L. (1952). *Color, class and personality.* Washington, DC: American Council on Education.

Wallace, M. (1993). Race, gender and psychoanalysis in forties film: *Lost boundaries, home of the brave,* and *The quiet one.* In M. Diawara (Ed.), *Black American cinema* (pp. 257–271). New York: Routledge.

Warner, W. L. et al. (1947). *Color and human nature: Negro personality development in a northern city.* Washington, DC: American Council on Education.

Werker, A. (Director) & De Rochemont, L. (Producer). (1949). *Lost boundaries* [Motion Picture]. United States. Louis De Rochemont Associates.

# 3

Women in Psychotherapy on Film

*Shades of Scarlett Conquering*

MARILYN CHARLES

Long afterward, Oedipus, old and blinded, walked the roads. He
smelled a familiar smell. It was the Sphinx. Oedipus said, "I want
to ask you one question. Why didn't I recognize my mother?" "You
gave the wrong answer," said the Sphinx. "But that was what made
everything possible," said Oedipus. "No," she said. "When I asked,
What walks on four legs in the morning, two at noon, and three
in the evening, you answered, Man. You didn't say anything about
woman." "When you say Man," said Oedipus, "you include women
too. Everyone knows that." She said, "That's what you think."
—Muriel Rukeyser, Myth

When we buy our ticket to the movies, we're not just buying a few hours'
entertainment. We are also, for that interim, buying a worldview and borrow-
ing an identity—trying it on for size. However, this is not merely a conscious
act, nor one we shed entirely with the final credits. There are many layers of
absorption into the film, and of identification with the camera's gaze and with
the characters being portrayed. On the screen we encounter societal strictures,
such as depictions of what it means to "be crazy" or to "find help." Explo-
rations of the workings of the human mind on the screen offer opportunities
for catharsis, but also blur the very problems they purport to explore (Wood,

67

1975). Depictions of women in psychotherapy on film have been complicated by the tendency to view woman as subject and to depict health in terms of societal roles rather than personal development. More recent films, however, show an auspicious shift in emphasis from "the Problem of Women" to "women's problems" (Walker, 1993).

In this chapter, I will be focusing on women as receivers rather than purveyors of therapy, the latter having been well covered by Gabbard and Gabbard in their 1987 volume *Psychiatry and the Cinema*. Further, I focus on characters in films that are all stylistically realistic. The impression of realism can be particularly dangerous because the technology lends itself so directly to this illusion. There is a confusion inherent in the sleight of hand engendered by this medium, through which illusion and truth can become hopelessly confounded (Johnston, 1977).

The cinema has become a forceful purveyor of cultural myths, implicitly promoting images (as icon or symbolic equation, and therefore as static). In contrast, symbols tend to be more fluid, their meanings changing over time in line with prevailing ideologies (Barthes, 1971). Johnston writes:

> Myth, then, as a form of speech or discourse, represents the major means in which women have been used in the cinema: myth transmits and transforms the ideology of sexism and renders it invisible—when it is made visible it evaporates—and therefore natural. (1977, p. 409)

Combating this process—making the invisible visible—has become a common theme in cinematic works about women in psychotherapy, much as it is an integral part of the therapeutic process itself.

The attempt to make what has been invisible manifest becomes an important part of the search for self, a recurrent theme in many movies in which the topic of women in psychotherapy is addressed. For example, after a traumatic incident, Esther, the main character in *The Bell Jar* (Peerce, 1979), desperately affirms selfhood, screaming "I am, I am, I am" against the impending dissolution of self that had been an integral part of her previous breakdown. In this film, it is the therapist's arms into which she falls and finds a containing environment. This theme becomes even more explicit in *Girl, Interrupted* (Mangold, 1999). In this film, the container has a somewhat harsher form: there will be no "loving arms" to sustain Susanna. She is told—in no uncertain terms—that she must become more proactive in seeking self-understanding. According to this dictum, there are no magic "cures," but only movements towards integrity in living—in Winnicott's (1971) terms, "becoming."

As a societal structure, psychotherapy is embedded in prevailing myths that define health and normalcy. As we look at how madness and psychotherapy are portrayed in film, we can trace important threads regarding presumptions of meaning in women's discourse. Without these presumptions of meaning, there is no therapy. Just as a dream makes no sense without understanding the individual's associations to the various parts of the dream, so, too, the individual's experience makes no sense unless we are able to track whatever sense there might be by listening with great absorption to what is being told. The therapist, in actuality, is entrusted with a life: with preserving and affirming the meanings of it, so that the patient might better understand and elaborate these meanings. As we analyze portrayals of this process in film, we can see how societal views can skew and obfuscate meanings, thereby impeding this fundamental task of understanding.

We begin to see a feminist agenda emerging in the Hollywood films of the 1970s, in such works as *Diary of a Mad Housewife* (Perry, 1970), *A Woman Under the Influence* (Cassavetes, 1974), and *An Unmarried Woman* (Mazursky, 1978). Each of these films brings into question the extent to which the woman's dis-ease is a function of disability or of growth. In *An Unmarried Woman*, for example, the therapeutic dialogue offers an invitation to live as an autonomous, pleasure-seeking individual, a far cry from earlier films, such as *The Snake Pit* (Litvak, 1948), in which cure was commensurate with abdicating the autonomous self and self-interest for the roles of wife and mother.

The film *An Unmarried Woman* brings up the further issue of the woman's pleasure as a legitimate end. In many previous films, the erotic aspect of the woman is vilified, relegated to the "bad" aspects of self in such films as *The Three Faces of Eve* (Johnson, 1957). However, the answers given in films such as *An Unmarried Woman*, which are written by men and display their fantasies about women, can also be called into question. For example, Paul Mazursky, the director of *An Unmarried Woman*, says, "I wanted to get inside a woman's head. . . . The only thing I could have done was to get a woman to help me write it. I thought about that for a while, but in the end I think it worked out" (quoted in R. Rich, 1994, p. 41). This failure to enter into a dialogue with those depicted as other becomes one more layer in the cinematic sleight of hand in which realism purports to convey truth through a vehicle that subsists on illusion. Without this dialogue, the filmmaker runs the risk of further obfuscating fantasy and reality. Ruby Rich suggests that too often, film presents "male fantasies of women—men's projections of themselves and their fears onto female characters" (1994, p. 41).

This can be an interesting depiction in and of itself, as long as we are clear as to what we are watching. However, in film, truth and illusion are subtly interwoven and it can be difficult to find sufficient perspective from which to ground oneself. Psychoanalytic theory has provided one means for deconstructing some of these cinematic "realities." Images are particularly apt vehicles for purveying value through condensations of meaning. For example, in

*The Snake Pit,* Virginia's madness is linked to her unkempt appearance: that is one of the ways in which the spectator is cued in to the extent of her disability. This type of equivalence has been termed a "symbolic equation" (Klein, 1930/1981; Segal, 1957), in which no distinction is made between the symbol and that which is symbolized. Cinema can also provide a means for highlighting implicit myths, thereby inviting us to consider alternative views or perspectives (Charles, 2003a). In *The Bell Jar,* for example, Esther breaks into our presumptions when she tells her boyfriend she is not willing to become a symbol of his dream. She is not willing to fulfill his expectations at the price of her own, leaving her own perceived needs to be indulged as asides within the larger context of his social agenda. Esther is determined to pursue her own ends, whatever the price.

Taken together, these movies underscore what a powerful force films can be for the promulgation of societal values. Because we are able to enter into the drama and experience ourselves (to some extent) as the subject within, movies become a part of our experienced reality, whether or not we are aware of their impact. Louise Bernikow (1980), for example, speaks of the tremendous impact that movies have had upon her, the most memorable of which is *Cinderella:* "I carry her story with me for the rest of my life. It is a story about women alone together and they are each other's enemies" (p. 18). For Bernikow this is a powerful lesson: "The echoes of 'Cinderella' . . . are about how awful women are to each other. The girl on screen . . . needs to be saved. A man will come and save her. . . . Women will not save her; they will thwart her" (p. 18).

## WOMEN IN FILM: THE SILENT SUBJECT

> Whatever is unnamed, undepicted in images, whatever is omitted from biography, censored in collections of letters, whatever is misnamed as something else, made difficult-to-come-by, whatever is buried in the memory by the collapse of meaning under an inadequate or lying language—this will become, not merely unspoken, but unspeakable.
>
> —Adrienne Rich, "It Is the Lesbian in Us,"
> *On Lies, Secrets, and Silence: Selected Prose 1966–1978*

History has been contaminated by a confusion between *humanity,* which includes both men and women, and *mankind,* which excludes womankind, thereby creating woman as "difference," as "other." Women have often been treated as objects and systematically excluded from many of the structures by which society is ordered and regulated (Penfold & Walker, 1983), leaving the feminine the unspoken, undervalued voice. This lack permeates all our cultural endeavors and yet has in many ways been invisible, depending on the prevailing cultural myths of the time. Woman's relationship with purveyors of mental health has been particularly problematic, because authoritative structures and institutions have been depicted as saving one from one's self, thereby trading external restraints for a new dogma of reward and punishment delivered by an internalized authority (Foucault, 1965). In this way, the goals of the self are only valued insofar as they support the goals of the system in power. To the extent that they do not, they become devalued and suspect, unspoken and unspeakable.

The history of the cinema has been punctuated by portrayals of women as passive objects caught in the clutches of an impersonal and demeaning therapeutic system or, alternatively, as misguided objects being helped towards the right path by a representative of a patriarchal system. The male voice and gaze have become privileged, making it difficult to understand the woman's story from her own frame of reference. Even when the female perspective is given, it is easily invalidated because it has no power (Kaplan, 1983). For example, in *Diary of a Mad Housewife*, Tina's reality is continually overridden, derided, or ignored by her husband.

In this film, we see the dilemma of the woman who will not be saved by either a woman or a man, but rather must learn to save herself. Therapy is not seen as helpful, but rather as one more vehicle for victimization. Perry gives us a glimpse of a woman caught between her own view of reality and the opposing views that are promulgated by others. The film takes place in the household of an upwardly mobile New York lawyer, Jonathan, who expects his wife, Tina, to be the perfect wife and mother. As Jonathan's needs escalate beyond his means, he ultimately brings the family to the brink of financial ruin. This creates an untenable tension between Tina's needs and those of the extremely narcissistic men with whom she finds herself involved. Even her daughters take sides against Tina in this drama, rather than running the risk of becoming aligned and identified with their demeaned and diminished mother.

The movie ends with Jonathan telling Tina that he has lost everything in his attempts to pull himself up the social ladder. "You're a fine human being, Tina," he concludes. "No, I'm not" she replies, "I'm just a human being." In keeping with the depiction of a woman at odds with other people's realities, in the final scenes we see Tina in group therapy, trying to explain her point of view as group members alternatively heckle her or side with her in the service of their own interests. No one really seems to hear her, or to care to. Even the therapist is silent and invisible, thereby implicitly colluding with the ongoing attacks.

In this film, we see how Tina becomes caught in the tension between her own view of reality and the opposing views that are promulgated by others. Meanings are derived within the larger social context, which defines what it means to adapt to or resist the prevailing myths of the time. In this way, even attempts to portray women as subjects become constrained by a social context that invalidates the truth of this very subjectivity. In a world in which the woman's voice is not valued, her story becomes incomprehensible when seen from her own perspective, because the very truths upon which society is structured and values are based are built upon images of the past that did not include her (Penfold & Walker, 1983). Paradoxically, these truths are often presented as explanations of "the natural order of things." This confusion between cause and effect obscures important distinctions between what is versus what must or might be, as the existence and functions of these structures go unquestioned, thereby providing a further rationale for the "way things are."

## CINEMA AND PSYCHOANALYSIS

> Hysteria was a theatre of femininity and revolt, a fantastic spectacle which delighted the onlookers at the Salpêtrière. What they saw were bodies in crisis. What they refused to see were women bound by constraints, wrapped in veils, carefully kept distant, pushed to the side of history and change; nullified; kept out of the way, at the edge of history.
>
> —Mindy Faber in *Delirium*

There has been an affinity between cinema and psychoanalysis that speaks in part to their concurrent developments historically, but also to fundamental processes they share, such as projection, identification, and reenactment. There are also similarities between film and dreams, such that each lends itself well to interpretive processes (Mayne, 1994). Projection may be the most salient similarity. In the cinema, just as in our everyday interpersonal relations, we are projecting images upon a screen. In daily life, this process is called "transference." To some extent, it is never truly the other we see, but only the other filtered through our preconceptions. In kind, at the cinema, we are not alone in filtering the reality given to us. This reality is itself prefiltered by the director, even when the medium is the documentary and therefore ostensibly objective or somehow more real (Renov, 1999).

These realities are also filtered in terms of our disidentifications. In psychoanalytic terms, the process of projective identification involves seeing in the other what we are loathe to acknowledge in ourselves. We project unacceptable aspects of ourselves onto the other as a way of getting rid of them. However, in so doing, we also provide an opportunity for better understanding and thereby making peace with the vilified qualities. The cinema provides a perfect opportunity for identifying qualities in the other that we might be reluctant to discover in ourselves. These qualities may either remain rejected—as in the villain whose annihilation we can enjoy—or may be processed in such a way as to make them more "digestible"—as in the ostensible villain who becomes humanized during the course of the film.

Psychoanalytic theory has been used as a tool for understanding many aspects of film. It has been used by feminists to explore the patriarchal nature of ideas about sexual difference and identity, the extent to which these differences are culturally derived (Mitchell, 1974), and how these views are reinforced through filmic representations (Walker, 1994). In addition, feminists have turned psychoanalytic thinking upon itself, to look at ways in which femininity has become problematized, as "the gaps and lacunae within (primarily Freudian) psychoanalytic theory become the site of the (missing) formulations of feminine psychic structures" (Walker, p. 83).

Ironically, by turning to analytic theory as a way of exploring these concerns, feminists have undermined their own efforts at understanding. Both Freud and Lacan posit woman as lack, as not-male. Emendations of analytic theory attempt to address this dilemma by bringing in more positive views of woman and addressing issues related to social context. For example, Benjamin (1998) argues the importance of moving beyond the artificial oppositions implied in the "social versus biological" and "male versus female" dichotomies. And yet, there is an essential paradox in that "the critique of gender complimentarity . . . at once upsets the oppositional categories of femininity and masculinity while recognizing that these positions inescapably organize experience" (Benjamin, p. 37).

It has been difficult for women to identify unambivalently with their representations on the screen. These representations have tended to be dichotomized into part images of the good (desexualized/compliant) versus the bad (sexualized/willful) woman. Identification may be particularly problematic for the woman spectator (de Lauretis, 1984). It has been defined in psychoanalytic terms as a process of assimilation, whereby attributes of the other are transformed and adapted into aspects of self, such that "it is by means of a series of identifications that the personality is constituted and specified" (Laplanche & Pontalis, 1973, p. 203). Cinematic identifications can become an important source of intrapersonal meanings as to what constitutes self versus not-self in the social world. For example, Alex, an African American woman depicted in the documentary *We Don't Live Under Normal Conditions* (Collins, 2000), laments her exclusion from the representations of culture that fail to mirror her image back to her. What she sees, instead, are myriad representations of not-self: she sees only whiteness reflected back in the cultural mirror. She is lost in a world in which she cannot see herself.

*Marilyn Charles*

MELODRAMA: INTERPLAYS OF ABSORPTION AND VISIBILITY

But there are times—perhaps this is one of them—
when we have to take ourselves more seriously or die;
when we have to pull back from the incantations,
rhythms we've moved to thoughtlessly . . .
No one who survives to speak
new language has avoided this
            —Adrienne Rich, "Transcendental Etude"

Many of the Hollywood films focusing on women in psychotherapy could be seen to fall under the rubric of the "melodrama" (defined in the Oxford Dictionary as "a sensational dramatic piece with crude appeals to the emotions and usu. a happy ending"). This term speaks to an expressiveness of form that makes "visible what is otherwise absent and ineffable in the narrative, by words alone" (Copjec, 1999, p. 250). Although the term "women's film" has tended to carry a pejorative tone, the conflicts inherent within these films are neither trivial nor superficial (Haskell, 1974), but rather explore the inherent tensions between self and other so intrinsic to women's experiences of being in the world. This devaluation speaks to a general tendency to valorize autonomy over interdependence in this culture.

Males are more often depicted as the protagonist or active voice. Even in those films in which the focus is on a female protagonist, our notions of gender and possibility color the narrative, which tends to be "patterned on a journey, whether inward or outward, whose possible outcomes are those outlined by Freud's mythical story of femininity" (de Lauretis, 1984, p. 139). These outcomes have to do with being "found" as the object of desire, rather than with becoming the subject of one's own desiring. Freud's (1931/1971, 1933/1971) notions of the ultimate goal of the woman as regards her own femininity are notably obscure, leaving the image of the woman (rather than the woman herself) the subject of the narrative. This entanglement seems to hold true even in those films that have been called variously "melodrama" or "women's films."

Joni Mitchell, in a 1975 song titled "Shades of Scarlett Conquering," recounts the dilemma of the woman who is so caught by her fictitious screen presence that she is unable to engage in real life relationships. We are invited into a dark world in which all might be possible, but the stories related there color our expectations of self and other. Fairy tales are promoted in which one is won because one is the object of someone else's desire. It is much more difficult to envision oneself as hero, and the price for pulling against the grain is often quite high. Think, for example, of Thelma and Louise, in the film of the same name (Scott, 1991), who band together against all odds and are left with the choice of a glorious death or ignominious defeat; or of actress Frances

Farmer, so determined to be herself in a world in which this has been defined as anathema. As we look at depictions of women in psychotherapy, we are taking in, at many levels, what it means to be a woman; what it means to be considered "mad"; what it means to be helped by another; and the various prices of accepting or not accepting that help.

The successful film absorbs us: it holds us in its thrall; we are captured by whatever is being depicted. Absorption is a term used by Diderot (1751) to describe a process in which "one gives oneself up to it with all one's thought without allowing oneself the least distraction" (in Fried, 1980, p. 184), so that one is enveloped, swept away, and even disappears through incorporation into something else. This is a very apt description of the identificatory process within the world of film, in which the viewer is invited in, as spectator and participant within the drama unfolding. Through this process, the beholder is both inside and outside the film, through identifications with the camera and director and with the characters being represented. However, the process of absorption also entails our disappearance: As we suspend disbelief and are carried into the drama, we disappear, to some extent, as a critical eye. As this happens, we are more susceptible to also absorbing ostensible realities being depicted within the film.

This process creates an odd sleight of hand, in which private and public selves become confounded, as we come to identify with, and thereby incorporate, dicta prescribing how one *should* be. According to Copjec (1999), the price of this universality is the annihilation of the particular, as the individual surrenders "the private kernel of his being, his *absolute* particularity, in order to enter a social reality in which he [is] comparable to others" (p. 251). Safety entails not being too different. This dichotomy—in which one's individuality is prized and privileged but also suspect—creates an illusion of a lack of difference that makes it difficult to speak about real differences. The crucial issue becomes to be able to affirm one's innermost self sufficiently that the pursuit of recognition does not result in inevitable misrecognitions.

This pursuit of recognition may be different for men and for women. Copjec (1999) suggests that whereas for the man the issue is of a lack, for the woman the issue is of an absence of lack. She sees this absence of lack as an essential aspect of melodrama, which "constructs not a diegetic reality in which one manages to gesture, however covertly, toward what one is forbidden to say, but . . . instead an *indeterminate* reality, one about which nothing definite can be said" (p. 258). This is so because the excess is not due to a prohibition, but rather to a failure to prohibit: a failure to close itself off. There is a lack of the type of definition that would prescribe specific boundaries (rather than a prohibition or exclusion based upon those boundaries) that makes it difficult to speak to important truths.

Copjec suggests that it is "because something has *not* been prohibited, has *not* been excluded from melodrama that it seems to comport an excess, an unspecifiable 'more,' something that reanimates it" (1999, p. 258). Paradoxically, melodrama addresses symbolic failure by attempting to make up for the lack causing it, thereby also affirming the lack. In this way, the melodrama, if we are able to embrace it, offers up to us an essential truth. Our dilemma comes in the difficulties we encounter in tolerating and being able to value this particular means of discovery.

Copjec (1999) describes this relationship with social reality as an hysterical one (defined in Lacan's terms as "the desire to have an unsatisfied desire" [1977a, p. 257]), in which imaginary resolutions are constructed. These resolutions are inherently fragile and merely mark the dilemma, rather than bringing resolution: "The hysterical solution intends not to *erase* the hysteric so much as to *mark her erasure* in order to hold open the possibility of some eventual recognition of her" (Copjec, 1999, p. 265). The misrecognition is a crucial aspect of this resolution, reflecting the essential plight of the hysteric. In presuming her own unacceptability, she affirms her own misconstruction through her misrecognition of self. Erasure marks the willful blindness of one who cannot be known without being disowned, thereby retaining the hope that one might be "other": one might be "more."

This type of absence is the essence of melodrama: that which is seen by the audience remains unseen by the characters. There is an essential misrecognition that guides the construction of the story. The melodrama affirms that there is more than can be seen. In this way, the dilemma of the characters mirrors our dilemma as humans. We are inevitably struggling towards an understanding that will remain, to some extent, beyond our comprehension. This "something more" has been described by Kant (1974) as the "absolute all": that which is beyond any given instantiation and yet, paradoxically, can only be made visible through that particular instantiation. Copjec (1999) links this idea to Lacan's depiction of love as going beyond any actual expression, so that it "can be posited only in that beyond, where, at first, it renounces its object" (Lacan, 1977b, p. 276). Copjec goes on to say,

> If Lacan chooses to retain the negation, to say as he does that in love 'something does not stop writing itself,' this is because negation and repetition are the very marks of the symbolic. Lacan's formulation means, then, that in love some part of the real is linked to the signifier, some part of the real is formalized. (p. 269)

This highlights the dilemma for the absent, unarticulated woman: it is always the love of the other that promises to save her.

In Lacan's terms, the absolute can only be approached in context, thereby vivifying that which is present and demarcating that which is not. This solution, the demarcation of erasure seen repeatedly in tales of the "madness" of women, would seem to represent an attempt to bring the real into the current social context, where it can resonate with the sensibilities of others and where it or one might be recognized. In this way, it may also be seen as a resolution to the dilemma posited by Freud in terms of the difficulty of locating the woman's desire and thereby positioning the woman as subject.

## FROM A DIFFERENT PERSPECTIVE: FILMS BY WOMEN

> To the person in the bell jar—blank and stopped as a dead baby—
> the world is a bad dream. I asked her if I would survive. She said
> yes. And with that, she at once freed me and condemned me back
> to life. If I am the arrow, I cannot fly through darkness.
> —Esther in *The Bell Jar*

Perhaps part of the difficulty in positioning the woman as subject in films about women in psychotherapy is that so few of these films have been made by women.[1] Those that do exist tend to be independent films with minimal public distribution (with notable exceptions, such as Jane Campion's *Angel at My Table* [1989]). Many of these are documentaries or biographies in which the woman's voice comes to carry an authority that seems to privilege the communication. In the documentary, most particularly, we are offered an additional illusion of truth, in that the speakers speak to us directly, ostensibly in their own voices. Citron has noted that "the autobiographical act is historically significant for women, and all others, who have traditionally lacked either a voice or a public forum for their speaking" (1999, p. 272). However, it is also as much of a motivated act as any other, so that the very terms "nonfiction" and "documentary" can obscure the fact that a point of view is being expressed in a medium that often uses intensity as a means for weighting the conviction of its message.

This line is particularly difficult to define in the biographical film, which structures itself around a real life without necessarily following the facts of it. Our willingness to believe in the constructed reality amplifies the illusion of truth (Charles, 2003b). This type of film has been one place where we see some of the impact of feminism and the feminine voice upon screen images. For example, in *Girl, Interrupted* (see Figure 3.1), the knight on the white horse is not the solution; the woman must save herself, in her own way. This film was directed by a man, but written largely by women from a woman's own experience (Kaysen, 1993).

The film begins with a view of Susanna Kaysen holding her friend Lisa in her arms after speaking angry truths. This shot presages the inherent dilemma of the characters in the film: can they survive confronting themselves, or will they break under the harsh light of "truth"? The screen image

FIGURE 3.1. Susanna (Winona Ryder) and her friend Lisa (Angelina Jolie) struggle with what it means to be female and "crazy" in a private psychiatric setting in this scene from *Girl, Interrupted* (Columbia Tri-Star, 2000). Courtesy of the Museum of Modern Art/Film Stills Archive.

mirrors the music playing in the background, which speaks about memories captured, like photographs. Then we hear Susanna's voice, inviting us to consider the memories that have culminated in this image. "Have you ever confused a dream with life?" Susanna wonders, "or thought your dream moving while sitting still? Maybe I was just crazy. Maybe it was the '60s. Or maybe I was just a girl, interrupted." The film chronicles then, in retrospect, Susanna's inability to move forward with her life, her suicide attempt, and her subsequent hospitalization at a private mental health facility. It also chronicles her ultimate deidealization of her friend, Lisa, whose own confrontations with life's exigencies shatter the self, rather than the illusion.

Susanna is initially hospitalized by a retired psychiatrist, who is also her father's friend. "You need a rest"; he says, "you're hurting everyone around you." This sets up an important theme in the movie: In whose interest are the participants acting? Much like her parents, Susanna's doctors do not seem to value her own perceived needs or desires, nor to recognize her as an autonomous human being. Her friends' intentions come into question, as well. Her boyfriend, Toby, plots her escape to ease his own isolation and Lisa calls her by a previous patient's name, apparently oblivious to the particulars of Susanna's being. Is she valued for herself or as one more self-object to be used in the service of the other's needs? Even Susanna's own agenda is called into question in a confrontation with a nurse on the ward. Susanna wants to take refuge in her "craziness," but the nurse admonishes, "You're not crazy. . . . You're a lazy, self-indulgent little girl who is driving yourself crazy. . . . You're just throwing it away."

In an attempt to better understand where she is caught, Susanna looks up her diagnosis in a textbook. It is an ominous sounding term: "borderline personality disorder." "'Instability of self-image, relationships, and mood,'" she reads, "uncertainty about goals; impulsive in activities that are self-damaging, such as casual sex. . . . Social contrariness and a general pessimistic attitude are often observed.' Well, that's me," she sighs. "That's everybody," replies Lisa.

There is a crucial transition in the film when Susanna begins to see a new therapist who engages with her more directly. When Susanna describes herself as ambivalent, the psychiatrist confronts her:

> "The word suggests that you are torn between two opposing courses of action."
>
> "Will I stay or will I go?"
>
> "Am I sane or am I crazy?"
>
> "Those aren't courses of action," objects Susanna.
>
> "They can be, dear, for some."
>
> "Well then, it's the wrong word."
>
> "No, I think it's perfect. . . . It's a very big question you're faced with, Susanna, the choice of your life. How much will you indulge in your flaws?

What are your flaws? Are they flaws? If you indulge in them, will you commit
yourself to hospital for life? Big questions. Big decisions. Not surprising you
profess carelessness about them."

Shaken after finding a friend dead at her own hands, Susanna observes:

When you don't want to feel, death can seem like a dream. But seeing death,
really seeing it, makes dreaming about it fucking ridiculous. Maybe there's a
moment growing up when something peels back. . . . All I know is I began to
feel things again. Crazy, sane, stupid: whatever I was, I knew there was only one
way back to the world and that was to use the place, to talk. . . . Was I ever crazy?
Maybe life is. . . . Crazy isn't being broken or swallowing a dark secret. It's you
or me, amplified.

For Susanna, her brush with "craziness" became an opportunity to find herself
and to make decisions about what she wanted her life to be. She was able to
do this within the context of a relatively benign institution, with a therapist
who was able to help her to define her own needs and values. Not everyone is
so lucky: this institution is in striking contrast to those portrayed in films such
as *Frances* (Clifford, 1982) or *Angel at My Table* (Campion, 1989).

The film *Angel at My Table* also highlights the dilemma of positioning
the woman as subject in her own life narrative. This film chronicles the life of
Janet Frame, a gifted writer who grew up in poverty in rural New Zealand in
the 1920s and 1930s. Campion portrays Frame as a dreamy and naïve adolescent, whose desires for recognition result in misrecognition. For example,
when she shares her writing (which includes the depiction of an overdose of
pills) with an admired and well-meaning teacher, his concern for her well-
being results in her incarceration in a mental hospital.

This first incarceration is relatively uneventful, aside from the diagnosis
given, which will haunt Janet for some time. She is told she suffers from schizophrenia, defined in her dictionary as "a gradual deterioration of the mind
with no cure." Then, in a fateful move, Janet follows, once again, the advice of
the adored teacher and goes to see the doctor he recommends. She asks for
help with her deteriorating teeth, but the woman also encourages her to admit
herself once again to a mental hospital, so that she might benefit from the lat-
est cure for her disorder. These women's misplaced faith in "the system" results
in the virtual loss of eight years of Janet's life. As she describes it: "Over the
next eight years I received more than 200 applications of electric shock treatment, each one equivalent in fear to an execution."

Meanwhile, Janet Frame's first book is published. Her mother, acceding
to the authority of the "experts," gives permission for a leucotomy, which is
narrowly avoided when Janet wins the Herbert Church Award for a book of
short stories. According to Campion's portrayal, Janet has no control over her

destiny and no real assistance in comprehending the dilemmas she faces. She seems to be lost in a world she cannot understand and in which no one seems to understand her in any way that does not undermine her. Janet continues to be troubled by her lack of understanding of her mental illness. Dismayed by the reaction to her diagnosis when she attempts to obtain a position as a nurse, she finally admits herself as a voluntary patient in London in order to get some answers to her questions. "Finally, it was concluded that I had never suffered from schizophrenia," she says. "At first, the truth seemed more terrifying than the lie. How could I now ask for help when there was nothing wrong with me?"

Janet finally does manage to find some help. Her new doctor appears to be able to see her as a whole human being. He tells her that her current problems are a direct result of the hospitalizations and will take some time to sort through. Meanwhile, he encourages her to write about her experiences in the hospital and to bring her writings to a literary agent. As the film continues, the doctor's recognition facilitates Janet's own and she begins to find acknowledgement of her talents and a place for herself—albeit an uncomfortable one—in the world of art and society. By the end of the film, Janet seems to have made her peace with herself and her world. The writing that had begun as an escape from a difficult world was also an attempt to communicate something of herself, as she experienced it, to others. Her writing also became a means for explaining self to self, thereby affirming both the inner self and her place within the external world.

In this film, some of the affective charge comes from our knowledge that we are watching the story of a real person. As we identify and disidentify with the character being portrayed, we are caught within the very excess that the film portrays. In this film, psychiatry is split between the impersonal, destructive world of medical intervention and the essentially human aspect of the man who eventually helps Janet Frame to make sense of self and experience. There is a dichotomization between the world that defines and destroys sickness, and the world that meets, affirms, and recognizes humanness.

The perils associated with the inability of the woman to define her own needs and control her own destiny are also explored in *Frances,* an account of the brief stardom and subsequent commitment to a mental institution of film actress Frances Farmer. This is a depiction of another true story with a less fortunate ending. The movie describes a torturous series of drugs, electric shock, rape, and even a lobotomy before Farmer's ultimate release from the hospital. As depicted in the film, Frances Farmer was a woman before her time. She incurred the ire of others through her unconventional attitudes and behaviors and through her unwillingness to conform to social standards. We are shown her intelligence, her irreverence, her deep social conscience and her complete lack of tact, a deadly combination that presages her doom. These qualities might have suited her better in the present day, but made her particularly ill suited to the role of movie star within the studio system of the time.

One perplexity in these dramas is the question of what comes to be defined as so unacceptable in the woman that it evokes such extreme measures in the world. This thread is perhaps depicted most clearly in *Frances*, whose main character is difficult in so many ways. The film shows Frances caught between the ambitions of her mother, who is determined to fulfill her dreams through her daughter, and her own needs. Her ultimate undoing comes through her inability to keep herself safely out of the clutches of her mother or the mental institutions to which she is remanded when she fails to comply with her mother's and society's strictures.

When Frances is first incarcerated, she is outraged at the presumptions of the psychiatrist who describes her as a "fascinating case" he is looking forward to solving. "Do you expect me for one moment to believe that you have greater insight into my personality than I do?" she rails at him. "I don't want to be what you want to make me," she continues, ". . . dull, average, normal." Frances is ferocious in her determination to maintain her self. Ultimately, however, she undermines this intention through her inability to survive either her mother or the mental health system intact. Her confrontations with her therapist bring down upon her the full wrath of "the system" and her refusals to back down result in her eventual destruction. The lobotomy represents a terrible compromise between self and environment, in which she pays the ultimate price for her freedom in terms of her subjectivity, her emotional world, and her creativity.

## WOMEN AND POWER

> You're trying to break my spirit: You're trying to turn me into you.
> —Frances Farmer to her mother in *Frances*

There is a harsh dichotomization in films about women's "madness" between those in power, who can create reality with some impunity, versus those without power, who come to be at the mercy of the powerful. This results in what Benjamin (1988) describes as a master-slave relationship, in which one's weakness becomes one's strength, as we propitiate the gods that be: "Women have been encouraged to participate in their own subjugation: the complement to the male refusal to recognize the other is woman's own acceptance of her lack of subjectivity, her willingness to offer recognition without expecting it in return" (p. 78). Benjamin suggests that real recognition of the other is only achieved through identification with whatever has been designated as other. Forced dichotomizations distend reality and encourage splitting and projection of whatever is deemed unacceptable into the other. The reciprocal of this projection is the need to protect oneself from the vilified other by affirming that the badness resides in the other, not the self. In this way, projective identification provides a means for possessing the object, while also keeping it at bay (Klein, 1952/1975).

This type of projective process enables us to hate in the other what cannot be recognized within the bounds of self. Unacceptable qualities such as weakness tend to get located in the woman, and feminine desire becomes demonized. For example, in *A Woman Under the Influence,* Mabel's husband's rage pushes her to renounce her adult self and her own desires and to recede further and further towards the less complicated, safer world of childhood (see Figure 3.2). "Tell me what you want me to be—who you want me to be! I can do that. I can be anything. You tell me, Nicky," she begs.

The potential misuse of power by those in the mental health system has been a theme in several documentaries in which women describe treatment used in retaliative and oppressive ways that fail to take the individual into account: "You learn to look normal," says Kris, in *We Don't Live Under Normal Conditions:*

> I've been held down, drugged, electroshocked. . . . The most serious abuse I've experienced in my life was in the mental health system. So I'm really experienced at figuring out what's perceived as normal and conforming to it. . . . It doesn't matter how you feel. Forget feeling.

It's about being safe.

Although the abuse of power is often linked with patriarchy, it is not only the power of the father that is to be feared, but that of the mother, as well. It has been difficult for mothers to inoculate their daughters, in a positive sense, by passing along their own wisdom. Wisdom has often taken the form of prohibitions against expressing oneself too fully or too boldly. "Standing out" has often been a vulnerable position, particularly without a strong empathic mother to facilitate one's progress. To the contrary, envy or overidentification with the potential vulnerability of the child can make of the mother a powerful and potentially lethal enemy (Charles, 2001a). In many movies depicting the "madness" of women, we see an embattled and often embittered mother attempting to save her daughter by molding her into some prescribed and proscribed form, often—as suggested in *Frances, The Bell Jar,* and *Girl, Interrupted*—in the interests of control rather than care.

A common theme running through these films is a lack of respect for the perspective or experience of the woman. Those individuals who are specifically charged with the woman's mental health are often so out of touch with her essential humanness that the encounter becomes traumatic. For example, in *Dialogues With Madwomen* (Light, 1993) Light describes an incident when she was first hospitalized:

FIGURE 3.2. Mabel (Gena Rowlands) dances on her living room couch in this scene from *A Woman Under the Influence* (Pioneer Entertainment, 1974). Courtesy of the Museum of Modern Art/Film Stills Archive.

Just before being admitted to the ward, I was asked to remove all my clothes, put a little paper across me, and wait for the doctor to come in. When he entered the room, I remember that he stood somewhat behind me and asked me my medical history. I told him that I was depressed and that I was afraid that I might hurt my children or myself. And then he suddenly asked me if I liked to kiss my husband's penis. I felt terribly embarrassed, and I knew that if I said no that he might think that I was there because I was not able to respond and not a sexual person and that in some way I was cold. I thought that if I said yes that he would think that I was bad, that he would think that I might be a nymphomaniac, that he would think—I was a whore. For twenty-five years, I've wondered why he asked me that question and what *he* got out of it. And if he had any idea what a question like that does to a woman sitting on a table with a strange man in a brightly lit room with no clothes on.

This lack of respect, lack of recognition, extended into the treatment, as well. When Allie Light was hospitalized, she obeyed whatever her doctor said, because "I thought he was there to get me well and to get me home, so I would do whatever that entailed." Ms. Light told her doctor:

I want to go to school . . . to make something of my life. . . . I need something of my own. . . . And he said to me, "If you can't stay home and take care of your children, then go and get a job. Don't waste everybody's time by going to school." I would like to say this to you, Dr. S.: I went to school, I got an education, I spent 10–11 years teaching in college. I became a filmmaker and now I'm making this film. And I did, in the long run, get a job and go to work.

## DOCUMENTARY FILMS: CONTEXTUALIZING "MADNESS"

The creative force was full blown then, because I'd taken the lid off. . . . I would enter into one of these ecstasies and I would just let the music that I'd hear in my mind out.
—R. B. in *Dialogues with Madwomen*

Portrayals such as those found in films such as *Frances* and *Angel at My Table* affirm the fears that many women have of being "locked up" if they reveal their true selves. We live in a world in which difference too easily becomes demonized. Documentaries such as *Dialogues with Madwomen* and *We Don't Live Under Normal Conditions* have offered women an opportunity to speak about how representatives of the mental health system had failed to recognize and affirm their experiences as unique individuals. Sandra, an Hispanic woman in *We Don't Live Under Normal Conditions*, says,

> Therapy has failed to give a context to my mom's illness, as though society had nothing to do with it. . . . People who grow up in an unjust system are unhealthy. . . . If you walk around with your eyes open and you don't feel the pain, I think that there is something wrong with you.

Sandra points to the irony of being held accountable for society's dicta in a world in which one is invisible, and yet somehow supposed to be balanced and happy: "How many philosophies and religions look for that, for the perfect balance? But, I mean, how can you be happy in a society like ours?"

*Dialogues with Madwomen* documents the stories of seven women whose experiences with the mental health system tended to exacerbate their distress, rather than helping them. Allie Light, the director, was hospitalized for depression at age twenty-eight:

> I thought all mothers frightened their kids. . . . She was ferocious. . . . She told me the story of Bluebeard . . . before I went to school. . . . These horrid stories that frightened me so much taught me to think about the meaning of the story and to apply it to myself and to try to figure out what it was that a story is really saying, and what I learned about that was I learned about metaphor. At a very early age, I learned that things stand for other things—that the bloody key stood for the fact that you can never go back again. And you can never undo the things that you've done. For some people, it's religion that keeps them going and for me it's metaphor. And how everything transcends what the reality of it is. You either go mad or you learn about metaphor.

Karen, an Asian-American woman in *Dialogues with Madwomen,* describes the rage that had resulted in her refusal to deal with the white people who had refused to deal with her. Growing up in an all-white middle class suburb, "it was just understood that I didn't exist. . . . When I went to Berkeley, all this anger, all this hatred. I just hated white people, but there was nowhere to go." She spent most of her adult life in a Chinese Marxist-Leninist group, but then "I had a breakdown in 1980, when I had symptoms that my doctor decided meant I was psychotic and wasn't going to be able to function." Her therapist prescribed Thorazine, which further distanced her from herself. "I think it was the Thorazine and the antidepressants that . . . really kills the hope. I mean I really think Thorazine creates despair. I think I was trying to get out of my life."

Karen describes reaching a point of desperation and calling her therapist, who put her off, offering to double the dose of Thorazine, but not willing to see her for almost a week. "That was the end of the Thorazine," she says. Desperate, she was finally able to find someone who was willing to see her that day

If someone hadn't listened to me then, I'm quite sure that I wouldn't be sitting here now. Because I wouldn't have known where else to turn. So that's a major thing that began to make things better: a therapist who was a *human being!* She said, "Well, I don't think that you're schizophrenic, but I think you question your own sense of reality." Somehow, I think that inner me, that death person walking around, was saying, "I want to be alive now."

Sharon, in *Dialogues with Madwomen,* affirms the importance of finding a real person with whom to engage: "I needed to be confronted and challenged. And I needed to be pissed off sometimes." Therapy provided her with a way of ending her own silence, and "learning to talk about what was wrong." This provided a means for internalizing not only more facilitative self-identifications, but also a process by which she could analyze and work through her own dilemmas:

The best thing that happened out of years of talking to my therapist is that my mind started to work like a conversation between the two of us. I would look at something I did and sort of in my mind I would start playing [him] for myself. He sort of inserted himself into my mind.

For Sharon, the affirmation she experienced in this therapeutic relationship was a prerequisite for being able to analyze herself and her actions sufficiently to be free to choose in the moment, rather than being so constrained by her history or the social context.

## CONCLUSION

I sat my mother down and said, "Mama, I need to know the stories of the women in your family." So it was reclaiming that legacy. That magic. I am *not* weird, or if I *am* weird, I come from a line of weird women who have made their way in this world.
—R. B. in *Dialogues with Madwomen*

In line with prominent psychoanalytic thinkers such as Bion (1962), de Lauretis (1984) notes the importance of experience in the ongoing construction of subjectivity. For de Lauretis, experience "is produced not by external ideas, values, or material causes, but by one's personal, subjective, engagement in the practices, discourses, and institutions that lend significance (value, meaning, and affect) to the events of the world" (p. 159). This is in accord with Bion's contention that we can only learn from our experience to the extent that we can be present with it. Previous opinions about the value of these experiences tend to undermine our ability to know what we know.

One way to deal with intolerable realities is to unlink the connections that give meaning to our experiences (Bion, 1967). In this way, painful realities can become unknown. Our need to not know aspects of self is exacerbated as values become fused with perceptions of sameness and difference, thereby fostering hierarchical relationships in which that which is "other" is measured in valenced terms of better and worse (Charles, 2001b). At times, the need to protect the self interferes with our ability to make contact. We fragment reality in attempts to decreate whatever is unknowable, and create "otherness" to keep a safe distance from unknowable aspects of ourselves. In the process, we condemn the other to outsider status via our unwillingness to make a simple act of recognition.

Meaning is constructed through a complex web of identifications, disidentifications, and counteridentifications. Sameness versus difference is the basic building blocks through which all meaning is constructed (Matte-Blanco, 1975, 1988). We try one another on for size in complex processes of constructing self and meaning, in a universe in which we are both like and unlike each "other" encountered (Charles, 2002). Much as we read people and contexts in terms of their meanings to us, and coconstruct realities vis à vis self and other, the film provides a context in which we can engage with another reality that is both ours and not ours. As the spectator, we are invited in as a participant/observer in someone else's reality. In this way, it is as if we had experienced the "realities" taking place in the film. The tensions between identification and disidentification constrain and limit the experience, and encourage reflective self-consciousness of the dialectic between self and other.

Otherness is a crucial issue for women, who have tended historically to be relegated to the "other" position. Film has collaborated in this construction of otherness in having been largely a male-dominated media in a society in which man and maleness have been the norm, the rule against which women have been described vis à vis their difference. As psychoanalytic thinking and theory have entered this stage, the issue of difference becomes compounded by one more affirmation of woman as difference, articulated by the male voice.

As we take an historical view of how women in therapy have been depicted in the cinema, we can see a progression from a view of women as a problem to be fixed by males, to a view of women's problems to be articulated, puzzled over, and worked through by the woman herself. This movement towards understanding rather than defining or labeling, and towards facilitating development (becoming) rather than fixing, reflects important historical changes as well. Ultimately, defining "woman" is inextricably tied to the experience of being and the process of becoming. In this way, semiosis meets psychoanalysis meets cinema. At its best, psychoanalysis is a process of becoming oneself through acceptance of one's being in the context of a relationship in which one's whole being is accepted. So, too, some of these films we have looked at explore this very process of becoming and those factors that facilitate, versus those that impede this process. Just as the psychoanalysis of an individual aids in understanding, and thereby in becoming, so too an analytic approach to film can aid us in better understanding factors that facilitate versus those that impede these two intertwined processes.

The repudiation of the feminine has been born out of the desire to keep at bay whatever cannot be held safely or comfortably within the representation of self. In psychoanalysis, this has resulted in an uneasy relationship with the female as the engulfing, seductive, or annihilating mother. In cinema, it has resulted in stereotyped notions of "vamp" versus "good girl." Much as Klein (1946/1975) notes, repudiated aspects of self become persecutors, terrorizing us by their very existence. Further, being cast as other loses us to ourselves. Films depicting women's confrontations with representatives of the mental health system and with societal values that question their authority to speak in their own voices point towards the erasure that has taken place in this society. The documentaries, in particular, place before us voices of the disowned aspects of self that have remained unknown, unspoken, unvalued, unspeakable.

The absence of affirmation is an insidious force, deconstructing reality and leaving us in a vacuum. Recognition is an invitation offered by both psychoanalysis and by the cinema: the idea that if one is willing to look beyond the given, if one is willing to see beyond the ostensible reality, greater truths might be revealed. Both psychoanalysis and cinema invite us into the world of another, through which we might come to better understand ourselves, if we are able to reflect on this reality. Through cinema, we become able to vicariously experience the life of another, with the promise of relief as the darkness fades, reconnecting us with our own lives, once again.

Our willingness to sit with uncomfortable realities and to reflect upon them creates the possibility of learning and growth. Film offers a unique opportunity to enter into the experience of the other and thereby offer up our recognition. It also offers us an opportunity to explore our own experience at a remove. This intervening space, this distance, helps us to tolerate what might be intolerable without the safety of difference. This is also the invitation of psychoanalysis: to be able to bring enough of ourselves into the space being constructed between oneself and one's analyst to be able to explore, with relative impunity, that which has been deemed too awful to even know.

Mairi, in *Dialogues with Madwomen*, notes, "In order to survive, you need to learn to forget." However, in order to heal, you need to learn how to remember, but to remember in a way that does not recapitulate the original trauma. As Susan, in *Dialogues with Madwomen*, puts it, "It was blindingly refreshing to find that I wasn't alone." Perhaps what these films tell us most profoundly is that our aloneness is in many ways an illusion. Versions of reality are continually intruding themselves into our minds and beings—which makes it very important, as we try to sort through who we are, what we believe in, and what we want, to pay attention to whose world we are being invited into, and what they might be trying to sell us.

## NOTES

The author would like to extend her deep appreciation to Chris Holmlund and Karen Telis for their thoughtful and illuminating readings of earlier versions of this chapter.

1. Women directed less than .2% of released feature films between 1949 and 1979; between 1983 and 1992 this figure was less than 5% (Green, 1998).

## REFERENCES

Barthes, R. (1971). *Mythologies.* London: Jonathan Cape.

Benjamin, J. (1988). *The bonds of love: Psychoanalysis, feminism, and the problem of domination.* New York: Pantheon.

Benjamin, J. (1998). Constructions of uncertain content: Gender and subjectivity beyond the oedipal complementarities. In *Shadow of the other: Intersubjectivity and gender in psychoanalysis* (pp. 35–78). New York: Routledge.

Bernikow, L. (1980). *Among women.* New York: Harmony Books.

Bion, W. R. (1962). *Learning from experience.* New York: Jason Aronson.

Bion, W. R. (1967). *Second thoughts.* Northvale, NJ: Jason Aronson.

Campion, J. (Director), & Ikin, B., & Major, G. (Producers). (1990). *An angel at my table* [Motion Picture]. New Zealand: Fine Lines Featuresw.

Cassavetes, J. (Director), & Shaw, S. (Producer). (1974). *A woman under the influence* [Motion Picture]. United States: Faces.

Charles, M. (2001a). Stealing beauty: An exploration of maternal narcissism. *Psychoanal. Rev., 88,* 549–570.

Charles, M. (2001b). Assimilating difference: Traumatic effects of prejudice. *Samiksa, 55,* 15–27.

Charles, M. (2002). *Patterns: Building blocks of experience.* Hillsdale, NJ: Analytic Press.

Charles, M. (2003a). Possibility versus foreclosure: Myth and female identity in film. Manuscript submitted for publication.

Charles, M. (2003b). A beautiful mind. *Amer. J. Psychoanal., 63*(1), 19–35.

Citron, M. (1999). Fleeing from documentary: Autobiographical film/video and the "ethics of responsibility." In D. Waldman & J. Walker (Eds.), *Feminism and documentary* (pp. 271–286). Minneapolis: University of Minnesota Press.

Clifford, J. (Director), & Sanger, J. (Producer). (1982). *Frances* [Motion Picture]. United States: Faces.

Collins, R. (Director/Producer). (2000). *We don't live under normal conditions* [Video]. United States: Fanlight Productions.

Copjec, J. (1999). More! From melodrama to magnitude. In J. Bergstrom (Ed.), *Endless night: Cinema and psychoanalysis, parallel histories* (pp. 249–272). Berkeley: University of California Press.

de Lauretis, T. (1984). *Alice doesn't: Feminism, semiotics, cinema*. Bloomington: Indiana University Press.

Faber, M. (Director/Producer). (1993). *Delirium* [Video]. United States: Women Make Movies (Distributor).

Foucault, M. (1965). *Madness and civilization: A history of insanity in the age of reason* (R. Howard, Trans.). New York: Random House.

Freud, S. (1971). Female sexuality. In J. Strachey (Ed. and Trans.), The *standard edition of the complete psychological works of Sigmund Freud* (Vol. 21, pp. 223–243). London: Hogarth Press. (Original work published 1931)

Freud, S. (1971). Femininity. In J. Strachey (Ed. and Trans.), The *standard edition of the complete psychological works of Sigmund Freud* (Vol. 22, pp. 112–135). London: Hogarth Press. (Original work published 1933)

Fried, M. (1980). *Absorption and theatricality: Painting and the beholder in the age of Diderot*. Berkeley: University of California Press.

Gabbard, K., & Gabbard, G. (1987). *Psychiatry and the cinema*. Chicago: University of Chicago Press.

Green, P. (1998). *Cracks in the pedestal: Ideology and gender in Hollywood*. Amherst: University of Massachusetts Press.

Haskell, M. (1974). *From reverence to rape*. New York: Holt, Rinehart & Winston.

Johnson, N. (Director/Producer). (1957). *Three faces of Eve* [Motion Picture]. United States: Twentieth Century Fox.

Johnston, C. (1977). Myths of women in the cinema. In K. Kay & G. Peary (Eds.), *Women and the cinema: A critical anthology* (pp. 407–411). New York: E. P. Dutton.

Kant, E. (1974). *Anthropology from a pragmatic point of view*. The Hague: Nijhoff.

Kaplan, E. A. (1983). *Women and film: Both sides of the camera*. New York: Methuen.

Kaysen, S. (1993). *Girl, interrupted*. New York: Turtle Bay Books.

Klein, M. (1975). Notes on some schizoid mechanisms. In *Envy and gratitude and other works, 1946–1963* (pp. 1–24). London: Hogarth Press. (Original work published 1946)

Klein, M. (1975). Some theoretical conclusions regarding the emotional life of infants. In _Envy and gratitude and other works, 1946–1963_ (pp. 141–175). London: Hogarth Press. (Original work published 1952)

Klein, M. (1981). The importance of symbol-formation in the development of the ego. In _Love, guilt and reparation and other works, 1921–1945_ (pp. 219–232). London: Hogarth Press and the Institute of Psycho-Analysis. (Original work published 1930)

Lacan, J. (1977a). _Ecrits: A selection_ (J.-A. Miller, Ed.; A. Sheridan, Trans.). New York: W. W. Norton.

Lacan, J. (1977b). _The four fundamental concepts of psycho-analysis_ (A. Sheridan, Trans). New York: W. W. Norton.

Laplanche, J., & Pontalis, J.-B. (1973). _The language of psycho-analysis_ (D. Nicholson-Smith, Trans). New York: Norton.

Light, A. (Director), & Saraf, I. (Producer). (1993). _Dialogues with madwomen_ [Video]. United States: Light-Saraf Films.

Litvak, A. M. (Director), & Zanuck, D. (Producer). (1948). _The snake pit_ [Motion Picture]. United States: Twentieth Century Fox.

Mangold, J. (Director), & Wick, D. (Producer). (1999). _Girl, interrupted_ [Motion Picture]. United States: Columbia Pictures.

Matte-Blanco, I. (1975). _The unconscious as infinite sets: An essay in bi-logic._ London: Duckworth.

Matte-Blanco, I. (1988). _Thinking, feeling, and being: Clinical reflections on the fundamental antinomy of human beings and world._ London and New York: Routledge.

Mayne, J. (1994). Feminist film theory and criticism. In D. Carson, L. Kittmar, & J. R. Welsch (Eds.), _Multiple voices in feminist film criticism_ (pp. 48–64). Minneapolis: University of Minnesota Press.

Mazursky, P. (Director), & Mazursky, P., & Ray, A. (Producers). (1978). _An unmarried women_ [Motion Picture]. United States: Twentieth Century Fox.

Mitchell, J. (1974). _Psychoanalysis and feminism._ New York: Random House.

Peerce, L. (Director), & Brandt, J. F. Jr. (Producer). (1979). _The bell jar_ [Motion Picture]. United States: Avco Embassy Pictures.

Penfold, P. S., & Walker, G. A. (1983). _Women and the psychiatric paradox._ Montreal, Eden Press.

Perry, F. (Director/Producer). (1970). _Diary of a mad hosuewife_ [Motion Picture]. United States: Universal Pictures.

Renov, M. (1999). New subjectivities: Documentary and self-representation in the post-verité age. In D. Waldman & J. Walker (Eds.), _Feminism and documentary_ (pp. 84–94). Minneapolis: University of Minnesota Press.

Rich, A. (1979). It is the lesbian in us. In _On lies, secrets, and silence: Selected prose 1966–1978_ (pp. 199–202). New York: W. W. Norton.

Rich, R. R. (1994). In the name of feminist film criticism. In D. Carson, L. Dittmar, & J. R. Welsch (Eds.), *Multiple voices in feminist film criticism* (pp. 27–47). Minneapolis: University of Minnesota Press.

Rukeyser, M. (1994). Myth. In J. H. Levi (Ed.), *A Muriel Rukeyser reader.* New York: W. W. Norton. (Originally published 1973)

Scott, R. (Director), & Scott, R., & Polk, M. (Producers). (1991). *Thelma & Louise* [Motion Picture]. United States: Metro-Goldwyn-Mayer.

Segal, H. (1957). Notes on symbol formation. *International Journal Psycho-Analysis, 38,* 391–397.

Walker, J. (1993). *Couching resistance: Women, film and psychoanalytic psychiatry.* Minneapolis: University of Minnesota Press.

Walker, J. (1994). Psychoanalysis and feminist film theory: The problem of sexual difference and identity. In D. Carson, L. Dittmar, & J. R. Welsch (Eds.), *Multiple voices in feminist film criticism* (pp. 82–92). Minneapolis: University of Minnesota Press.

Winnicott, D. W. (1971). *Playing and reality.* London: Routledge.

Wood, M. (1975). *America at the movies.* New York: Basic Books.

Wood, R. (1977). *Hitchcock's films.* Cranberry, NJ: A. S. Barnes.

# 4

# Psychotherapy as Oppression?

## The Institutional Edifice

JANET WALKER

The bars of the mental institution have long served as a convenient physical expression of psychiatry's perceived authoritarian impulse. Classical Hollywood offerings such as *Bedlam* (Robson, 1946), *Spellbound* (Hitchcock, 1945), *The Snake Pit* (Litvak, 1948), and *The Cobweb* (Minnelli, 1955); 1960s and 1970s films including *Lilith* (Rossen, 1964) and *One Flew Over the Cuckoo's Nest* (Forman, 1975); and, recently, *Girl, Interrupted* (Mangold, 1999), and *A Beautiful Mind* (Howard, 2001) have translated the thematics of authority to the dramatic mise-en-scène of the asylum, hospital, state mental institution, or clinic. Often such films begin with a few introductory shots featuring the outside of the inevitably large and imposing concrete edifice. In *Bedlam* and *The Snake Pit*, for example, brick fortresses loom, daunting from the outside and fitted on the inside with a labyrinth of vacant corridors, dark cells, and strange devices of restraint and sometimes torture. The metaphoric "locked doors of [the] mind" invoked by a character in *Spellbound* are also literalized there and elsewhere, as cell doors clang shut and keys are turned and pocketed. In other words, Hollywood films set in mental institutions offer a critique from a humanitarian perspective of the ostensibly repressive nature of American psychiatry. The institution of psychiatry, conceived in the Foucauldian sense as a publicly and legally recognized social authority—an institution with its own rules and etiquette and its own group of medical practitioners (Foucault, 1965, 1973, 1982)—is reconstructed in cinematic terms as institutional psychiatry of an authoritarian stripe.

However, a number of contemporary film scholars have exposed the disingenuousness of cinema's antipsychiatry impulse. The filmic representation of psychiatry, they have argued, including that of films set in institutions as well as those featuring the many psychodynamic aspects of treatment that are less obviously controlling than physical restraint, is not that of a punitive system against which liberal social forces are bound to chafe. Rather, it is that of a system wholly in concert with mainstream, conformist, and conservative social patterning. Dana Polan (1986), for example, has linked Freudian psychoanalysis in films of the 1940s to a postwar tendency to depend unquestioningly on science as "humanist rationality." The psychiatric professions grew tremendously during World War II when military psychiatry expanded to handle an enormous caseload of new recruits and soldiers returning from the battlefront suffering from "combat fatigue." After the war, the popular perception was that psychology could use its "vast new body of knowledge . . . to free the individual [from vaguely perceived social malaise] and to benefit society" (Havemann, 1957, front cover). It is not surprising, therefore, that fictional psychiatrists would be recruited eagerly by popular cinema to resolve the conflicts of fictional patients and film plots. Hollywoodian psychiatry, like its social referent, was celebrated as being central to the achievement of "the sense-filled journey through chaos to the stasis of an ending, the erection of a system" (Polan, 1986, pp. 162–164).

Feminist scholars Diane Waldman (1981), Mary Ann Doane (1987), and Kaja Silverman (1988) have demonstrated further and in detail how psychoanalysis (still at the heart of psychiatric training in the 1940s and 1950s) assimilated beautifully to the patriarchal workings of the society of that time and to classical Hollywood narrative, operating in films about mental illness, "to validate socially constructed modes of sexual difference which are already in place" (Doane, 1987, p. 46). Popular and psychiatric professional discourses of the postwar period often blamed women, and, in particular, "overprotective," "rejecting," or "dominating" mothers and those who worked for pay outside the home, for the destruction of family life and the concomitant failure of young men to succeed in battle. As sociologist Ferdinand Lundberg and psychoanalyst Marynia Farnham reasoned speciously in their bestseller *Modern Woman: The Lost Sex* (1947):

> The conclusion seems inescapable, therefore, that unhappiness not directly traceable to poverty, physical malformation or bereavement is increasing in our time. This subtly caused unhappiness is merely reinforced and intensified by such factors. The most precise expression of that unhappiness is neurosis. The bases for most of this unhappiness, as we have shown, are laid in the childhood home. The principle instrument of their creation are [sic] women. (p. 71)

Eugene Meyer, chairman of the National Committee on Mental Hygiene, and psychiatrist Edward Strecker also blamed mothers for the "alarming number of so-called 'psycho-neurotic' young Americans" revealed by "our war experiences":

> No one could view this huge test tube of manpower, tried and found wanting, without realizing that an extremely important factor was the inability or unwillingness of the American mom and her surrogates to grant the boon of emotional emancipation during childhood. (Strecker, 1947, pp. 219–220)

Film plots resonated with these wider sociocultural values. Waldman's central insight is that "adjustment," glossed in psychiatry as the "functional, often transitory, alteration of accommodation by which one can adapt himself better to the immediate environment" (American Psychiatric Association, 1980, p. 2) became gender normative "adjustment therapy" when Hollywood films incorporated psychoanalytic plot lines. As will be discussed with regard to *The Snake Pit*, male psychiatrist characters "cure" their women patients by reconciling them to gender-stereotypical roles. And, as a matter of fact, male patients in movies have a way of rehabituating female psychiatrists to nonprofessional femininity, as I have discussed elsewhere with regard to *Spellbound, She Wouldn't Say Yes* (Hall, 1945), and *Knock on Wood* (Panama, 1954), among other examples (Walker, 1993, pp. 122–138).

But how are we to decide the significance of films set in mental institutions if the meanings attributed to them by popular reviewers and scholars are different, opposite, or, in any case, seemingly subject to critical caprice? Does the asylum film, or any single asylum film, highlight the outrageous affronts to human freedom to which institutionalized patients are subject, or does it participate in social consensus about the need for and the appropriate configurations of a well-ordered society? Or, from an alternate perspective, can the asylum film sometimes extend into the popular realm anticonformist impulses found within psychiatry itself? Obviously, different films encompass different meanings or different meanings for different critics. But I do not believe it would be correct to explain this variability of interpretation as being a feature of meaning itself, conceived as an endless field of play where every reading is possible and all are equally valid. Instead, I would suggest that 1) the psychiatric institution in the postwar era was neither monolithic nor fully self-satisfied; 2) the adjustment tendency in psychiatry was subject to a critique from within the psychological professions themselves; and 3) a given film could therefore reflect and contribute to the full, complex, and even contradictory range of practices and discourses that constituted postwar American psychiatry.

With regard to the first two propositions, it is appallingly true, as I have discussed elsewhere, that in-patient treatments such as electroconvulsive

therapy and psychosurgery—standard set pieces in films set in mental institutions—were sometimes applied in real life against the conscious desires of
patients and to women disproportionately (Walker, 1993, pp. 23–50).[1] But it
is also true that within professional psychiatry itself there was debate on the
desirability and ideology of the adjustment orientation. In the 1950s and
1960s, and in conjunction with the rise of various egalitarian social movements including the Civil Rights and women's movements, the face of American psychiatry became less dictatorial and more self-critical. The theoretical
question of whether psychoanalysis was (or should be) nondirective or directive was broached time and time again in core psychoanalytic journals of the
1950s. Words including "clarification," "uncovering," "working through,"
"insight therapy," and "interpretive," along with "nondirective," were sought to
describe antiadjustment psychotherapeutic practices regarded as advisable.[2]
Countertransference, a term rarely used by Freud, received a great deal of
attention in American psychoanalytic literature, and the concept catalyzed
thoughts about the analyst's own human foibles and presumptions to superior
knowledge (Orr, 1959; Wolstein, 1959). As psychoanalyst Lucia Tower wrote
in 1956, "No analyst has ever been presumed to have been so perfectly analyzed that he no longer has an unconscious, or is without the susceptibility to
the stirring up of instinctual impulses and defenses against them" (p. 264).

Normative gender roles were also subject to reanalysis. For example, at
the same time that marriage manuals by psychologists were advocating
women's "sexual surrender" (Robinson, 1959), Norman Reider, chief of psychiatric service at San Francisco Hospital, evaluated what he saw as society's
bias toward marriage, including "those irrational elements, highly emotionally
tinged, that make us automatically consider possible divorce or separation
with a certain amount of discomfort and anxiety" (1956, p. 311). He urged
psychiatric practitioners to resist a limited view of family, asserting that "to
continue some marriages, given certain irresolvable conditions, may be a disservice to both the marital partners and to the children as well" (p. 312). By
the mid-1960s, humanistic psychology, which Abraham Maslow named the
"Third Force" (after Freudianism and Behaviorism), had explicitly linked conformity to Nazi rhetoric, oppressive social values, and misapplied American
psychiatric practices:

> Adjusted to what? To a bad culture? To a dominating parent? What shall we
> think of a well-adjusted slave? . . . Clearly what will be called personality prob-
> lems depends on who is doing the calling. The slave owner? The dictator? The
> patriarchal father? The husband who wants his wife to remain a child? It
> seems quite clear that personality problems may sometimes be loud protests
> against the crushing of one's psychological bones, of one's true inner nature.
> What is sick then is *not* to protest while this crime is being committed.
> (Maslow, 1968, p. 8)

Notions that social problems sprang from female maladjustment and that they could be stemmed by therapeutic attention to same were being very seriously questioned and overhauled.

It is the variability of this wider cultural context, I submit, that makes legible the corresponding variability and historical changes that characterize our culture's cinematic offerings. The following analysis of *The Snake Pit, The Cobweb,* and *One Flew Over the Cuckoo's Nest* in relation to the famous Frederick Wiseman documentary *Titicut Follies* (1967) is intended to examine closely the ambiguities that abide in, and in fact define, cinematic representations of social and psychiatric authority in relation to attributions of madness and sanity, masculinity and femininity. Such issues come into crisp focus when psychic borders between illness and health and directive and nondirective psychiatric practices are expressed as the trappings of the mental institution and its inhabitants.

## THE SNAKE PIT

*The Snake Pit* has generally been regarded as a socially conscious critique of the inhumane nature of mental hospital conditions.[3] Regimentation, straitjacket restraint, electroconvulsive therapy, and hydrotherapy seem to be depicted as undesirable and even cruel methods of treatment. Virginia (Olivia de Havilland) waits terrified, not knowing what to expect, on the bench outside the room where the shock treatments are administered. Her name is called and she is ushered inside. She is forced onto the table, held down by three nurses, and her protests are cut off by a phallic mouthguard. She is given three more shock treatments, each of which is shown in a systematic montage of three shots. The first shot is always of the dials of the ECT machine; the second of Virginia, post-ECT, lying on the gurney with the gag still in place; and the third is of a typewriter rolling out the record of the therapy and its result. The mechanical devices of restraint and the technique of visual repetition underline the physically punishing nature of the treatment. I am moved by this melodramatic rendition of the extremes of adjustment psychiatry, and further on in this chapter I will detail its components.

But first, in the tradition of feminist scholarship, I would like to consider how the film does partially uphold the strongly directive and gender-normative psychiatric practices that it seems merely to critique. There is a softening of the rigors of institutional conditions that is evident in the film. 20th Century-Fox studio executive Darryl Zanuck himself advised against going overboard in *The Snake Pit* with "the intimate details of life in an insane asylum," saying that to portray them was "neither courageous nor clever" and probably "most uninteresting and dull."[4] These instructions were undoubtedly

meant to make the film more palatable to the wide audience Zanuck aspired
to reach. However, the resulting lack of "intimate details" in *The Snake Pit*
meant that none of the shocking images that would appear nearly twenty
years later in *Titicut Follies* (images of inmates being forcefed through nasal
tubes, shaved perfunctorily and made to bleed, kept naked in their cells and
taunted by guards) would be a part of this earlier, fictional portrayal of institutional life. Zanuck's rendering made institutional psychiatry appear more
benign than it could have.

The indictment of forced ECT is also qualified in certain ways so that
these procedures appear, on another level, as acceptable manifestations of psychiatry's claims to mastery. For one thing, it is the wise and paternal Dr. Kik
(Leo Genn) who prescribes shock treatment for Virginia in order to "reach
her" for psychoanalytic psychotherapy. Moreover, an interesting enunciative
device exemplifies the film's positive identification with the apparatus of
shock treatment. The results of Virginia's final treatment are slightly different.
She is not shown on the gurney, but up walking, and this improvement is
reported on a chart that rolls out of the typewriter: "Patient more alert but still
confused in surroundings." But surprisingly, another line is added to the chart,
a line not attributed to any fictional doctor or nurse, but stemming instead
from the film's narrational register. The chart reads, "On the following
evening, about. . . ." After the word "about" there is a dissolve to a clock and
then another dissolve to Virginia's face centered on her pillow. Thus, the film
has introduced a narrational device that links shock treatment with visual storytelling, organically connecting ECT, cinematic narration, and the look at an
immobile woman.

The potential indictment of ECT and of the hospital's regimentation
in general is also undercut by the film's tendency to blame existing inhumane conditions on aberrant individuals. Nurse Davis (Helen Craig)
employs shock treatment on Virginia as a punitive measure because the
nurse is secretly in love with Dr. Kik and jealous of the attention he lavishes
on Virginia. We recognize her as a "bad" character by her severe hairstyle
and through the comments of another nurse who implies that Nurse
Davis's rules are overly strict. Nurse Davis fits within the Hollywood convention of the "masculinized" (unfulfilled) woman (like the female curator
of the Thatcher library in *Citizen Kane* and the infamous Nurse Ratched
from *One Flew Over The Cuckoo's Nest*). In *The Snake Pit*, another nurse
shown in the process of administering hydrotherapy against Virginia's will
is also portrayed as unfulfilled and so more brusque than need be. Virginia
asks whether she is single and the nurse replies ruefully, "Don't rub it in."
The implication is that if only the personnel were kind, caring, and fulfilled
as women through marriage, they would administer kindlier electroconvulsive shocks.

The hybridized psychoanalytic therapy Dr. Kik practices on Virginia unfolds as a review of her past relationships with men. According to Kik, Virginia's "main problem happens to be complete inability to accept his [her husband's] love." As Mary Ann Doane (1987) explains, "Her symptom is the erasure of the male figure but not of the social situation entailed" (p. 46):

> DR. KIK: You've told me many times you were married, and how can you be married without having a husband?
>
> VIRGINIA: Yes, that's strange, isn't it?
>
> DR. KIK: Virginia Stuart Cunningham.
>
> VIRGINIA: Cunningham
>
> VIRGINIA: Mrs. Robert Cunningham.
>
> VIRGINIA: Robert.
>
> DR. KIK: Your husband.
>
> VIRGINIA: My husband.
>
> DR. KIK: Isn't it better to know?

The sign of the cure will be her acceptance of the therapeutically affirmed spouse, Robert (Mark Stevens), whom Virginia no longer recognizes. In general, at Juniper Hill women are treated according to a social definition of normalcy that enforces attitudes of obedience and passivity. One patient, Margaret, wants to see her baby, but Dr. Kik refuses to release her to her husband, John, because her domestic situation does not conform to the ideal of the nuclear family:

> DR. KIK: He can't take you home to that crowded house with all his folks around, you know that Margaret. That's why you're almost well, because you know it. . . . John's trying to find a place just for you and him.
>
> MARGARET: And the baby?
>
> DR. KIK: Of course.

In this example too, the goals of psychoanalytic psychiatry are consistent with those of traditional marriage and with cinematic storytelling conventions.

The film's narrational conceits reinforce this balance of power. Virginia's past is reframed by her husband and her analyst, the two working in concert. It is Robert who delivers his wife into treatment with Dr. Kik by narrating the story of their courtship, which becomes our first glimpse of Virginia's past. "She needed me like a child needing protection," asserts Robert. In another memory that he relates in voice-over, he and Virginia are in the kitchen arguing over her mental state. Filmic techniques draw our attention to a knife lying on the kitchen counter. We notice that Virginia stares at it as if to take it up and threaten her husband, but he himself does not notice. Later, in Dr. Kik's office, Virginia glances down at a letter opener as if thinking of using it to harm Dr. Kik. He does notice, saying, "You want to hurt me, why? You'd want to hurt anybody who tried to stop you from doing away with a very important day in your life. Wouldn't it be better to try to face it?" Here we may note the transferential element in which conflicts from the patient's past life are replayed in the analytic setting. But what I would point to is that the woman is endowed with misanthropic urges that the narrative, having first attributed to her, then proceeds to manage. The result is a scenario in which a woman's behavior toward her spouse is regulated by psychoanalysis.

When the film does present Virginia herself narrating a sequence of events from the past, her story is shown to be authorized by Dr. Kik and even, at one point, elicited by narcosynthesis. Virginia's account of her childhood relationship with her father is provoked by Dr. Kik's inquiry when he finds her cradling a doll. "Are you a good mother?" he asks. Virginia replies, "Every woman wants to have [a baby]." She then recounts her childhood flirtations with her father, her jealousy of her pregnant mother, and the death of her father. Her father died on the heels of an angry act in which she crushed a doll dressed in a soldier's uniform that had been established previously as representative of him. According to the analysis provided by the film, Virginia unconsciously believes that she is responsible for the death of her father.

The film weaves still another layer of enunciative control in the form of Dr. Kik's flashback to Virginia's past. His account begins as far back as Virginia's infancy, a part of her story even she cannot relate. We see a crying baby, and hear Dr. Kik's voice describing how babies need love. Dr. Kik's narration later repeats the image of Virginia crushing the little soldier doll, and Kik explains that "children are afraid to grow up because they're afraid to let go of the love they felt for their father." Finally, Dr. Kik explains how Virginia's love for her husband developed out of her love for the kind and thoughtful parts of her father's character. In the course of the analysis, Dr. Kik teaches Virginia a proper reading of the events of her past. He teaches her to stop blaming herself for the death of her father, and to transfer her love for her father to the appropriate spousal object. She learns to crave the baby of her husband, not the baby of her father.

This account conforms to an aspect of classical psychoanalytic theories of female psychosexual development in which the path to proper femininity converges with the path to maternity. Interestingly, in *The Snake Pit* the fictional analyst assumes an especially universalizing authority in that Dr. Kik was not even present at the events from Virginia's infancy that he narrates over on-screen images. He simply knows they occurred as part of a psychoanalytic generalization about human development. Dr. Kik asks Virginia if she understands his interpretation, and she replies that she knows what *he* thinks. Finally, in her successful prerelease interview, another doctor asks if she is "aware of the origin of [her] illness." She replies modestly, disclaiming her own authority to speak in the very act of accepting psychoanalytic authority: "I'd have to be a doctor to put it into the right words," she starts, and then continues with the account she has been taught.

To speak, then, is not to control one's own subjectivity, but to parrot the proper words one has been taught. In this light, a supposedly happy event near the end of the film must be qualified. Ready to leave Juniper Hill, Virginia goes to say good-bye to Hester, a mute girl she has befriended. She does so, but as she leaves, Hester grabs her arm. "Good-bye Virginia," says Hester hesitantly. Virginia exclaims, "Oh, Hester, you've talked. I knew you would. You're going to get well now, I know you will." In the context of the reading I have been proposing, this pat link between speech and cure is not that of liberating analysis, but that of the adjustment impulse, for speaking is homologous to articulating patriarchal authority.

The verbal expression of psychoanalytic wisdom also takes the form of auditory hallucinations: Virginia hears voices. In the opening scene of the film an unseen man's voice is heard asking, "Do you know where you are, Mrs. Cunningham?" A close-up captures Virginia looking startled, and on the sound track in a nonsynchronous voice-over, we hear her speak: "Where is he? It's as if he were crouching behind me." At the end of this opening sequence we learn that the voice is that of Dr. Kik, whose face Virginia fails to place but whose voice carries an eerie familiarity. That the cinematic manifestation through voice-over of the male speaking voice is coterminous with Virginia's imagination of a male voice of authority implies a unique collusion of cinema and psychoanalysis. Cinema facilitates the introjection of psychoanalytic inquiry and control into a woman's psyche.

The development of authority in this sequence and in *The Snake Pit* as a whole may be described with reference to Foucault's *Madness and Civilization* (1965). According to Foucault, the Quaker Samuel Tuke did not really liberate the insane when he unchained them. What he did to create the nineteenth-century asylum from the prison was to substitute "the stifling anguish of responsibility" for the stifling anguish of physical restraint. Corporeal restraint imposed by chains and bars was displaced by self-restraint, the internal, moral version of the prison cell. In Foucault's terms:

> Instead of submitting to a simple negative operation that loosened bonds and delivered one's deepest nature from madness, it must be recognized that one was in the grip of a positive operation that confined madness in a system of rewards and punishments, and included it in the movement of moral consciousness. (pp. 247–250)

Likewise in *The Snake Pit*, the straps and wires of the ECT machine and the seamless immobilizing embrace of the straitjacket give way to the moral confines of a male voice in the patient's head. The speaking subject Virginia hears is simultaneously that of her analyst, her superego, and her moral consciousness: psychiatry, the family, and society. After all, the word "confinement" refers both to imprisonment and to "lying in," to being jailed and to giving birth—the double prescription of the feminine mystique.

Nevertheless, in addition to its strong patriarchal thrust, *The Snake Pit* does offer some countercurrents of resistance both on the level of ideological machinations (that might have contributed to the film's reception as an advocacy tool for mental hospital reform) and on the level of textual discontinuities (that put into question the rationality of dominant psychiatric discourse). The rules of Juniper Hill, as enforced by various individuals who work within the institution, are often portrayed as arbitrary or even sadistic and psychotogenic. Virginia is bound to obey Nurse Davis no matter what. At one point, however, Virginia has a sudden realization that Nurse Davis is in love with Dr. Kik and says so to her face. Nurse Davis becomes enraged and punishes Virginia by returning her to the upper wards where her illness deepens. Virginia's other removal to the upper wards is also caused by insensitive treatment at the hands of a member of the staff, this time a doctor, who is portrayed as rather eccentric himself. Because in each case Virginia is punished for acting out in response to what the plot presents as unjust treatment, the institution is implicated in the compounding of her madness.

The film's idiom of resistance is strengthened when Virginia is joined in her rebellious actions by other more minor characters. As the patients are being led back in from outside at the opening of the film, one patient breaks rank and sinks to the floor in a kind of sit-down strike. Later Virginia copies this act when she plops herself down on the out-of-bounds rug on Ward 12. When told to get up and off she does so, but another patient leaps forward onto the rug in a wild, erratic Charleston. Even though sanity is defined by the film as learning to accept authority, it is simultaneously defined as the natural, joyful desire to break the rules and to act jointly in doing so. Near the end of the film, Dr. Kik praises Virginia's loyalty to the mute Hester. Virginia replies to the effect that patients can understand each other better than doctors understand patients.

The film may also be read as providing a subtle commentary on social conditions that contribute to mental illness. The tidbits we learn about the lives of two characters who return home during the course of the film are illustrative. As indicated previously, Margaret is held until a home can be arranged just for her, her husband, and the baby. But there is also Grace. Grace's view of going home is rather different: "Before long I'll be on my own, wondering where the next meal's coming from." As one of the film's few references to the outside world, this represents the acknowledgement of adverse social and economic conditions, an acknowledgement that is particularly pointed in a era touted as affluent. From this perspective, even Margaret's situation may be reread. Why, after all, was she living with a group of people who drove her crazy in the first place if not out of economic necessity?

But perhaps the film's most intriguing critique of adjustment psychiatry may be read not at the level of the plot, but at the level of cinematic signification. In this context, the voices Virginia imagines connote something more in addition to the internalized patriarchal value described above. When Virginia's husband Robert comes to take her for a picnic on the grounds, a female voice supports her fears that the man she sees is not really Robert. The voice warns, "Watch yourself, honey. Everything counts against you." On one level, this is the voice of paranoia. But on another level, this warning is an appropriate response to conditions we have already seen Virginia experience as she was lied to and unjustly treated by the staff. Dr. Kik calls this distrust of Robert "the patient's main problem." But in Robert's account of Virginia's breakdown, Virginia shrieks an important line that goes unheard by the psychoanalytic work of the fictional doctor. In accordance with Kik's diagnosis, she does scream, "No, you can't make me love you." But she also screams, "No, you can't make me *belong* to you." This subversive brand of "madness" cannot be acknowledged nor contained by the overt psychoanalytic explanation provided, but it does allow a point of spectator identification at odds with adjustment psychiatry.

Another aspect of the film's sympathetic textual madness is its solicitation of our identification with Virginia's hallucinations, which are manifested in the film both visually and auditorily. The image of ocean waves sweeping over Virginia's inert body and the optically altered aerial shot of a miniature Virginia caught in a teeming "snake pit" of inmate serpents interrupt the film's realist visual scheme to function on the emotionally evocative level as fugitive images from the avant-garde (see Figure 4.1). Auditory hallucinations take us back to the film's opening. Above, it was suggested that the voice Virginia hears connotes the introjection of psychiatric authority into her ego boundaries. But further reflection suggests an alternate meaning. Virginia is mad precisely because she hears and heeds that voice of authority. In other words, the authoritative voice is a pathogenic symptom. The audience is encouraged in this sequence to identify with a symptom that should, if the film were thoroughly in concert with its adjustment impetus, set Virginia apart from us, the healthy. But when we hear Dr. Kik's query in the opening scene of the film, we are no more sure than Virginia whether the man is speaking from a proximate position just offscreen or whether his voice is, as we confirm a moment later, imagined by Virginia. It is only when the camera pulls back from the close-up of Virginia to an establishing shot of the bench on which she is

FIGURE 4.1. Virginia (Olivia de Havilland) in "the snake pit." Courtesy of the Academy of Motion Picture Arts and Sciences.

seated that we have the information to determine that the voice we heard was in fact imaginary. By that time Virginia has also figured it out. Moments later the doctor really will hail Virginia, from off-screen at first and then from on-screen in a subsequent shot. Crucial, though, is that initial moment of indeterminacy when we share Virginia's auditory hallucination. In that instant, the cinematic voice-over is to the audience what the delusional voice is to the character, and our identification with the film's main character is thus articulated through identification with the symptoms of her so-called madness.

These opening dialogs between the supposedly mad and the certifiably sane may be considered in reference to Shoshana Felman's (1985) elegant and Lacanian interpretation of a story by Balzac.[5] The story involves a conversation between a salesman and a madman whose claims to be a banker are mistakenly believed by the salesman because the madman is able to talk the talk. Felman argues that the conversation itself, rather than any individual character, is "methodically mad" because it teaches us through the device of the madman's discourse "that language has no master" (1985, pp. 105–106). This, according to Felman, amounts to a "displacement of discourse" away from the conventional communicative function of speech and toward a "radical interrogation" of language. Similarly, *The Snake Pit* opens with the "displacement of discourse" from unreflective standard conversation to the question of place, the enigma of a seemingly mad topography, and the troubling discontinuity of identities. Who is speaking and where is he? Who is replying and how? The film's particular stylistic choices interrupt a smooth circuit of identity and locution before it has even begun.

Moreover, like the madman, Virginia invents a more fully blown, even novelistic, context for her plight: "Why, yes of course. I'm writing a novel about prisons and I've come here to study conditions and take notes." According to Felman's reading of the Balzac story, the device of a character in a short story or a novel who fictionalizes himself puts into question psychological realism itself:

> [The madman's] delirious confabulation does not point to a referent of a psychological order, but rather to the dynamics of the language game. He is not defined by his motivation, but by his role in the narration and his place in the discourse. (p. 110)

Likewise, Virginia's delusion is at the same time a symptom of her illness and an aspect of the film's discursive play. Virginia's stated misrecognition of the mental hospital as a prison and the supporting subjective shots of crowded-together inmates behind restraining bars call into question the fictive pretense that Virignia is wrong to read her surroundings as a prison. The film gives us to see that the "madwoman" is right: the asylum really is a prison.

Specific dialog also sets "the dynamics of the language game" against authoritarian psychiatry. As she files in from the yard along with the other inmates,
Virginia has the following conversation with her sympathetic companion,
who hears Virginia's words but fails to understand them:

> VIRGINIA: I don't like regimentation.
>
> GRACE: Please, Virginia. [Talking in line is not allowed.]
>
> VIRGINIA: I may have to make a speech against it.
>
> GRACE: Against what?
>
> VIRGINIA: Regimentation, of course. But I can't make a speech without writ-
> ing it.

In this conversation the two women talk at cross-purposes, all the more
crossed for the fact that the object of Grace's dialog is to stop Virginia from
speaking. And Virginia herself acknowledges the effective failure of speech in
the absence of writing, an absence against which she struggles.

Going beyond the comparison with the Balzac story, but offering a felic-
itous comparison with Felman's other findings, the relationship of language
and madness in *The Snake Pit* is focused very specifically as a problem of language, madness, and femininity. When the camera finally pulls back to an
establishing shot of the bench where Virginia is seated at the opening of the
film, Grace is revealed sitting next to Virginia. This woman is visible to Virginia even when the latter is under the power of her delusions and imagining
the voice of Dr. Kik. Virginia suspects at first that Dr. Kik has transformed
himself into Grace: "He's clever, but he can't fool me with his magic. It's an old
trick, changing into a girl." But she immediately makes the appropriate distinction between the two: "Oh, she can't be he, she doesn't ask questions."

The basis on which Virginia makes her distinction between male and
female conversationalists is revealing. To acknowledge that "she can't be he"
because of a mode of speech is precisely to acknowledge the binary logic
described by Lacan, under which a biologically gendered subject is obliged to
take up one or the other of two possible psychosexual positions to enter into
symbolic language and identity. Even under her delusions, the supposedly
mad Virginia is capable of taking account of sexual difference, but the distinction she manages has nothing to do with normative gender roles.

In fact the film makes evident the inherent contradictions in normative
femininity. Virginia's error in giving her maiden name rather then her married
name may be read, in contradistinction to the film's authoritative insistence on
conformity to patriarchal patterns, as a covert strategy of dissidence, a lin-
guistic dissension from the unquestioned normalcy of the patriarchal nomina-
tion of married women. In general, the character of Virginia functions not
only to lead the way down the road to proper femininity, but, in its split sub-

jectivity—in the interstices between the world as it is and the world as it is imagined or hallucinated—the character of Virginia functions also to suspend the domination of the pedantic discourse of reason.

## THE COBWEB

The melodrama genre has been regarded as a site where certain ambiguities and even contradictions of patriarchal capitalism are brought to the fore.[6] As a melodrama set in a psychiatric clinic, *The Cobweb*, like *The Snake Pit*, draws on psychiatric symbolism to figure these contradictions. Of the two films, *The Cobweb* is the more taken up with the misalignment between marriage and authoritative psychiatry, a misalignment that is represented as inevitable given 1950s social configurations. The film is structured by the division of the narrative into two interconnected plots. One plot line concerns Dr. Stuart McIver's (Richard Widmark) work at the luxuriously endowed psychiatric clinic, and the other his relationship with his wife Karen (Gloria Grahame) and their children (Rodowick, 1982). Having established these parallel plots, the narrative proceeds by intercutting between them so that elements of one plot are continually translated into the terms of the other. Ultimately, however, irresolvable contradictions are pressed to the surface as the two plots bump up against each other. As far as I am concerned, this is all to the good. *The Cobweb* is a remarkable film, but not because it represents psychiatrists as the "secular saints" of what has been called the Golden Age of movie psychiatry (Gabbard & Gabbard, 1987, p. 253). Rather, the film rises in my estimation—and I would deem it more progressive than *The Snake Pit*—because its psychiatrist characters are fallible and they, and psychiatric authority itself, are subject to what I consider to be a very appropriate critique, given the power and history of these elements.

The "therapeutic family" seen in *The Snake Pit* (with Dr. Kik representing the father, Nurse Davis as the "bad" mother, and Virginia as the daughter) is even more explicit in *The Cobweb*, as Nowell-Smith (1977) argues (see Figure 4.2). Dr. Stuart McIver is the virile, dedicated modern father. He attends meetings with patients and encourages them to take responsibility for their own governance. The child and primary patient in the clinic family is Stevie (John Kerr), whose infantilized position is made clear by the diminution of the name of this boy in his midteens. As doctor and patient, McIver and Stevie are involved in a modified Oedipal conflict, consolidated by Stevie's attraction to McIver's wife, whom he has met accidentally. McIver's protest, "I'm not your father, Stevie," only serves to underscore the extent to which the narrative does structure him as such. Meg Rinehart (Lauren Bacall) is the nurturing mother to whom Stevie opens up. In this

FIGURE 4.2. *The Cobweb*'s "therapeutic family." Courtesy of the Academy of Motion Picture Arts and Sciences.

plot, not only do Meg Rinehart and Dr. McIver work to make Stevie well, they actually have an affair that "consummates" the clinic family marriage. "We're different, we're good parents," says Meg to Stuart. The harmonious personal and therapeutic goals of the clinic family are encapsulated in one image in particular: that of the rustic, homey, Italian supper Stuart and Meg share with an artist friend and his pregnant, contented wife.

However, the harmony of the clinic family is disturbed by the presence of Dr. McIver's actual family—a narrative complication obviated in *The Snake Pit* by the fact that Dr. Kik makes it clear that he has no real family. The presence of the family members in this second plot discomposes the first plot's interdependency on patriarchy and cure by suggesting that 1) mental problems may exist outside of treatment centers—it is not only patients but people in general who are disturbed; 2) these problems may be the result of the heightened sensibility of disturbed individuals—an appropriate response to a disturbed world; and 3) even psychiatrists are subject to problems of interpersonal relations. The family, then, becomes an outside, unregulated site of perturbation.

McIver's wife, Karen, represents a central source of disturbance, in keeping with Rodowick's (1982) claims about the excess of feminine sexuality in 1950s melodrama.[7] Near the beginning of the film, a title that reads "The Trouble Began" is written out across the screen as Karen drives up to the clinic. The immediate "trouble" is that Karen has stopped to give Stevie a lift and that she has taken the initiative to order draperies for the common room of the clinic without going through channels. Plotwise, "the trouble" is Karen's performance of wifely duties. Stuart says, "I'd be home more if there were something to come home to . . . a real woman."

At a deeper level, however, "the trouble" is Karen's sexual desire, which her husband cannot or refuses to fulfill. In this way, female sexual desire comes to embody textual trouble. One scene in particular links the heat of Karen's desire to her lack of sexual relations with Stuart. In the right foreground we see Karen, perspiring, lying restive in her bed. At the left of the frame in deep space, we see Stuart open an adjoining door and look at her. But he doesn't enter, and the sense of incompletion is enormous.[8]

On a more abstract enunciative level, Karen's physical, feminine presence overwhelms the codes of dress and gets expressed as saturated color and art direction, according to the melodramatic principle whereby highly charged psychological states are symbolized as opulent décor.[9] When she picks up Stevie, the entire back of the station wagon is filled with brightly colored flowers, and Stevie remarks upon them. Karen replies sensuously, "Isn't it enough that they have color and form, and that they make you feel good?" Stevie then speaks of a French painter who died in a hospital room "in a white bed in a white room with doctors in white standing around. The last thing he said was,

'Some red, show me some red. Before dying I want to see some red and some green.'" Here color, and color film stock, as prominent aspects of Karen's visual representation are given a higher valuation than the white morbidity of the hospital setting. But perhaps the clearest decorative allusion to Karen's unfulfilled desire is the draperies. When Karen shuts herself in a phone booth to arrange for the drapes, her perspiring and radiant image appears explosive. But both staff and patients reject the rich brocade with which she has attempted to furnish the clinic and make her presence felt.

The final sequence of the film attempts the joint resolution of the two plots through the therapeutic pacification of the two sources of trouble, Stevie and Karen. On a stormy night, Stevie has fled the clinic, and search crews drag the river for his body. Meg breaks off her relations with Stuart and he and Karen reconcile. Apparently, Karen has taken the advice of an older counselor: "Don't nurse your wounds, nurse his." As they pull up to the house, their headlights flash on a bedraggled Stevie, alive and waiting for his doctor. The last shot of the film is of Stevie, lying on the McIvers' couch, covered with the rejected draperies. Stuart supervises from the rear, and Karen prepares to spoon hot milk into Stevie's mouth—the maternal role embodied. The superimposed title reads, "The Trouble Was Over." A maternal Karen is no longer a threat to Stevie, nor an unbridled sexual disturbance. Karen's draperies have become a comforter.

Neat as this ending seems at first, another look reveals that the mutual dependency of the subplots encourages the elision rather than the resolution of the problems raised in each. Stevie's disturbance can only be resolved by the constitution of a family that desexualizes the woman, for her sexuality poses the threat of an Oedipal feud between father and son, whereas the resolution of Karen's personal disturbance would require the expression of sexual desire in the relationship with her husband. However, the scene of the reconciliation between Karen and Stuart is repressed in the film both temporally and cinematographically. Only the tail end is included, and what is shown is photographed in extreme long shot. We never learn what issues were raised and discussed, so that the peace afforded by the ostensible reconciliation is unexpected and uneasy, and the memory of Meg remains current.[10]

Another way of looking at it would be to see it as a problem of McIver's insufficiency. He has a bigamous relationship to the narrative structure. If he devotes himself to Meg, to the world of the clinic, he shortchanges his own wife. His energies are also insufficient to the needs of the children. Just as Karen and Meg are doubled, Stevie and his young friend Susie (Susan Strasberg) are doubled in McIver's son and daughter. But, as the film's dialogue and its mise-en-scène make clear, conscientious attention paid to the clinic offspring necessitates the neglect of the biological offspring. Karen reports that when their daughter was asked what she wanted to be when she grew up, she answered, "a patient." The editing and the composition of the film's final sequence describe the actual son's abandonment by his father. When McIver pushes open the swinging door of what he takes to be an empty kitchen to warm some milk for Stevie, the door initially blocks his view and ours of McIver's own son, Mark, who is seated at the kitchen table. Mark is occluded by his father's errand of mercy for the other boy. We only see him after the door swings shut again. Once McIver notices Mark, he attempts a mumbled apology, "Sometimes it's easier for a doctor to take care of his patients than someone of his own." His son interrupts him, saying, "I know, Dad, that's your *job*," and McIver exits, his guilt assuaged. But the gloom of the boy, dressed inexplicably in a dark, even funereal suit and sitting alone late at night, belies the supposed satisfaction of this solution. Instead of reinforcing a social ideal in which the man's breadwinner role suffices as his duty to his family, this film suggests than an overemphasis on career deprives a man's family of the quality of his attention.

In *The Cobweb*, the emotional stability of the psychiatrist himself is impugned. In the car with Karen at the beginning of the film, Stevie implies that doctors are as ill as patients: "Everybody's tilted here. You can't tell the patients from the doctors." Karen's reply goes even further, questioning not only the mental health of doctors but their prognosis as well: "Oh, but I can. . . . The patients get better." Even Dr. McIver's monologue at the opening of the film contributes to this doubt about the mental health of doctors. Dictating a letter to his secretary, he speaks the following words, which are interrupted by the arrival of a patient: "In dealing with the . . . ah . . . borderline patient, that is to say the people who find it difficult to cope with the normal strains of living, in whom the danger of a psychotic break is always present. . . ." Although motivated by the narrative and ostensibly a discussion of borderline psychotics, this speech, delivered directly to the camera, could be read alternatively as an account of the psychiatrist's own role in the narrative, for *The Cobweb* is about McIver's own difficulty coping with the "normal strains of living." In a sense he is the perfect borderline patient—on the border between authority and its critique.

*The Snake Pit* acknowledges that institutional psychiatry can malfunction, but the film offers the corrective of a good, omniscient, and sane psychiatrist in the main role who represents the institution at its ideal best. *The Cobweb*, on the other hand, deepens *The Snake Pit*'s complaints against psychiatry by locating mental disturbance in the central authority figure himself, the best psychiatrist at the clinic, whose own words constitute a revealing self-analysis.

## ONE FLEW OVER THE CUCKOO'S NEST AND TITICUT FOLLIES

Comparing *The Snake Pit* and *The Cobweb* would seem to suggest that the popular critique of adjustment psychiatry was gaining momentum decade by decade. And, indeed, the surface level anti-institutional impetus that, in *The Snake Pit,* is moderated by the ministrations of the avuncular Dr. Kik returns with a vengeance in *One Flew Over the Cuckoo's Nest.* In the later film, patients are routinely shamed, shocked, restrained, and even, in one case, involuntarily lobotomized. Critics have pointed out that Ken Kesey's 1962 novel from which the 1975 film version was adapted "disparages psychotherapy," and that the profession's portrayal "may have contributed to the growing trend away from viewing insanity as a disease best treated by incarceration" (Sullivan, 1992, p. 49; Rosenwein, 1992, p.46). Gabbard and Gabbard (1987) add to this sense of the story as an exposé, explaining that in the film *One Flew Over the Cuckoo's Nest* (as in *Frances* and certain other institutional films), "ECT is used malevolently to produce socially appropriate behavior, lobotomy standing in reserve as the final solution to the nonconformist problem" (p. 36).

It is certainly true that the mental institution and its personnel are rendered in both the novel and the film as an appalling ménage, and it is no surprise to learn from Gabbard and Gabbard among others that families and patients themselves withdrew their consent for ECT after seeing *Cuckoo's Nest* (Gabbard & Gabbard, 1987, pp. 167–168). However, I would argue that, as in *The Snake Pit,* the film's critique of institutional psychiatry is not quite what it seems. In *Cuckoo's Nest* the excesses of institutional psychiatry are not realized when psychiatrists exert their power, but rather when they cede it to someone who is not a male medical doctor nor a credentialed psychiatrist. In the final analysis, it is not psychiatric or psychotherapeutic practices that are indicted here, but rather an evil individual who makes improper use of the instruments of psychiatry and who is therefore to blame for the harm that comes to the inmates of Oregon State Hospital at Salem. Furthermore, even though the film is what we would think of as realistic in its trappings (for example, ECT is presented in all its particulars and the film employs an actual psychiatrist in the role of Dr. Spivey, the institution's director),[11] it is nevertheless distorted in its rendering of mental illness and psychotherapeutic practice when it comes to the lead characters Randall McMurphy and Nurse Mildred Ratched (played by Jack Nicholson and Louise Fletcher, both in Academy Award winning performances). Hence the quotes around the word "therapeutic" in discussions of the film's "celluloid psychiatry" (MacDonald, 1992). As Gabbard and Gabbard point out, the narrative suggests that mental institution inmates are "not really crazy." Furthermore, the treatment Nurse Ratched provides realizes its primary function in the film as "a metaphor for emasculation" (Gabbard & Gabbard, 1987, p. 139). As critics before me have observed, novel and film both turn the uses and abuses of power in the mental ward into a microcosmic representation of society's suppression of its noncomformist and dissident members (Safer, 1992),[12] which in turn contributes to the film's shift away from culpable psychiatry. I am not prescribing authenticity for films about psychiatry. Rather, I am suggesting that here, as with other fictionalized treatments of social or historical themes, the onus is on us to read the implications of the text's inauthenticity. Precisely by sidelining Dr. Spivey and substituting Nurse Ratched, and by giving the institution a strongly symbolic dimension, the film abrogates to a certain extent its own ostensible critique of authoritarian psychiatry.

Critics have pondered a perceived contradiction between the narrative's liberal humanitarian values and its sexism and racism (since all the orderlies on the ward and at Nurse Ratched's disposal are black). For example, Gabbard and Gabbard (1987) remark that its "misogynist ideology . . . did not prevent the film," which they see as exemplifying cinema's attempted exposé of punitive psychiatry, "from garnering four major Academy Awards" (p. 140).[13] Another noted contradiction is that film and novel disparage psychiatry while at the same time presenting a thoroughly psychoanalytic set of characters and conflicts (Sullivan, 1992; Sodowsky & Sodowsky, 1991). I would argue however, that the film is not as liberal humanist, and therefore not as paradoxical, as it seems. In scapegoating the central woman character—a female professional—and in blaming her for the emasculation of the male patients on her ward, the film actually supports gender-normative values that the institution of psychiatry itself had a definite hand in inculcating into postwar sociocultural mores.

The woman's treacherous ambush of psychiatric authority is expressed with great economy in one sequence in particular: the case meeting at which it is decided to keep McMurphy on the ward instead of sending him back to the work farm. Previously, we have seen McMurphy interviewed by Dr. Spivey alone and, later, by a group of doctors. In the first two-person sequence, the editing proceeds in a classical shot/reverse shot pattern, as Dr. Spivey levels with McMurphy about the findings in the latter's chart, acknowledging to McMurphy that work farm personnel do not find him to be mentally ill, but only malingering. Dr. Spivey seems ready to accept this possibility and seeks McMurphy's consent to be observed. The second interview sequence, however, is blocked and shot so as to suggest visually as well as narratively that McMurphy has become a problem. The sequence opens with a medium shot of McMurphy, slouched chin in hand with a troubled expression on his face. The next few shots alternate between Spivey and McMurphy as they discuss McMurphy's lack of adjustment to the institution. So far, the sequence is handled in a classical manner. Then, suddenly, we are given a medium shot of another man whom we take to be a psychiatrist. This is followed by a medium shot of still another doctor. The sequence proceeds as a series of shots of doctors and their disturbing patient, each man isolated from the others as they puzzle over McMurphy. What is odd about this sequence is that we're never given a master shot. We aren't privy to the spatial relationship among the men, except to the extent that we can piece it together through the directions of their glances. Even the angles of some of the shots are unusual. One of the doctors, a distinguished looking man with glasses, appears in a canted shot, the rakish angle of which suggests unrest. I would not be surprised to find that these shots were made individually, at another place and time, and that these two other doctors were never really in the room with Nicholson. In any case, the point is that a sense of great dis-ease and disconnection is conveyed through the shooting and editing style, and that this lack of grounding is linked to frustrated speculation about McMurphy's mental state and deliberations about what action to take. What McMurphy contributes to the conversation is his opinion that "Nurse Ratched is a cunt. . . . She likes a rigged game."

The disturbance enacted by this second sequence is chillingly settled by Nurse Ratched in the film's third and last sequence featuring Dr. Spivey. Initially, this sequence, like the second one, lacks a master shot. Two more doctors who are new to us appear in over-the-shoulder individual medium shots, and these shots are intercut with shots of the two doctors introduced in the previous sequence. From what they say, speaking of McMurphy in the third person, we surmise that the latter is not in the room. One doctor says, "I think he's dangerous; he's not crazy but he's dangerous. The second doctor replies, "I don't think he's overtly psychotic, but I still think he's quite sick." Suddenly, we see that Dr. Spivey *is* there, seated between two of his colleagues. He expresses his opinion as to how to handle McMurphy: "I'd like to send him back to the work farm, frankly."

But this is not to be. As Dr. Spivey speaks we realize with a start—and a cut—that Nurse Ratched is in the room: a substitution of Ratched for McMurphy has been effected. She grimaces, hearing Dr. Spivey's opinion. A second shot of Dr. Spivey and his colleagues follows in which Spivey looks over his right shoulder toward Nurse Ratched, saying, "The person the closest to him is the one he most dislikes." We now realize that Nurse Ratched is not seated at the table with the others, but rather apart and behind. For the first time in the sequence, the camera moves, executing a little dolly in on Nurse Ratched, whose eyes are illuminated by the light from an adjacent window (an effect possibly achieved by movie lighting). Her countenance glows diabolically as the camera approaches her. The static and isolated shots of the second sequence and the beginning of this one are now abolished as classical shooting and editing patterns are reestablished. Nurse Ratched takes her stand:

> Well, gentlemen, if we send him back to Pendleton or we send him up to disturbed, it's one more way of passing on our problem to somebody else. You know we don't like to do that, so I'd like to keep him on the ward. I think we can help him.

Although we don't see the approbation, we realize later that her clever ploy to reassert control over McMurphy by playing to the doctors' professional pride has worked. McMurphy is sent back to the ward. Later he is lobotomized. Still later, he is suffocated by Chief Bromden, who can't stand to see McMurphy drained of energy and volition. McMurphy does not die, therefore, as a result of the inhumanity of psychiatric practice. Rather, he dies because psychiatric practice has been wrested from the hands of the proper authorities. McMurphy would not have met his dire fate had the woman not been in charge.

That *Cuckoo's Nest* actually recoils from its ostensible critique of psychiatry is also illuminated through the comparison with a strikingly similar—but fundamentally different—sequence in the documentary *Titicut Follies*. Each of the two sequences depicts a case consultation regarding a difficult patient who would like to be returned from the mental institution to the prison. Each is attended by handful of men and one woman. Each is constructed as a series of shots of individual "talking heads." In each, the woman makes a statement explicitly contextualizing this case in relation to others and reflecting on psychiatric practice. Each ends with the affirmation that the patient should remain. However, the rhyming sequence in *Titicut Follies* does accomplish the critique of psychiatry that *Cuckoo's Nest* ultimately avoids.

The major theme of *Titicut Follies*, and of the numerous other documentaries Wiseman has made about various institutions (especially the fourteen produced between 1967 and 1980, including *High School* [1968], *Hospital* [1970], *Welfare* [1975], and others), is that institutional life is inherently grating and brutish. This is not due, according to Wiseman's filmwork, to malevolent or power-hungry individuals, but rather to the nature of institutional organization itself. As Stephen Mamber summarized in his 1974 classic, *Cinema Verite in America*, "[Wiseman's] institutions are conservative in both philosophy and approach. They reflect the status quo and do not sponsor innovation" (p. 247). Dan Armstrong (1988) concurs. In Wiseman films, "the 'system' is most pernicious when it works the way it is supposed to, not when there is a gap between institutional ideology and practice or a breach of professional ethics" (p. 183).

Throughout *Titicut Follies* we see interactions between staff and inmates that leave us pondering the thin line between mental illness and health. For example, an interview between a convicted child molester and a Viennese psychiatrist makes it clear that the molester has uncontrolled and dangerous sexual impulses, but at the same time the psychiatrist's interest seems to extend beyond professional parameters to "a certain lewd suggestiveness" (Mamber, 1974, p. 218). Later in the film, when this same psychiatrist is waylaid on his rounds by another inmate named Vladimir, it is no surprise that the latter fails to convince the doctor that the psychological tests condemning him to his indefinite stay at Bridgewater State Hospital are irrelevant and nasty, and that the stay itself is doing him harm.

As the case meeting sequence makes clear in retrospect, the psychiatrist from the previous scenes, however inept, applies logic and treatment practices fully commensurate with those of other staff doctors and the institution at large. But, as is also suggested by the handling of this sequence in context of what has gone before, this logic and these practices are largely misguided.

What we see is Vladimir attending a staff meeting where he makes his case for return to the prison. At the prison, he explains, there is suitable work for him, sports to enjoy, and respite from the cacophony of the mental hospital, where he's "thrown in with over a hundred of them . . . [who] yell and walk around [and] televisions are blaring." Here, he petitions, medication "has harmed my thoughts." "How can I improve," he inquires, "if I am getting worse?" "I have a perfect right to be excited," he attests. "I've been here for a year and a half and this place is doing me harm." A young male doctor, whom we have just observed in a previous sequence joking about his head cold and how it might be the death of him, is seen here again interacting with Vladimir. "You felt the coffee was poisoned; you felt that people were messing you up in your thinking," the doctor reminds Vladimir. Indeed, Vladimir persists in thinking not only that the institution is harming him but that the harm is intended: "If you leave me here, that means that you want me to get harmed. . . . That's logic and that proves I am sane." "Isn't that perfect logic?" he asks. "No it isn't Vladimir," the doctor replies with an evident measure of sympathy.

At that point Vladimir is removed from the room and the staff consult among themselves. The young doctor and the woman doctor, or perhaps nurse, agree:

> YOUNG MALE DOCTOR: He's been much better than this and he's now falling apart; now whether this is some reaction to his medication is something we'll have to look at. However, he was looking a lot more catatonic and depressed before and sometimes we find that on the anti-depressants you remove the depression and you uncover the paranoid stuff and we may have to give him larger quantities of tranquilizers just to tone this down.

> WOMAN: He argues in a perfect paranoid pattern. If you accept his basic premise then the rest of it *is* logical. But the basic premise is not true.

> WOMAN: He's terrified of leaving.

> YOUNG MALE DOCTOR: And the louder he shouts about going back, the more frightened he indicates that he probably is. Well, I think what we have to do with him is put him on a higher dose of tranquilizers and see if we can bring the paranoid elements into a little better control and see if we can get him back on medication—if he's taking it now and I'm not sure he is.

DOCTOR WITH MUSTACHE: Testing showed paranoia.

YOUNG MALE DOCTOR (into dictaphone): Diagnosis: schizophrenic reaction, chronic undifferentiated type with prominent paranoid features.

If Vladimir were being harmed by the prescribed treatment, would he qualify as paranoid? Or, how can a patient with paranoia seek redress for inappropriate treatment? What if it is the "basic premise" of the physicians—that the patient is paranoid—and not that of the patient—that he is being harmed—that is incorrect? Or, what if the patient *is* paranoid and yet the treatment is also exacerbating that illness? All of these questions arise as a result of the film's consistent blurring of the line between doctors and patients, and because the doctors' conclusion is collective. In contradistinction to *Cuckoo's Nest*, where Nurse Ratched is isolated by camera, editing, mise-en-scène, opinion, and intent, in *Titicut Follies* it is through no fault of any ill-intentioned or inept individual, but through the machinations of the system itself, that patients can be confined against their will and possibly harmed by incorrect diagnosis and treatment. The fact that Wiseman's right to screen the film was legally restricted for more than twenty years, and that the court proceedings were initiated and continued by state officials and not Bridgewater inmates, serves to confirm that the film was widely read as a critique of the institutional practices depicted therein (Taylor, 1988; Benson & Anderson, 1989, 1992).

## CONCLUSION

Individual films portraying mental institutions, therefore, can cut both ways in evaluating the legitimacy and efficacy of psychiatric confinement. The most compelling ones in this regard, as exemplified here by *The Cobweb* and *Titicut Follies*, are complex meditations on the delicacy and transience of sanity in relation to the challenges presented to psychiatrists, patients, and the psychiatric institution itself. Even *The Snake Pit*, although produced at the time of American psychiatry's rise to prominence and before the advent of second-wave feminism, manages at a certain level to articulate a critique of the excesses of adjustment psychiatry. In this film's first "going to staff" sequence, the doctors other than Dr. Kik are predisposed to recommending Virginia's release with the hope of freeing up a bed looming large in their considerations. But they work against their own interests with one doctor inadvisedly shaking his finger in Virginia's face until she is driven to confusion and must be kept on site for further treatment. The second staff meeting unfolds smoothly with doctors and patient on best behavior. Nevertheless, the first of the two sequences, like that of *Titicut Follies*, may help inspire in viewers a healthy skepticism toward the notion that psychiatry—or any social institution for that matter—is never beyond reproach.

These films are able to couch a reasoned critique of institutional psychiatry precisely because they take mental illness seriously. In addition, they take seriously the promise and potential of psychiatry and the related service professions to help those who suffer from psychological disorders. Here there is an acknowledged role for psychiatry, a role made more rather than less significant by the film's simultaneous acknowledgement of 1) the frustrating intractability of certain disorders (Virginia's internal voices in *The Snake Pit*, Stevie as a borderline patient in *The Cobweb*, the disturbances of the child molester and Vladimir in *Titicut Follies*), and 2) the fallibility of psychiatry and psychiatrists (Dr. McIver's own shortcomings and possible adjustment disorder in *The Cobweb*, and the exaggerated prurience of the Viennese psychiatrist in *Titicut Follies*).

*One Flew Over the Cuckoo's Nest*, on the other hand, while undoubtedly a masterful dramatic work, is much less attuned both to mental illness and to the inevitable imperfections of psychiatrists, which the film pawns off on a lesser trained malicious individual. McMurphy is at best a free spirit and at worst a social misfit, but he is not, according to Dr. Spivey, mentally ill. A measured and knowledgeable individual, Dr. Spivey makes just the one error, that of his misplaced trust in the professionalism of Nurse Ratched.

This comparative analysis of films from the 1940s through the 1970s suggests the fallacy of assuming that cinema's ability to offer a nuanced critique of authoritarian psychiatry and the authoritarian elements within institutional psychiatry has developed over the years. In fact I judge *The Snake Pit* and *The Cobweb* as well as *Titicut Follies* to be more supple in their approach to the representation of psychiatry and mental illness than the later and much acclaimed *One Flew Over the Cuckoo's Nest*.[14] To my mind, the most productive and interesting representations of psychiatry are not those that feature white-coated benevolence and the luxury of one-on-one care on one hand or psychiatry-as-torture on the other. I would opt instead for portrayals of institutions and their patients that acknowledge the potential, the mutuality, and the frailties of the psychotherapeutic setting.

## NOTES

1. My discussion of these matters in *Couching Resistance* (1993) owes a debt to the work of Valenstein (1986) and Showalter (1985). The literature of psychosurgery stresses over and over again that the most important criterion for selection was not diagnosis, but rather the existence of a proper environment for care to which the patient could be returned. See, for example, Kalinowsky and Scarff (1948, pp. 81–85).

In accordance with vestigial Victorian sentiments about women's dependency and patriarchal protective responsibility, it was thought that while few postoperative lobotomy patients could ever return to outside jobs, lobotomized women could be returned to the protection of the home and to the routinized domestic duties that society often delegated to them. See Freeman and Watts (1950), quoted in Valenstein (1986, pp. 228–229).

2. For summaries of this debate, see Rangell (1954, pp. 152–162) and Zetzel (1953, pp. 526–537).

3. Starr (1982) cites *The Snake Pit* as evidence of public concern over mental hospital conditions. Also see reviews by Spears (1955, pp. 436–444) and Dworkin (1954–1955, pp. 484–491).

4. Script conference notes on *The Snake Pit*, December 2, 1946, Special Collections, Doheny Library, University of Southern California. Zanuck's words are paraphrased in these notes by his secretary, Molly Mandaville.

5. The story analyzed is Balzac's "L'Illustre Gaudissart," in *La Comédie humaine* (1966).

6. This discussion of *The Cobweb* has been greatly influenced by prior work on the film done in the context of studies of melodrama and its specific Hollywood incarnation. See Elsaesser's seminal "Tales of Sound and Fury: Observations on the Family Melodrama" originally published in 1972 (1987, pp. 443–469); Nowell-Smith (1977, pp. 113–118); and Rodowick (1982, pp. 40–45).

7. Rodowick cites Nowell-Smith's claim that the problem of melodrama is always that of the acquisition of individual identity within the symbolic order of patriarchal society, and he quotes a line from the film as support: "In all institutions, something of the individual gets lost." Rodowick then goes even further to indicate that the "problem is especially crucial in the representation of women," and that "feminine sexuality is always in excess of the social system which seeks to contain it" (1982, p. 42).

8. Elsaesser's article (1987) in its initial appearance (Monogram no. 4 [1972], pp. 2–15) is illustrated with a still from this scene carrying the caption, "Dappling the Dawn with Desire."

9. Elsaesser tells us that the melodramas of Douglas Sirk, Nicholas Ray, and Vincente Minnelli in particular are characterized by a "heightening of the ordinary gesture and a use of setting and décor so as to reflect the characters' fetishist fixations" (1987, p. 56), or that psychological symbolization emerges from the decor and from "vertiginous drop[s] in the emotional temperature" (p. 60).

10. Nowell-Smith describes this scene as a "hysterical" one in which the "realist convention breaks down" (1977, p. 119).

11. See, for example, the discussion by Safer (1992). The film's realism is also very frequently contrasted to the novel's subjective narration, since the novel is told from the perspective of Chief Bromden, whose confused but wise thoughts and fantasies are rendered abstractly.

12. The Searles text (1992), in which the commentaries by Safer, McMahan, and MacDonald appear, also provides an extensive bibliography of critical essays on book and film.

13. This particular contradiction between the story's liberalism and its misogyny is also a noted feature of the novel. For example, McMahan, originally writing in 1975, pointed out that *Cuckoo's Nest* is a "really teachable novel" since students are "eager to explore the ramification of the partial allegory" which offers a "compelling presentation of the way society manipulates individuals in order to keep the bureaucracy running smoothly." But she also stated in no uncertain terms that "*Cuckoo's Nest* is a sexist novel" (McMahan, 1992, p. 145).

14. This reversal of expectations is borne out in the recent Academy Award winning best picture, *A Beautiful Mind*. Because the film takes as its subject an actual person, the mathematician John Nash who was diagnosed with paranoid schizophrenia and went on to win a Nobel Prize, considerations of the film have centered on its various omissions and departures from historical fact. Most relevant to the current discussion, however, is the question of the film's representation of mental illness, psychiatry, and, in particular, shock therapy. In *The Snake Pit*, we see Virginia being prepped for electroshock treatment, but the convulsions themselves are elided by cutaways to the square black generator with its various gauges and dials. In *A Beautiful Mind*, as in *Cuckoo's Nest*, we are shown the patient's convulsions. Nash, like McMurphy before him (though what the former receives is insulin, rather than electroshock), writhes on the table in front of our eyes. However legitimate the procedure—and contemporary psychiatry does generally continue to hold it in high regard—it is a procedure that is difficult to watch without experiencing a measure of distaste for the contorted human form pinned in spots like a specimen to the table. By representing shock treatment explicitly and in a lurid manner, the later films encourage its equation with torture, thus furthering their simple liberal humanist critique of psychiatry.

## REFERENCES

American Psychiatric Association. (1980). *A psychiatry glossary* (5th ed.). Boston: Little, Brown & Co.

Armstrong, D. (1988). Wiseman's *Model* and the documentary project: Toward a radical film practice. In A. Rosenthal (Ed.), *New challenges for documentary*. Berkeley: University of California Press, 1988).

de Balzac, H. (1966). L'Illustre Gaudissart. In *La Comédie humaine*. Paris: Editions du Seuil, Collection L'Intégrale.

Benson, T., and Anderson, C. (1989). *Reality fictions: The films of Frederick Wiseman*. Carbondale: Southern Illinois University Press.

Benson, T., and Anderson, C. (1992). The freeing of *Titicut follies*. In D. Herbeck (Ed.), *Free speech yearbook*, Vol. 30. Carbondale: Southern Illinois University Press.

Doane, M. (1987). Clinical eyes: The medical discourse. In *The desire to desire*. Bloomington: Indiana University Press.

Dworkin, M. (1954–1955). Movie psychiatrics. *Antioch Review*, 484–491.

Elsaesser, T. (1987). Tales of sound and fury: Observations on the family melodrama. In C. Gledhill (Ed.), *Home is where the heart is: Studies in melodrama and the woman's film* (pp. 443–469). London: British Film Institute.

Felman, S. (1985). *Writing and madness: Literature/philosophy/psychoanalysis* (M. Evans and S. Felman, Trans.). Ithaca, NY: Cornell University Press.

Forman, M. (Director), & Douglas, M. (Producer). (1975). *One flew over the cuckoo's nest* [Motion Picture]. United States: Fantasy Films and N. V. Zvaluw.

Foucault, M. (1965). *Madness and civilization* (R. Howard, Trans.). New York: Random House.

Foucault, M. (1973). *Birth of the clinic* (A. Sheridan Smith, Trans.). New York: Random House.

Foucault, M. (1982). *The archaeology of knowledge and the discourse on language* (A. Sheridan Smith, Trans.). New York: Pantheon.

Freeman, W., and Watts, J. (1950). *Psychosurgery: In the treatment of mental disorders and intractable pain* (2nd ed.). Springfield: Charles C. Thomas.

Gabbard, G., and Gabbard, K. (1987). *Psychiatry and the cinema*. Chicago: University of Chicago Press.

Hall, Alexander (Director), & Van Upp, V. (Producer). (1945). *She wouldn't say yes* [Motion Picture]. United States: Columbia Pictures.

Havemann, E. (1957). *The age of psychology*. New York: Simon & Schuster.

Hitchcock, A. (Director), & Selznick, D. (Producer). (1945). *Spellbound* [Motion Picture]. United States: Selznick Studios.

Howard, R. (Director), & Grazer, B. and Howard, R. (Producers). (2001). *A beautiful mind* [Motion Picture]. United States: Imagine Entertainment.

Kalinowsky, L., and Scarff, J. (1948). The selection of psychiatric cases for prefrontal lobotomy. *American Journal of Psychiatry, 105*(1), 81–85.

Kesey, K. (2002). *One flew over the cuckoo's nest*. New York: Viking.

Litvak, A. (Director), & Bassler, R. and Litvak, A. (Producers). (1948). *The snake pit* [Motion Picture]. United States: 20th Century-Fox.

Lundberg, F., and Farnham, M. (1947). *Modern woman: The lost sex*. New York: Harper Brothers.

MacDonald, G. (1992). Control by camera. In G. Searles (Ed.), *A casebook on Ken Kesey's "One flew over the cuckoo's nest."* Albuquerque: University of New Mexico Press.

McMahan, E. (1992). The big nurse as Ratched: Sexism in Kesey's *Cuckoo's nest*. In G. Searles (Ed.), *A casebook on Ken Kesey's "One flew over the cuckoo's nest."* Albuquerque: University of New Mexico Press.

Mamber, S. (1974). *Cinema Verite in America: Studies in uncontrolled documentary.* Cambridge, MA: MIT Press.

Mandaville, M. (1946). Script conference notes on *The snake pit,* December 2. Special Collections, Doheny Library, University of Southern California.

Mangold, J. (Director, & Konrad, C. and Wick, D. (Producers). (1999). *Girl, interrupted* [Motion Picture]. United States and Germany: 3 Act Entertainment, Columbia Pictures, Global Entertainment Productions, GmbH & Company, Medien KG, and Red Wagon Productions.

Maslow, A. (1968). *Toward a psychology of being.* Princeton: Van Nostrand.

Minnelli, V. (Director), & Houseman, J. (Producer). (1955). *The cobweb* [Motion Picture]. United States: MGM.

Nowell-Smith, G. (1977). Minnelli and melodrama. *Screen, 18*(2), 113–118.

Orr, D. (1959). Transference and counter-transference: A historical survey. *Journal of the American Psychoanalytic Association, 2*(4), 621–670.

Panama, N. (Director/Co-producer), & Frank, M. (Co-producer). (1954). *Knock on wood* [Motion Picture]. United States: Paramount.

Polan, D. (1986). *Power and paranoia: History, narrative and the American cinema, 1940–1950.* New York: Columbia University Press.

Rangell, L. (1954). Scientific proceedings: Psychoanalysis and dynamic psychotherapy—similarities and differences. *Journal of the American Psychoanalytic Association, 2*(1), 152–162.

Reider, N. (1956). Problems in the prediction of marital adjustment. In V. Eisenstein (Ed.), *Neurotic interaction in marriage* (pp. 311–325). New York: Basic Books.

Robinson, M. (1959). *The power of sexual surrender.* New York: Signet.

Robson, M. (Director), & Lewton, V. (Producer). (1946). *Bedlam* [Motion Picture]. United States: RKO Pictures.

Rodowick, D. (1982). Madness, authority, and ideology in the domestic melodrama of the 1950s. *The Velvet Light Trap, 189,* 40–45.

Rosenwein, R. (1992). A place apart: The historical context of Kesey's asylum. In G. Searles (Ed.), *A casebook on Ken Kesey's "One flew over the cuckoo's nest."* Albuquerque: University of New Mexico Press.

Rossen, R. (Director and Producer). (1964). *Lilith* [Motion Picture]. United States: Columbia Pictures.

Safer, E. (1992). "It's the truth even if it didn't happen": Ken Kesey's *One flew over the cuckoo's nest.* In G. Searles (Ed.), *A casebook on Ken Kesey's "One flew over the cuckoo's nest."* Albuquerque: University of New Mexico Press.

Searles, G., ed. (1992). *A casebook on Ken Kesey's "One flew over the cuckoo's nest."* Albuquerque: University of New Mexico Press.

Showalter, E. (1985). *The female malady: Women, madness and English culture, 1930–1980.* New York: Pantheon.

Silverman, K. (1988). *The acoustic mirror: The female voice in psychoanalysis and cinema.* Bloomington: Indiana University Press.

Sodowsky, G., & Sodowsky, R. (1991). Different approaches to psychopathology and symbolism in the novel and film *One flew over the cuckoo's nest. Literature and Psychology, 37*(1/2), 34–41.

Spears, J. (1955). The doctor on the screen. *Films in Review, 6*(9), 436–444.

Starr, P. (1982). *The social transformation of American medicine.* New York: Basic Books.

Strecker, E. (1947). *Their mothers' sons: The psychiatrist examines an American problem.* New York: Lippincott.

Sullivan, R. (1992). Big mama, big papa, and little sons in Ken Kesey's *One flew over the cuckoo's nest.* In G. Searles (Ed.), *A casebook on Ken Kesey's "One flew over the cuckoo's nest."* Albuquerque: University of New Mexico Press.

Taylor, C. (1988). *Titicut follies. Sight and Sound, 57,* 2.

Tower, L. (1956). Countertransference. *Journal of the American Psychoanalytic Association, 4*(2), 256–265.

Valenstein, E. (1986). *Great and desperate cures: The rise and decline of psychosurgery and other radical treatments for mental illness.* New York: Basic Books.

Waldman, D. (1981). Horror and domesticity: The modern gothic romance film of the 1940s. Unpublished doctoral dissertation. University of Wisconsin.

Waldman, D. (1984). "At last I can tell it to someone!": Feminine point of view and subjectivity in the gothic romance film of the 40s. *Cinema Journal, 23*(2), 29–40.

Walker, J. (1993). *Couching resistance: Women, film, and psychoanalytic psychiatry.* Minneapolis: Minnesota University Press.

Wiseman, F. (Director and Producer). (1968). *High School* [Motion Picture]. United States: Osti Productions.

Wiseman, F. (Director and Producer). (1970). *Hospital* [Motion Picture]. United States: Osti Films.

Wiseman, F. (Director and Producer). (1967). *Titicut follies* [Motion Picture]. United States.

Wiseman, F. (Director and Producer). (1975). *Welfare* [Motion Picture]. United States: Zipporah Films.

Wolstein, B. (1959). *Countertransference.* New York: Grune & Stratton.

Zetzel, E. (1953). The traditional psychoanalytic technique and its variations. *Journal of the American Psychoanalytic Association, 1*(1), 526–537.

# 5

---

# Woody Allen and Freud

## ALAIN J.-J. COHEN

### INTRODUCTION

There are certain things that make [life] worthwhile. . . . Groucho
Marx, Willie Mays and, uh, the second movement of the Jupiter
Symphony, and . . . Louie Armstrong's recording of "Potatoehead
Blues" . . . Swedish movies, naturally . . . *Sentimental Education* by
Flaubert . . . Marlon Brando, Frank Sinatra . . . those incredible
apples and pears by Cézanne . . . uh, the crabs at Sam Wo's . . .
Tracy's face . . .

—Ike in *Manhattan*

One of the most creative contemporary American directors, Woody Allen
has created a vast and distinct body of work of about thirty-five odd films
which are manifestly intertwined with the history of cinema, literature, philosophy, and psychotherapy. To a remarkable extent, this accomplishment may
be tied to Allen's comic talent, which runs the gamut from wit and humor to
slapstick (derived as well from the stage and the art of the stand-up comic).
His uncategorisable comic talent earns him a particular place in the history of
comic films, comic actors, and directors (besides Chaplin, Keaton, Lloyd,
W. C. Fields, G. Marx, J. Lewis, and so forth). Too, Woody Allen may have
succeeded in proposing his particular version of "New York," "neurotic," "Jewish," and "intellectual" into a compelling universality abroad as well as in the
United States. Upon analysis, it appears that most of his work is characterized
by an engaging (recursive, sometimes obsessional) set of techniques marked by

a dual self-referential stylistic trademark: 1) A playful and deliberate oscillation and slippage between his existential director persona and his fictional actor persona: the effect of this now-expected reflexivity provokes a creative confusion and specular synergy that has evolved and been refined throughout his work. In the recent *Celebrity* (Allen 1998) the main protagonist, played by Kenneth Branagh, imitates Woody's mannerisms and verbal and gestural tics (and pure lust for Charlize Theron). 2) The playful reference to the history of cinema, for example, among so many others Curtiz's *Casablanca* (Curtiz, 1942) in *Play it again, Sam* (1972), or Welles's *The Lady from Shanghai* (Welles, 1948) in *Manhattan Murder Mystery* (Allen, 1993), not to mention the lingering presence of the work of Ingmar Bergman from *Interiors* (Allen, 1975) to *Deconstructing Harry* (Allen, 1997). *Stardust Memories* (Allen, 1980) combines both features, as Allen plays at being a film director within his own film. In the diegesis,[1] the director attends a weekend festival wherein his life opus is being shown and celebrated. The film begins with a lengthy dream-nightmare sequence of about four and a half minutes that is itself a postmodern remake and tribute to Fellini's own two-and-a-half-minute opening dream-nightmare sequence in *8 1/2* (Fellini, 1960). However, whereas Fellini gave himself distance and ontological slippage by having the actor Mastroianni play his own role as an anxious film director, Woody Allen, instead, gave himself both roles and thereby entrapped his spectators into the confusion mentioned above.

There is, however, a deeper structure at play in all of Allen's films. It consists of a psychoanalytic savoir faire that lies at the heart of his filmmaking. It is ubiquitous. Freud, Oedipus, incest, anxiety and depression, neurosis and psychosis, guilt and shame, paranoia and narcissistic wounds, therapy sessions, analysis terminable/ interminable, the logic of case studies, *Witz*, Freud's mind model and his writings: all these elements appear as Allen's natural ether and everyday discourse. They make manifest the lifelong dialogue that Woody Allen, as a filmmaker, has systematically entertained with the world of psychoanalysis. From his early films in the 1970s to the present, his characters are either in treatment or therapy or refer to it, allusively or persistently. For a while the protagonist in *Zelig* (Allen, 1983), who impersonates everyone with whom he comes into contact, impersonates an analyst facing his own therapist (Mia Farrow); a writer who has rented a flat in Manhattan undergoes a cathartic self-revelation upon overhearing another woman's sessions through the building's heating ducts in *Another Woman* (Allen, 1988); in *Everybody Says I Love You* (Allen 1996), a daughter gives her father a few tips on seducing the protagonist, played by Julia Roberts, after listening in on her dreams and fantasies conveyed during her sessions with her own analyst mother.

In addition, as we shall see, Allen's remarkable contribution to psychoanalysis is to have illuminated psychoanalytic questions through filmic form, and we may add chiasmatically, to have infused film form with psychoanalytically distinct material. Psychoanalysis keeps transforming itself as a polymorphous signifier, abundantly at play as a verbal reference, a figure of discourse, a trope, a topos, a thematic, an image or a set of images, a process, simple shots or complex sequences, and the object of a film narrative, among other things. All these elements have rarely been so adroitly melded in Woody Allen's work as in *Annie Hall* (Allen, 1977) or in *Deconstructing Harry* (Allen, 1997). This research will be restricted to these two films, in which the signifier "psychoanalytic couch" will serve as parameter and guarantee of even stricter restriction. Before addressing these two films, it would be helpful to revisit the questions of psychoanalytic methods and the psychoanalytic clinical case studies insofar as they obtain in fiction films.

## MODELS AND METHODS: FREUD'S CASE STUDIES AND FICTION FILM

Regarding the methods of psychoanalytic interpretation, they are threefold in their application to literary texts, and by extension to the field of film analysis as they deal with a) the psychoanalytic investment specific to a cast of characters, b) the ensuing psychoanalysis of the author/director, and c) the psychoanalytic effect upon the reader/spectator.

The first approach is fairly traditional in literary analysis, provided that the caveat be foregrounded that we are never dealing with a single protagonist (the point is not to put Hamlet on a couch) as much as with a network of interwoven protagonists. For example, Hamlet is interdefined in a network that includes Ophelia, Gertrud, Claudius, Polonius, Laertes, and so on; together, they all reconfigure an oedipal system which replays and models Sophocles for Freud and which became thence taken for granted by the rest of the twentieth century. The second approach is also well known in psychoanalytic approaches, with the added caveat that we are not looking for Shakespeare on the couch any more than Hamlet. Rather, our research focuses upon recursive signifiers and recursive topoi, thematics, and problematics. Whereupon the superimposition of several plays (or sonnets) may point to, or reveal, haunting metaphors and problematics by sheer juxtaposition. Regarding these first two approaches, it becomes evident that Woody Allen's synergystic oscillations between direction and performance in his own films, as both protagonist and film director as mentioned above, complicate immeasurably the psychoanalytic analysis of his work.

As for the third type, that of the research on the psychoanalytic effect, it is the most difficult to assay: the point is not to enter one's own subjective reactions for the benefit of one's reader, as much as to point to the markers and vectors of entry into the text and the film for the reader or spectator. This also points to the harder psychoanalytic effect, to wit, the way in which we are psychoanalyzed by a film instead of psychoanalyzing it. In this Lacan (1975) was illuminating when he pointed to how viewers are studied by the art works at which they may be gazing.

It would be well worth our while to evoke the history of mimesis (and catharsis) from Aristotle to present-day semiotics to acknowledge the haunting power of fiction. Freud highlighted the continuum from play to dreaming to daydreaming to art (albeit transmuted by the innermost secrets of *ars poetica*): "The aesthetic pleasure we gain from the works of imaginative writers is of the same type as forepleasure. . . . The true enjoyment of literature proceeds from the release of tension in our minds" (Freud, 1908, 1953–1971, p. 156). A psychoanalytic case study does not a fiction film make. Nor does, mutatis mutandis, a fiction film a case study make. Only montage and the art of film-making can transform the diegesis of a ninety-minute film into the signifier of an analysis that evolves over several years. A brief scanning of pertinent aspects in one of Freud's case studies, along with specific fragments highlighted prior to Woody Allen by Hitchcock, another filmmaker inspired by psychoanalysis, may illuminate Woody Allen's achievement on this score.

Elsewhere (Cohen, 1996a), I have linked Hitchcock's filmmaking to Freud's art and technique in the elaboration of his renowned psychoanalytic case studies (Dora, Little Hans, The "Rat Man," Schreber, The "Wolf Man"). In his legendary 1918 case study of the Wolf Man Freud proceeds, syntagm by syntagm in his footnotes (Freud, 1918, 1953–1971, 42–44), from the analysis of the dream and the patient's primal scene to the fragmentary resolution with fresh materials (89–103). Freud's focus upon a concatenation of signifiers in the Wolf Man illustrates the bipolar aspects of language (the metaphoric versus the metonymic poles). It is a formidable lesson in psychoanalytic detective-like work (Freud did refer more than once to Sherlock Holmes) as well as in semiotic methods. It was to inspire Jakobson (1956) in the well-known application of the Saussurian paradigm/syntagm opposition to the opposition of metaphor/metonymy in rhetoric, and it was to be used by Lacan in mapping it onto the psychoanalytic opposition of condensation/displacement. Metz (1977) is luminous in his own application of this tradition to filmic language.

In Freud's most famous case study, the fear of a yellow-striped butterfly (a "babushka" in Russian) opening and closing its wings, the stripes of a "Wasp," or (W)espe (S. P. are the initials of the Wolf Man's real name) are linked to a yellow-striped pear (a "grusha"). Grusha (the name of his nursery maid) and Matrona, the later-to-be-desired peasant woman, were both in the same sexual position as the mother in the primal scene at five o'clock (a Roman *V*). Freud even comments, somewhat filmically, that the parents' position (in a *coitus a tergo*) would have been particularly favorable for observation for the infant in his remembered, or fantasized, or probably later reconstructed, "primal scene." Freud is never trenchant about it. The imaged signifiers are made to relate in the hallucinating connections of an unfolding sexual scenario, the great syntagmatic narrative account of the Wolf Man to Freud, of what were heretofore poetic ciphers, or paradigmatic metaphors. Leclaire (1966) highlighted the concatenation (Roman *V/ W/* wolf's pricked ears? or the reversal of *W* into *M* (atrona), etc). The playfulness of which resides in the fact that it can be read linearly and narratively, by stochastic (or random) free association, or with the sheer power of poetic affect. Whatever the case, such examples illuminate the bipolar nature of language, and raise the fascinating question of its application to a rhetoric of images, endowed with a similar bipolarity.

In *Spellbound* (1945), his most directly psychoanalytic film (this may be debatable for the Hitch specialists of *Psycho* (Hitchcock, 1960), *Vertigo* (Hitchcock, 1958), *Marnie* (Hitchcock, 1964), *The Birds* (Hitchcock, 1963), and so on), Hitchcock, who knew his Freud (and his Aristotle) rather well, displayed the same versatility in constructing a suspenseful diegesis, which will be so illuminating—*après-coup*. The concatenation of image signifiers and of recursive figures is well known by film scholars and by Hitch aficionados, as it extends in various close-ups, from the shape of a fork's tines upon a tablecloth, the stripes of a dress or those of a blanket, the parallel lines of a railroad track, a parallel pair of skis in motion, to the bars of a wrought-iron fence. They are strategically crafted to provoke an anxiogenic reaction upon the amnesiac patient (Gregory Peck), and the psychoanalytic solicitude of his would-be therapist (Ingrid Bergman). They interweave with a solution brought out in the Dali-designed sets for a dream-à-clef sequence (see Figure 5.1), with an asymmetrical wheel soon to be associated with the (repressed) barrel of a gun, used a second time by a criminal psychiatrist who will revolve and "shoot" the camera-gun upon himself when found out by the psychoanalyst (semiotician and protecting lover-to-be-Bergman) in the renowned point-of-view shot of the penultimate sequence of the film.

With the benefit of fiction, the analytic work dissolves (and absolves of responsibility) the patient's guilt associated with the death of his brother. The atrocious death was after all an accident, though the patient's unconscious may have desired his brother's demise. The concatenation of figures is to be viewed linearly and proleptically, in heuristic procedure and with psychoanalytic "floating attention," especially on first screening of the film, or analeptically so as to provoke the necessary *après-coup* effect of psychoanalytic (and cathartic) recognition, simultaneously for the diegetic interactants and for the spectatorship in film analysis. The *après-coup* effect, and affect, is to link with poetic necessity what had at first appeared randomly composed. A network of recursive figures

FIGURE 5.1. The dream sequence designed by Salvadore Dali for Hitchcock's *Spellbound* (Selznick International Pictures, 1945). Courtesy of the Museum of Modern Art/Film Stills Archive.

is now apparently tied, whereas the same configuration had enjoyed heretofore nothing but limited meaningfulness. Film analysis, just as psychoanalysis, moves forward and backwards, downstream and back upstream. This is how a downstream stochastic unfolding of recursive figures meets with an upstream analysis; therein lies the recognition of patterns and isotopes strewn in the filmmaker's composition.

## ANNIE HALL

*Annie Hall* (1977) opens on a tight shot of Alvy, the main protagonist of the film, played by Woody Allen (is it Woody who plays at being Alvy, or Alvy who plays at being Woody?), who looks straight at the camera, as if it were a documentary rather than a narrative film, where such shots are considered antithetical to the codes of mainstream filmmaking. In this respect Woody Allen uses the same unconventional approach as did the French "New Wave" filmmakers in the 1960s. He thus addresses both an internal audience while doing a stand-up comedy routine, as well as the cinematic audience, since he faces the camera directly, and he refers to a joke enjoyed by Groucho Marx: "I'd never belong to any club that would have someone like me for a member" (Allen, 1977). Alvy-Woody traces the joke explicitly back to Freud's *Wit and Its Relation to the Unconscious* (1905/1955–1971). This explicit reference to Freud's text would convoke the spectator's intelligence to practice an immanent rather than extraneous Freudian interpretation of the dialogue were it not for the fact that the character is already ahead of the interpretive game. He readily applies, with gusto and self-deprecation, Groucho's and Freud's joke to his own relationship to women, and then proceeds to revisit his childhood, his past two marriages and his just-failed relationship with Annie Hall. The relationships appear in crosscut flashbacks throughout the first half of the film. The crosscut mimics his apparent random memory recall.

Flashbacks are situated at the intersection of film art and technique and psychoanalytic insight: flashbacks in myriad styles depend, of course, upon the art of editing and mise-en-scène; however, in so doing, flashbacks relate as if in cause-and-effect the transference of the there-and-then into the here-and-now (Cohen, 1996b, 2000b). The trajectories of relationships are nonlinear, the rules of the unconscious are dominated by the rules of affect rather than by the chronological sequencing of events. In cinematic terms, the unconscious may be viewed as a labyrinthic sequencing of myriad-tracked editing; in psychoanalytic terms, studying the principles of editing may be another royal road to the unconscious (Metz, 1977). In clinical terms, sessions may link distant and present affects as therapy explores the mysteries of associations. Just as Annie Hall invites Alvy to a drink upstairs, he informs her that he has been in analysis for the past fifteen years. Once again, the alert spectator is convoked to overinterpretation, but is already confused between Alvy's psychoanalyzed persona and Allen's persona and fame with regard to his own long-standing analysis, dazzled by the drift of fact and fiction. This time, again ahead of the spectator, it is Annie who comments upon his "fifteen years" (Metz, 1977, p. 38), with tender irony at his first slip of the tongue and stammering, then with sarcasm at their first screen fight in bed (50). When Alvy complains during their lovemaking that she is removed, Annie's "inner self moves up from the bed and sits down from the chair, watching" (51). Later in the film, the same simulacrum-splitting between the protagonists and their clonelike spirits is used with shrewd reflexivity whether Alvy and Annie visit the scene of her seduction by her previous lover, or whether they also both visit his own childhood scene, in the company of his parents.

Woody Allen plays freely with various film form experiments throughout *Annie Hall*. For instance, when Annie and Alvy engage in their first conversation, their inner thoughts appear as subtitles (39–40): Just as Alvy comments awkwardly upon the emergence of new criteria in the art of photography, "I wonder what she looks like naked," appears at the bottom of the frame. Similarly, her reply, "It's all instinctive. I try to feel it," while discussing outwardly her photographic art sense is juxtaposed to the subtitle, "I hope he doesn't turn out to be a *shmuck* like all the others." In this Allen follows the grand tradition of the film gag that goes back to the origins of cinema.

However, it is in the use of the split-screen technique that he reaches the most dramatic and psychoanalytic effect. The rhetoric of the split screen in cinema convention has a rich history as varied in significance as for instance Abel Gance's *Napoléon* (Gance, 1927) or Andy Warhol's *The Chelsea Girls* (Warhol, 1966)—the former, at the end of the film, in triple split screen, as if to enhance the victorious battles and growing triumph of Napoleon on his way to become emperor, and the latter to create a postmodern disjunct of meaning systems between left and right screen. Woody Allen seems to have a more entertaining agenda. At first, the technique is used to highlight a chasm of social and class differences. The sequence where Alvy is invited to spend Easter weekend at Annie's parents highlights a contrast between the present dinner table and that of his own upbringing—between the staid Waspish Halls versus the loud Jewish Singers. In crosscut, under the stereotyping gaze of Annie's grandmother, Woody Allen has the Alvy character mutate into a complete orthodox Jewish image of himself from the grandmother's point of view. Afterwards, the two families' dialogues are overlapped and juxtaposed, and eventually the families start talking to one another across the split screen (57) which produces a comic effect, as well as an imaginative counterpoint to the psychoanalytic displacement of the there-and-then upon the present. This playfulness on Woody Allen's part may be associated with similar tropes in literary fiction as, for example, in the work of Philip Roth.

It is, however, in his next use of the split screen to highlight "his" and "her" therapies in a memorable one-minute sequence that Allen reaches far greater accomplishment (see Figure 5.2). Annie occupies the left side of the split screen. She is involved in face-to-face therapy within a modern luminous interior depicted on her side of the frame, whereas Alvy, on the right side of the split screen, lies on the couch, but still looks directly at the camera and convokes the viewer. His reclining position on the leather couch with his analyst seated behind him in a more traditional tall armchair, within a much darker interior, indicates that they are involved in what appears as classical psychoanalysis. Despite the deliberate clashing psychoanalytic styles, both of their analysts nevertheless address in turn exactly the same question to their patients: "How often do you have sex?," and they obtain the same factual answer, "three times a week," albeit modified in a tone of hysterical frustration by Alvy—"Hardly ever. Maybe three times a week"—and in obsessional exasperation by Annie "Constantly. I'd say three times a week."

The sequence deserves further filmic analysis. Woody Allen's mise-en-scène convokes the spectator to witness the painful point-of-no-return in the relationship between Annie and Alvy. Neither of them seems able to transcend the limitations of their own neuroses, yet both of them can communicate across the screen through their analysts. Thus, the filmmaker can have them metacommunicate that they can no longer communicate. The spectator is further convoked to responsible interpretation so as to provide a synthesis in the back-and-forth between the two parts of the screen. As a result, a closer analysis of the dialogue shows the clear double bind in which Annie's character is caught: on the one hand, she is aware that Alvy is paying for her analysis and feels guilty for it; on the other hand, given the progress of her analysis, she is not willing to yield to Alvy's sexual demands when she does not feel inclined. This progress is delineated with great care in the screenwriting, and its effect is to convoke spectatorial empathy for the female character. Furthermore, the effect of such a focus upon Annie's double bind is to make Alvy's character far less attractive. Through and despite the humor of the sequence, Woody Allen's mise-en-scène establishes clearly that the director is not empathetically aligned with the Alvy protagonist. There is thus a refined disjunction between the directorial prerogative and his protagonist.

The split screen convention borrowed so successfully from the history of cinema proves to be an astute instrument of laughter and play. In addition, it may represent a psychoanalytic advance for the characters, for the spectatorial position and perhaps for the director caught in the logic of his mimesis of action: in so far as the mirroring provoked by the two sides of the screen illuminates a psychoanalytic dilemma for the characters, it entices the spectatorial

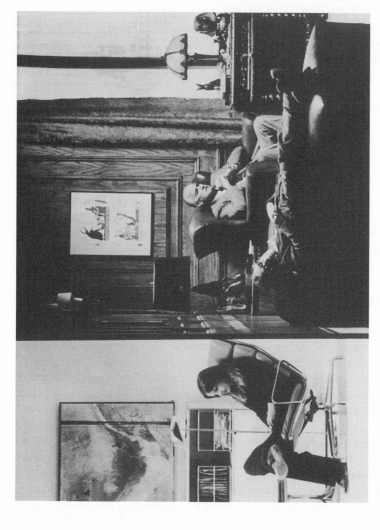

FIGURE 5.2. Alvy Singer (Woody Allen) and his girlfriend, Annie Hall (Diane Keaton), pictured here in split-screen as they complain to their respective analysts about their sex life in this scene from *Annie Hall* (MGM, 1977). Courtesy of the Wisconsin Center for Film and Theater Research.

position to participate in the working through of meaning processes. This process may psychoanalyze the spectatorial position along with the psychoanalyzed protagonists.


### DECONSTRUCTING HARRY: DECONSTRUCTING WOODY

> Your books all seem a little sad on the surface. . . . Which is why I like deconstructing them, because . . . underneath they're really happy. It's just that you don't know it.
> —Mary in *Deconstructing Harry*

As we have seen in *Annie Hall,* Woody Allen enjoys playing with the slippage between the directorial function and the actorial one, where functions appear to analyze each other, on the edge of an ambiguity which has become constitutive of his art. In *The Purple Rose of Cairo* (Allen, 1984), wherein Allen is not a protagonist in his own film, the slippage occurs instead between different types of world illusions. The everyday world of fiction is represented in color whereas the world of cinema and escape is represented in a black and white film-within-the film. Tom, the main protagonist in the black and white film-within-the-film, steps out of the screen to meet Cecilia, the diegetic spectator in the color film and the colored world. After making the necessary changes, Tom invites Cecilia to step back into the screen with him. In this back and forth between two universes, one may appear as fact and everyday and the other as fiction, though they are technically both fictional universes and one could be called metafictional whereas the other would be the referential universe. To Allen's credit, the two worlds end up overlapping and the most poignant moment occurs when Cecilia has to choose between the two universes and the two men who love her—especially as both men are played by the same actor.

*Deconstructing Harry* (1997) is part homage to, or pastiche of, or postmodern remake of Bergman's *Wild Strawberries* (Bergman, 1968). Harry is embarked on an odyssey similar to that of Bergman's Professor Borg to receive an honorary degree from the school from which he had been expelled when he was young. To add elements of slapstick to Bergman's metaphysical vision, the odyssey of Woody's protagonist includes a visit to a Dantesque or Sadean vision of the Inferno; he arrives at his destination in the company of a prostitute, the corpse of a friend who died during the car trip, and the son whom he has kidnapped from his ex-wife's jealous guard. In this film Woody Allen explores further the same oscillation between life and fiction, and the creative instability that the friction between the two worlds may provoke.

Once again, we shall limit ourselves to the evaluation of the occurrences of the signifier "psychoanalytic couch." Suffice it so say that Harry Block is a writer whose rather transparent transposition from the cast of characters in his everyday life into his fiction provokes the ire of his friends and relatives, and that one of his ex-wives in the referential universe was a psychoanalyst, Joan (played by Kirstie Alley), transposed as Helen, also a psychoanalyst (Demi Moore) in Harry's fictional world. In a carefully crafted series of embedded narratives, punctuated by rythmically timed jump cuts, Harry speaks to his present analyst. Once again, the analyst's sessions are the locus of all temporalities, where all affects associate freely in the transference of the there-and-then into the here-and-now, from existence to fiction and vice versa: "Nothing's changed. I had a shrink then, I have a shrink now. I'm six shrinks later. I'm three wives down the line." Harry recounts how one of his irate lovers (Lucy, played by Judy Harris) tried to kill him—the opening dramatic sequence of the film, viewed at first in jump cuts and now replayed verbally for his analyst. With further irony, the opening credit sequence in jump cuts is rythmed to the soundtrack of a song aptly titled "Twisted," which begins with the lines "My analyst told me that I was out of my head. . . ." The analyst reminds Harry of a story he had written about an actor who was "out-of-focus." The story anticipates symmetrically and self-referentially the end of the film as Harry suffers from the same disease shortly before receiving an honorary degree from the school from which he had been expelled when he was young. Allen's invented neurosis of "being out-of-focus" is performed in perplexing anxiety by Robin Williams. The film form may transpose an entertaining form of postmodern neurosis, a form of entropy, but it could also be associated as a recursive topos linked with the loss of vision (or age?) from which the redux director suffers as well in his last film, *Hollywood Ending* (2002).

The relationship with his analyst ex-wife is of an explosive type, whereas Demi Moore instead portrays a calm and seductive analyst who repeatedly terminates her patients' sessions, professionally, while initiating, unprofessionally, a future possible relationship. Upon the third repetition, with her third patient within the film, of the amusingly delivered suggestive reply dealing with termination, decent interval, and the suggestive mention of a future possibility of "seeing each other again . . . socially" (Allen, 1998, p. 62), it becomes evident that Harry the writer, or rather Allen the filmmaker, is keenly interested in pushing the limits of countertransference into acting out and transgressing the taboo of psychoanalytic treatment. In so doing, albeit in the exploration of fiction, he may also be deconstructing the psychoanalytic treatment, deconstructing the refined tension studied as countertransference aside from deconstructing the protagonist called Harry. The deconstruction of the fiction analyst (Demi Moore) cumulates with her conversion to orthodox Jewish religious practices, as she offers prayers before every action about anything and everything, ultimately and farcically, before performing oral sex on her ex-patient-now-husband.

The deconstruction of the referential ex-wife analyst is also farcical albeit far more sadistic than the preceding description with the fiction analyst. Harry has a flashback of his last argument with Joan before their final separation. Their quarrel about an affair that Harry had with one of her patients is crosscut with the arrival of Mr. Farber for his session with Joan. The session is interrupted several times as a gag: Joan keeps getting up to continue the screaming argument with Harry, then goes back to sit behind Farber, and then goes back to screaming in extended rage at Harry's bad faith until, unhinged, she orders him out of her house from behind the couch of a broken down Farber. We may note that, just as with Alvy in *Annie Hall*, the spectatorial principle is not aligned with Harry, any more than it is with Joan. This is a painful scene to recall for protagonist Harry as well. The spectatorial principle may rather be aligned with the patient's reaction in this sequence: he seems caught in his own primal scene, among angry and jealous parents who are not paying attention to him—and he starts crying.

## MOURNING AND IDEALIZATION

The quote from *Manhattan* (1979) placed in epigraph in the introduction refers to a sequence in which Ike-Woody is lying on the couch, depressed, after the end of his relationship with Mary (Diane Keaton) and his failed relationship with Tracy as well (see Figure 5.3). By lying on the couch and speaking into the microphone, he finds his voice for the novel that he wants to write, of which we heard several false starts to the tune of Gershwin's "Rhapsody in Blue" at the beginning of the film until he found the style with which he was pleased. In a Proustian manner, it corresponds to the film which has been unfolding and is now about to end. The evocation of art and life continues in constant Mœbius until life seems to take over with the phrase "Tracy's face," charged apparently with greater intensity than the rest of the impressive list that Ike has committed to his writing. At almost the end of the film, he discovers his metaphysical edge, expressed as a voice to himself, a survey of his aesthetics, and in this film the primacy of the existential over the aesthetic: he is transformed as he evokes the face of the woman; he realises how massively he had denied to himself his love for her. But this would be a profound misreading of the utterance "Tracy's face": first it may be an homage to Proust's metonymic reference to Albertine's cheek, but in *Manhattan* it is too late, for Tracy's face is already committed to art.

By lying on the ubiquitous couch, without an analyst in the shot, the character finds therapy in his writing and, at the same time, positions the

FIGURE 5.3. Writer Isaac Davis, like the actor who portrays him (Woody Allen), seems quite comfortable assuming the recumbent position in this scene from *Manhattan* (United Artists, 1979). Courtesy of the Museum of Modern Art/Film Stills Archive.

spectatorial principle into the role of the absent analyst. The list is haunting and also profoundly ambivalent: on the one hand the consolation of art, on the other hand the existential intensity. The latter shakes him from his despondency and makes him run to the other side of Manhattan to find Tracy on her way to a six-month stay in London: "Six months is not so long. . . . You've got to have faith in people," she says with nostalgic Gershwin's notes muffled in the background. The notes are in sync with his delight at a view of Manhattan with fireworks over the skyline intertwined with "Rhapsody in Blue" at the beginning of the film. The spectatorial principle redoubles now as the psychoanalytic principle registers at this point the overlap between the psychoanalysis of the character and that of the director and the (cathartic) analysis to which it is itself submitted thereby.

In *Annie Hall*, we have previously observed Allen's couch and his obsession with sex and creativity through psychoanalysis, albeit combined with his wonderful play with film form: the split screen and the split therapy. Allen's art combines mourning the lost relationship with Annie and the process of aesthetic creation which metamorphoses the idealized lost object. He has played spectacularly with film form throughout his work. I pointed out in other research (Cohen, 2000a) the iconic quotations from the history of cinema present in *Zelig* (1983), which offers a stunning transposition of the 1920s quality of photography and ways of filming and editing, along with a 1920s voiceover documentary sound. In an interview with Björkman (1993), Woody Allen pays homage to Gordon Willis, his long-standing director of photography, and also corroborates punctually the research for the ideal filmic simulacrum:

> We got old lenses from the 1920s, old cameras and old sound equipment. . . . We filmed it in exactly the kind of lighting we would have had at the time. We made flicker-mattes, so that our film would have flickering light like the old films. And we put scratches in the negative. We didn't want to overdo it. . . . Gordon and I knew what kind of style we would imitate. We've seen so many of these films in our lifetime. (pp. 137–140)

This attention to details points to the construction of the film's spectator as being aligned to apprehend and enjoy in a 1980s film the re-creation of 1920s techniques, in constant back-and-forth slippage from one era to another. Allen and Willis retrieved archival footage as much as they painstakingly simulated archival footage from the era. Yet Woody's greatest aesthetic success had to do with the jump cuts so dear to Godard and the French "New Wave" to which we referred regarding *Deconstructing Harry*. The narrative in jump cuts to his analyst and the arrival of a would-be vengefully murderous

Judy Davis in the opening credit sequence both mimic Woody's staccato speech delivery and the staccato search for his writerly style at the beginning of *Manhattan*.

⊙⊹⊙

In conclusion, albeit without a couch shot, it is in *Stardust Memories* that Woody played with spectacular jump cuts. These shots consist of the female portraiture of Doris (Charlotte Rampling) in a virtuoso black-and-white film. Allen as director aligns film form, evanescent stylized shots, and the narrative flashback of the nostalgic failed love of his life in the throes of a mental breakdown. Now in a psychiatric institution, Doris looks directly into the camera as she poses a series of insufferable questions. Therein, gorgeously beautiful, beyond the power of the couch, in the solitude of her psychotic universe, she is too close yet so distant, and the questions remain unanswerable. At that punctual moment, the jump cuts correspond filmically to the deep structure of the (polysemic) breakdown—hers, theirs, and that of the filmic apparatus. The sequence places the spectatorial principle in a conflict between ethics and aesthetics: the clash of the spectacle offered by the beauty of the shot, the light, the art of photography, not to mention the raw sensuality of Charlotte Rampling, versus our ethical fear, compassion, and guilty voyeurism at witnessing a character undergoing a mental breakdown. As we have seen, the psychoanalytic principles at work in Allen's film may deconstruct systematically all the interwoven orders of cinema: the director, his characters, and the spectator. Yet this deconstruction seems to work in sync with a profound understanding and feeling for the cathartic effect of transsubstantiated emotion in his art.

## NOTE

1. Souriau (1951) refashioned the term "diegesis" in aesthetics, which was to become everyday in film studies and literary semiotics. Jacobson coined "meta-diegetic" (1972) and Genette added the terms "homo-diegetic," "hetero-diegetic," and "pseudo-diegetic" (1972) for use, for instance, when a voice-over belongs to a character within the narrative diegesis, or to an (omniscient) narrator in a documentary or in fiction film.

## REFERENCES

Allen, W. (Director), & Jacobs, A. (Producer). (1972). *Play it again, Sam* [Motion picture]. United States: Paramount.

Allen, W. (Director), & Gallo, F. (Producer). (1977). *Annie Hall* [Motion picture]. United States: United Artists.

Allen, W. (Director), & Rollins, J., Joffe, C. (Producers). (1978). *Interiors* [Motion picture]. United States: United Artists.

Allen, W. (Director), & Rollins, J., Joffe, C. (Producers). (1979). *Manhattan* [Motion picture]. United States: United Artists.

Allen, W. (Director), & Greenhut, R. (Producer). (1980). *Stardust memories* [Motion picture]. United States: United Artists.

Allen, W. (1982). *Four films of Woody Allen: Annie Hall* (with Marshall Brickman), *Manhattan* (with Marshall Brickman), and *Stardust memories*. Screenplays. New York: Random House.

Allen, W. (Director), & Greenhut, R. (Producer). (1983). *Zelig* [Motion picture]. United States: Orion.

Allen, W. (Director), & Greenhut, R. (Producer). (1984). *The purple rose of Cairo* [Motion picture]. United States: Orion.

Allen, W. (1987). *Three films of Woody Allen: Zelig. Broadway Danny Rose. The purple rose of Cairo.* Screenplays. New York: Random House.

Allen, W. (Director), & Greenhut, R. (Producer). (1988). *Another woman* [Motion picture]. United States: Rank.

Allen, W. (Director), & Greenhut, R. (Producer). (1993). *Manhattan murder mystery* [Motion picture]. United States: Tristan

Allen, W. (Director), & Greenhut, R. (Producer). (1996). *Everyone says I love you* [Motion picture]. United States: Sweetland.

Allen, W. (Director), & Doumanian, J. (Producer). (1997). *Deconstructing Harry* [Motion picture]. United States: Fine Line Cinema.

Allen, W. (Director), & Doumanian, J. (Producer). (1998). *Celebrity* [Motion picture]. United States: Buena Vista.

Allen, W. (Director), & Aronson, L. (Producer). (2002). *Hollywood ending* [Motion picture]. United States: Drearnworks.

Bergman, I. (Director), & Ekelund, A. (Producer). (1957). *Wild strawberries* [Motion picture]. Sweden: Svensk Filmindustri.

Björkman, S. (1993). *Woody Allen on Woody Allen. In conversation with S. Björkman.* New York: Grove Press.

Cohen, A. J.-J. (1996a). Stochastics of sex and death in *Basic* (filmic) *instinct. Semiotica. Special Issue: Christian Metz 112*(1/2), 109–122.

Cohen, A. J.-J. (1996b). Freud's paradox of temporality. Freud's *Nachträglichkeit*. Lacan's Schema 'R.'" *Interdisciplinary Journal of Germanic Linguistics and Semiotic Analysis 1*(1), 21–40.

Cohen, A. J.-J. (2000a). Woody Allen's *Zelig*. A simulation documentary. In S. Simpkins, C. W. Spinks, & J. Deeley (Eds.), *Semiotics 1999* (pp. 315–331). New York: Peter Lang.

Cohen, A. J.-J. (2000b). Semio-Cybernetics of visual memory. *Interdisciplinary Journal of Germanic Linguistics and Semiotic Analysis, 5*(2), 230–244.

Curtiz, M. (Director), & Wallis, H. (Producer). (1942). *Casablanca* [Motion picture]. United States: Warner.

Fellini, F. (Director), & Rizzoli, A. (Producer). (1963). *Eight and a half* [Motion picture]. Italy: Cineriz.

Freud, S. (1953–1971). *The interpretation of dreams.* In J. Strachey (Ed. and Trans.), *Standard edition of the complete psychological works of Sigmund Freud* (Vols. 4 and 5). London: Hogarth Press. (Original work published 1900)

Freud, S. (1953–1971). Dora: An analysis of a case of hysteria. In J. Strachey (Ed. and Trans.), *Standard edition of the complete psychological works of Sigmund Freud* (Vol. 7). London: Hogarth Press. (Original work published 1900)

Freud, S. (1955–1971) *Wit and its relation to the unconscious.* In J. Strachey (Ed. and Trans.), *Standard edition of the complete psychological works of Sigmund Freud* (Vol. 8). London: Hogarth Press. (Original work published 1905)

Freud, S. (1953–1971). *Creative writers and day-dreaming.* In J. Strachey (Ed. and Trans.), *Standard edition of the complete psychological works of Sigmund Freud* (Vol. 9). London: Hogarth Press. (Original work published 1908)

Freud, S. (1953–1971). *The rat-man. A case of obsessional neurosis.* In J. Strachey (Ed. and Trans.), *Standard edition of the complete psychological works of Sigmund Freud* (Vol. 10). London: Hogarth Press. (Original work published 1909)

Freud, S. (1953–1971). *An infantile neurosis (the "wolfman").* In J. Strachey (Ed. and Trans.), *Standard edition of the complete psychological works of Sigmund Freud* (Vol. 17). London: Hogarth Press. (Original work published 1918)

Gance, A. (Director). (1927). *Napoleon* [Motion picture]. France: WESTI.

Genette, G. (1972). *Figures III.* Paris: Sevil.

Hitchcock, A. (Director), & Selznick, D. (Producer). (1945). *Spellbound* [Motion picture]. United States: Selznick Studios.

Hitchcock, A. (Director/Producer). (1958). *Vertigo* [Motion picture]. United States: Paramount.

Hitchcock, A. (Director/Producer). (1960). *Psycho* [Motion picture]. United States: Shamley.

Hitchcock, A. (Director/Producer). (1963). *The birds* [Motion picture]. United States: Universal.

Hitchcock, A. (Director/Producer). (1964). *Marnie* [Motion picture]. United States: Universal.

Jakobson, R. (1956). Two aspects of language and two types of aphasic disturbances." *Fundamentals of language.* The Hague: Mouton.

Jakobson, R. (1972). *Questions de poétique.* Paris: Sevil.

Lacan, J. (1975). *Four fundamental concepts of psychoanalysis*. New York: Norton.

Leclaire, D. (1966). A propos de l'analyse par Freud de l'homme aux loups. *Cahiers pour l'Analyse, 5*.

Metz, C. (1977). *The imaginary signifier: Psychoanalysis and cinema*. Bloomington: Indiana University Press.

Souriau, E. (1951). La structure de l'univers filmique et le vocabulaire de la filmologie. *Revue internationale de filmologie*, No. 7–8 (May), 231–240.

Warhol, A. (Director/Producer). 1966. *The Chelsea girls* [Motion picture]. United States: Andy Warhol.

Welles, O. (Director), & Wilson, R., Castle, W. (Producers). 1948. *The lady from Shanghai* [Motion picture]. United States: Columbia.

# 6

## Freud at the Movies, 1907–1925

### From the Piazza Colonna and
### Hammerstein's Roofgarden to
### The Secrets of a Soul

SANFORD GIFFORD

### INTRODUCTION

This is the story of the only two movies that Freud was known to have seen, in 1907 and 1909, and a third film that he refused to see in 1927, declaring that psychoanalytic concepts were unsuitable for "plastic representation." This "educational film" *(Lehrfilm)*, intended to show the general public how analysis worked, was proposed by two of Freud's most faithful followers, Karl Abraham and Hanns Sachs. It was also rejected by Eitingon and Ernest Jones, who supported Freud, although none of them had seen the film. Called *The Secrets of a Soul* (Pabst, 1925), it was directed by G. W. Pabst, a master of the German silent film. It was not a sensational film, and had a modest popular success. The later history of the movies suggests that this obiter dictum of Freud's was not one of his great prophecies, in view of the hundreds of films that followed, good, bad, and indifferent, attempting to apply psychoanalytic theories, or their directors' idea of analysis.

Without attempting a systematic review of the literature on film and psychoanalysis, Freud's close follower, Otto Rank, had suggested in 1914 that "cinematography, which . . . reminds us of the dream-work, can also express certain psychological facts and relationships—which the writer is often unable to describe with verbal clarity—in such clear and conspicuous imagery that it facilitates our understanding of them (Rank, 1914/1971, pp. 4–7). Hugo Münsterberg, not an analyst but a popular psychiatrist in the tradition of William James, had written a whole book (1916) in praise of moving pictures. He valued films especially for their educational possibilities, and their capacity for creating an illusion of space and depth. In describing the "plastic impression" created by the stereopticon, he suggested that films might create the same effect by using two cameras and projectors, foreshadowing three-dimensional techniques of many years later. He proposed that memory and imagination could be better represented in film than on the stage, because "the photoplay obeys the laws of the mind rather than those of the outer world." He commented on the "heightened suggestibility" of the movie audience, and acknowledged the exaggerated emotions required by the silent screen, where "a New England temperament, forced into Neapolitan expressions of hatred and jealousy . . . too easily appears a caricature."

Among recent critical writings, Laura Marcus (2002) makes an important contribution to the interrelationships between film and psychoanalytic theory, both before and after Freud's 1925 edict against film representations of analysis. She recalls many other analysts who were fascinated by films besides Otto Rank, who explicitly equated cinematography with dream work. She quotes his comments on the film *The Student of Prague* (Rye, 1913) as the starting point for Freud's famous essay on "The Uncanny" (1919/1973), although Freud refers to the book by Ewer, not the film. Other analysts interested in film were Lou Andreas-Salomé, Ella Freeman Sharpe, and Bertram Lewin, besides Hanns Sachs. Many film critics were also fascinated by psychoanalysis, including Walter Benjamin, Siegfried Kracauer, and Christian Metz.

An important enthusiast for film as an art form was one of Freud's favorite analysands, the British poet HD, who, with her companion, "Bryher," were also analysands of Hanns Sachs. Both Sachs and HD had written extensively for the film journal *Close Up*, and HD had even acted in a film, *Borderline*, that was closely modeled on *Secrets of a Soul*. And yet, in one of her various tributes to Freud, HD stated that she had never discussed her film work with Freud! According to Marcus, "It seems likely that she saw her sessions with Freud as continuing, or perhaps replacing, the work of film." Marcus concludes her essay with the stunning assertion that HD

> helps us to understand [how] Freud's silence on the question of film . . . conceals the profundity of the relationship between psychoanalysis and film. *Psychoanalysis is itself cinema* [italics added]. . . . In this reading, the absence of filmic

analogies in Freud's writings does not signal an indifference toward cinema. In the absence of analogy, a more fundamental relationship—the identity between psychoanalysis and film—begins to emerge. (Marcus, 2002)

## FREUD'S ONLY VISITS TO THE MOVIES

Freud was probably unaware of a rough parallel in the evolution of the psychoanalytic movement and the development of the film industry. Freud and Breuer's *Studies on Hysteria* (Freud, 1893–1895/1955) had appeared in 1895, Freud's pioneering theoretical and clinical papers in the first decade of the twentieth century, and his fully developed structural theory in the 1920s. Edison had patented the Kinetograph, a primitive device weighing half a ton that produced short, comic one-reelers in the peepshow format of the Nickelodeon, in 1893. Longer feature films developed gradually, and the great German silents appeared in the early 1920s (Abel, 1998, pp. 215–245). This parallelism was no accident, in that both Freud's theories and Edison's inventions were manifestations of the modern era, along with Cubism and avant-garde music and poetry. Quite independently, all modern artists seemed to be obeying Virginia Woolf's imaginary date: "On or about December 1910 human character changed. . . . And when human relations change . . . there is a change in religion, conduct, politics and literature" (1924, pp. 4–5). This marked the end of the Edwardian Age in England, and the beginning of modern times in the Western world. Roger Fry's pioneer exhibit of French Impressionists took place in 1910, and its American equivalent, the Armory Show in New York, in 1912.

Freud saw his first movie in 1907, when he was enjoying a solitary trip to Rome, after being assured by Jung that their recent Congress had been a success. He was writing his family, "to my dear ones," in a happy mood, describing a delightful evening in the Piazza Colonna, where crowds congregated, band concerts were given, and "the air is really delicious" (E. Freud, 1960, pp. 261–263). Besides the music, a screen had been erected on a rooftop, on which lantern slides and movies were projected, mingled with ads for a stomach medicine called Fermentine. Freud made fun of the ads, but

> to beguile the public these are interspersed with pictures of landscapes, Negroes of the Congo, glacier ascents and so on . . . and short cinematographic performances, for the sake of which the old children (including your father) suffer quietly the advertisements. . . . I usually remain spellbound.

The entire letter, however, is one of Freud's eloquent testimonials to the charms of Italy, rather than a critique of the movies themselves, and a lovely summer evening in Rome may well have predisposed him to enjoy the film.

Freud saw his next movie on Sept 4, 1909, at Hammerstein's Victoria Theatre in New York, on his way to deliver the Clark Lectures in Worcester, Massachusetts. A. A. Brill had taken Freud, Jung, and Ferenczi, later joined by Ernest Jones, for dinner at Hammerstein's Roofgarden, where vaudeville skits began at 8:30, interspersed with short films. Freud's reaction to the films was described by Jones (1955): he (Freud) was "going on to a cinema to see one of the primitive films of those days with plenty of wild chasing. Ferenczi in his boyish way was very excited at it, but Freud was only quietly amused" (p. 56). This comment reflected Jones's mild disparagement, even jealousy, of Ferenczi more than a clear impression of Freud's reaction, and Jones did not indicate his own or Jung's reactions to the films.

As to what kind of film they saw, Hammerstein's Victoria Theatre was known for presenting evenings of vaudeville and films, and close by was the Eden Musée, showing short comic films exploiting fast action and chases, like the later Keystone Cops of Mack Sennett. The projectionist at the Eden was Edwin Porter, a pioneer in the transition between shorts and features who had already created *The Great Train Robbery* (Porter, 1903). Although the prototype of the film camera had been invented by Edison, the French were far ahead of the Americans in the early 1900s, from the Lumière Brothers, Méliès, and Charles Pathé. In 1909 Freud probably saw one of Pathé's many farces, perhaps with comedians like Max Linder or Migé, a "conscientious buffoon . . . whose gags and masterful pratfalls . . . lead to an escalating orgy of destruction" (Abel, 1998). Perhaps Freud's reserve merely meant that slapstick was not to his taste.

## THE FILM PROPOSAL FROM ABRAHAM AND SACHS

Freud's next and more significant encounter with film occurred in 1925, with Abraham and Sachs's proposal, at a time when Freud's popularity with the general public was at its peak. Karl Abraham (1925) had written Freud, "The discussion of psychoanalysis in newspapers and magazines can no longer be kept quiet. . . . Naturally there is no lack of antagonism. But without doubt the interest has never been so strong" (as quoted in Fallend & Reichmayr, 1992, pp. 132–152). The postwar period in Germany was also a time of social disorganization and increased interest in psychoanalysis, prompted in part, as in the United States after World War II, by experiences with posttraumatic war neuroses (Eppensteiner, Fallend, and Reichmayr, 1987). Freud was gratified by the professional acceptance of his theories but he was also uneasy about their popularity and the risk of their being oversimplified and distorted. Two years before, Freud had rebuffed Samuel Goldwyn, who had offered him $100,000 to consult on film as "the foremost expert on love," and Goldwyn had hoped Freud would even "write a story for the screen" (Gay, 1988, p. 454). As in rejecting Colonel Robert McCormick's invitation to psychoanalyze the youthful killers, Leopold and Loeb, Freud had consistently refused to make financial use of his popularity, in spite of his concern about money to support the International Psychoanalytic Press.

Freud's lifelong mistrust of popularization, however, could never protect him from the public's need to use analytic concepts for their own purposes. These included Dadaist poets like André Breton and dozens of writers and film makers who created crude and sensational representations of madness. Analysis was sometimes represented as hypnosis, in which dreams and memories were recalled, and a hypnotist would induce his hypnotized subject to commit crimes. The two best and most famous films of this era, *The Cabinet of Dr. Caligari* (Wiene, 1919) and *Dr. Mabuse the Gambler* (Lang, 1922) were dramatic examples of this genre (Kracauer, 1947; Eisner, 1973).

In the summer of 1925 Karl Abraham, one of Freud's oldest and most loyal followers and a founder of the Berlin Psychoanalytic Institute, proposed an "educational film" based on a clinical case and supervised by senior analysts (Abraham and Freud, 1963). Freud rejected the idea, and the complex controversy among his closest associates that followed was called "the Film Affair." The complications were brilliantly described by Paul Ries (Ries, 1995, pp. 759–791) in great detail, and I am heavily indebted to his paper, which I will try to summarize. For other reasons, the early 1920s were also very difficult years for Freud, including the painful finale of Otto Rank's break with him and the discovery of his mouth cancer in 1923. These events overshadowed the "Film Affair," and the analytic establishment may have wished to minimize its importance.

The original film proposal had came to Abraham from Hans Neumann (quoted in Ries, 1995, p. 763), an independent film maker in Berlin who had some familiarity with analysis. He had suggested "an educational film about analysis, with an introduction illustrating examples of repression, the unconscious etc., and a clinical case, showing the cure of nervous symptoms." The film would be accompanied by a short, "easily comprehensible, popular paper on psychoanalysis," to be offered to the audience like an opera libretto. Abraham wrote Freud (June 7, 1925) enthusiastically about this proposal, as "a popular, scientific, psychoanalytic film with your authorization and supervision of recognized colleagues." He admitted that "this kind of thing is not really up my street" but "so typical of our times that it is sure to be carried out, if not with us then with people who know nothing about it." Abraham mentioned the ubiquitous "wild analysts" who would be eager to exploit the idea, and he emphasized Neumann's knowledge of Freud's work, adding some ideas of his own for the introductory pamphlet. He predicted that Freud would probably have "no great sympathy for the plan as a whole" but he hoped that he would "come to acknowledge the force of the practical argument." Abraham wrote this from his sickbed, suffering from what he called a "feverish bronchitis." As Abraham had guessed, Freud was "not happy about your magnificent project." Though swayed at first by the risk of "wild analysts" exploiting such a film, Freud said such travesties could always be repudiated when carried out by others. He emphasized instead the authorization, which only he could give: "My chief objection is still that I do not believe that satisfactory plastic representation of our abstractions is at all possible." Nevertheless he expressed his confidence in Abraham's judgment, and suggested that he convey to Neumann his disbelief "in anything good and useful coming out of the project." Though Freud would not give his authorization, he left the door open by saying that if Abraham later found the script acceptable, Freud might be more willing to consider it.

Subsequent correspondence between them chiefly concerned Abraham's continuing respiratory symptoms. Then, on July 18, Abraham wrote Freud that he and Hanns Sachs "believe we have every guarantee that the [film project] will be carried out with genuine seriousness." A month later, however, he wrote, "I am sorry to hear that there has been some upset to do with the film. . . . But the work is progressing well and I feel sure that one day you will come round to agreeing with Sachs and myself." On August 20 he reiterated his impression of good progress on the film and said, "Sachs was devoting himself to it and proving very competent." But he admitted his dislike for the film's advertisement, agreeing with Freud's remark that "one should have nothing to do with these people." Intervening letters chiefly concerned Abraham's deteriorating health and his attendance at the Bad Homburg International Psychoanalytic Association Congress, where he was elected president of the IPA.

Abraham reported to Freud that he had heard Rank deliver a rapid, incomprehensible paper, and that Rank seemed "sick," in a way that suggested "a new manic phase." In spite of his own illness, Abraham wrote a paper on "The Impostor," and in late October he wrote to Freud, in answer to a letter in the (October 27, 1925) *Rundbriefe:*

> You know, dear Professor, that I am very unwilling to enter once again into a discussion of the film affair. But because of your reproach of harshness (in your circular letter) I find myself in the same position as on several previous occasions. In almost twenty years, we have had no differences of opinion except where personalities were concerned, whom I, very much to my regret, had to criticize. The same sequence of events repeated itself each time; you indulgently overlooked everything that could be challenged in the behavior of the person concerned, whilst all the blame was directed against me. In Jung's case it was . . . "jealousy"; in Rank's, "unfriendly behavior" and, this time, "harshness." (Abraham, 1963)

In conclusion, Abraham asked Freud if each time Freud had disagreed with him, had he not been reacting to criticism that was basically his own, but that he could not admit into consciousness? Abraham acknowledged his pain at having "aroused [Freud's] displeasure once again" and hoped that he would "one day reconsider his judgment." Freud answered quickly (November 5, 1925):

> I cannot convert myself to your point of view on the film affair. There are a good many things that I see differently. . . . You were certainly right about Jung but not quite so right about Rank. . . . But should you turn out to be right this time too, nothing would prevent me from once again admitting it.

On this unhappy, uncompromising note, their correspondence ended; these were the last letters exchanged between two very old friends. Abraham died a month later, on Christmas day, 1925, of a lung cancer that none of his physicians had correctly diagnosed, including Felix Deutsch and Wilhelm Fliess, both of whom had treated Freud on occasion.

## ABRAHAM'S DEATH AND THE MAKING OF THE FILM

Freud was devastated by this loss, as reflected in his correspondence with Jones (Paskauskas, 1993) and with Abraham's widow. During these six short months, from Abraham's first film proposal to his death, a great deal had transpired. The shooting of the film was almost completed by mid-November, but a clear picture of these events is hard to obtain, according to Ries (1995), who had examined many highly specialized film journals, archives, and unpublished correspondence. One problem was the omissions from the Freud-Abraham correspondence, perhaps made by the editors to minimize an embarrassing episode. Another problem was an unpublished biography of Pabst by his son Michael, quoted by many critics, including Atwell (1977), but recently proved to be quite unreliable (Ries, 1995, p. 763, n.10). Nevertheless, Ries clearly describes how Neumann's original *Lehrfilm* was taken over by UFA, the giant, once state-supported German film company, and converted into a commercial film, to be called *The Secrets of a Soul*. This was the point where G. W. Pabst became the director of the film, and Neumann the producer. Ries points out that more detailed information is needed to avoid two simplistic conclusions: 1) that Abraham and Sachs should be blamed for disobeying Freud's warnings against popularization, or 2) that UFA should be blamed for "hoodwinking a couple of naïve psychoanalysts into cooperating on something they did not understand," meaning commercial film production on a large scale.

On July 18, when Abraham had written Freud his most reassuring letter, he and Sachs had already provided Neumann with the case history of a
young physician, whose name was known but disguised in the film. At that
time neither Pabst nor UFA were involved, and the ad for the film that had
disturbed Freud and Abraham probably referred to "the treatment of nervous
diseases by psychoanalysis according to Professor Freud." This was contrary
to Freud's express desire that his name not be mentioned. Neumann was a
small independent film maker, in a highly competitive market, at a time
when German firms were confronted with the increasing popularity of
American films. Other *Lehrfilme* were being made about all kinds of specialized medical subjects, from gynecology and hypnosis to a film on psychoanalysis, unsupervised by analysts. When Neumann had proposed to place
the project in the cultural section of UFA, Sachs had agreed. He wrote to
Freud that to refuse would have been "monstrous," a disservice to the psychoanalytic movement. A new ad for the film, as a UFA *Kulturfilm*, did not
imply Freud's authorization, but referred to Freudian theory as "a courageous
experiment." Abraham and Sachs, "two of Freud's best known pupils," were
named as "scientific directors," and Hans Neumann as producer and G. W.
Pabst as director.

Pabst was then emerging as a major director, when the Expressionism
of films like *Dr. Caligari* and *Nosferatu* (Murnau, 1921) were being superseded
by films reflecting *Die Neue Sachlichkeit*, or the New Objectivity (Eisner, 1973;
Kracauer, 1947; Atwell & Rentschler, 1990). Pabst had just completed *The
Street Without Joy* (Pabst, 1925), in which Greta Garbo made her debut, with
a realistic emphasis on poverty and the everyday life of the streets. His great
successes were yet to come: *The Threepenny Opera* (Pabst, 1931) with music by
Kurt Weil and *Pandora's Box* (Pabst, 1929) with Louise Brooks. Pabst had
requested a coherent plot, besides the dream-sequences Abraham and Sachs
had offered, and the final script was probably written by Colin Ross. Pabst
chose well-known actors for the film: Werner Krauss who had played the lead
in *Dr. Caligari*, and Pawel Pawlow for the psychiatrist (see Figure 6.1), a Russian who had been an associate of the great Stanislawsky. Pawlow could not
speak German, but Pabst insisted that he read Freud in Russian, in order to
understand his part. He was coached by Sachs, "who was wonderful in teaching us his theories" (Bachmann, quoted in Ries, 1995). Filming lasted twelve
weeks, beginning in September, and afterward Sachs was no longer involved
in the final editing of the film.

After Abraham's death in December, Sachs was left alone to face the
combined criticism of Freud, Eitingon, and Ernest Jones, who had been leading the attack upon Sachs long before. Ferenczi had joined Freud in opposing
the film project by sending him an offensive newspaper clipping. Meanwhile
in Vienna, Siegfried Bernfeld and A. J. Storfer were working on a rival film,

FIGURE 6.1. Werner Kraus and Pawel Pawlow as patient and psychoanalyst in the earliest known cinematic portrayal of the psychoanalytic process, from G. W. Pabst's *Secrets of a Soul* (UFA, 1926). Courtesy of the Museum of Modern Art/Film Stills Archive.

in the name of the International Psychoanalytic Verlag (Vienna), but clearly directed against Abraham and Sachs (Ries, 1995; Fallend & Reichmayr, 1992); the project will not be discussed here, because Bernfeld left his script unfinished and the film was never made.

On August 14, 1925, Freud wrote to Ferenczi:

> Stupid things are happening in matters of film. The company that beguiled Sachs and Abraham has naturally not been able to refrain from proclaiming my "assent" to the world. I remonstrated forcefully to Sachs and today, already, the *Neue Freie Presse* brought out a disclaimer. In the meantime Bernfeld is caught up in a similar undertaking with Storfer. I won't stop them, for film-making can be avoided as . . . little as bobbed hair. But I myself won't get mine cut, and don't intend to be brought into personal connection with any film. (Falzeder & Brabant, 2000, p. 222)

Jones later wrote Freud (December 5, 1925) about discussing the film with Sachs, Storfer, and Bernfeld at the Bad Homburg Congress, and sanctimoniously proclaimed his viewpoint as "identical with your own. . . . I regard it as unprofessional to depict one's own medical work in any such way before the public." He believed that Abraham "committed an error of judgement . . . [but] I cannot blame him. . . . The error was dictated by just that innocence and optimism that are otherwise such valuable traits in his character." Others he found less blameless, specifically Storfer, editor of the psychoanalytic *Almanach*, whom he considered "a pathological personality," and Sachs and Bernfeld, who "allowed their artistic ambitions and jealousies to triumph in a most narcissistic way" (Paskauskas, 1993, pp. 584–586).

Ries suggests that the split between Abraham and Sachs on one side and Freud and his other close followers on the other was prompted less by the film itself than by Abraham's behavior at the Bad Homburg Congress. But what this behavior was is not very clear. Max Schur's suggestion, that Freud's attitude toward Abraham was displaced anger at Abraham's earlier criticism of Fliess, is not very convincing (Schur, 1972, p. 388). A letter from Eitingon to Freud was critical of Sachs and the film, but sought some compromise in pointing out that Sachs's pamphlet accompanying the film could earn money for the *Verlag* and help defray the expenses of Abraham's lengthy illness. Freud wrote a conciliatory note to Jones (December 13, 1925) acknowledging that he disliked the idea of making a film "from the beginning. But I did not want to impose my feelings on others by laying down the law." He saw "an unexpectedly favorable turn" in selling the pamphlet, and concluded, "Perhaps we are all too conservative in this matter; one really ought to have made some sort of concession to the film fever." But these more tolerant sentiments came too late to reach Abraham, who died twelve days later.

THE FILM OPENS AND THE CONTROVERSY CONTINUES

Abraham's funeral, with all of its heartfelt grief and unstinting admiration, buried all criticism, and, as Ries suggests, his colleagues may well have wished to bury "the Film Affair" as well. The film itself, however, had its first previews in Berlin, during the very week of Abraham's funeral, on December 28, 1925. Jones saw the film in January, along with Eitingon and Ferenczi, but he described only the "consternation" caused by its being authorized by the president of the IPA (Abraham himself), and the "wave of abuse" against psychoanalysis that "took full advantage of the story" (Jones, 1957). Jones never described the film itself, nor his own reaction to it. He singled out Sachs as "mainly responsible" for the film, despite Abraham's repeated assertions that they had shared equally in the script, writing "Sachs and myself" even in his last letter to Freud.

Ferenczi continued the attack on Sachs, writing Freud (January 14, 1926) that "Sachs more and more covers himself with Abraham's mantle" and "does not really belong on the Committee," the secret inner circle Jones had created in 1910 to protect Freud from his enemies. Later Sachs was in fact dropped from the Committee at the Innsbruck IPA Congress in 1927 (Grosskurth, 1991), when it was reorganized and no longer secret. Eitingon had shared Ferenczi's displeasure with the film, and succeeded in having all the authors' names removed at the second (prerelease) preview of the film. Freud's mistrust of Sachs continued: "I have little confidence in Sachs's conscientious performance of duty, [and] do not like his recent development in the direction of the Cinema and of brutal personal hostilities" (Freud to Eitingon, July 21, 1926, as quoted in Ries, 1995).

By 1929, Sachs seemed no longer affected by Freud's disapproval when he wrote a cheerful essay on the psychology of film (Sachs, 1929) discussing the symbolic importance of gesture in Einstein's *Potemkin* and other films. Shortly after, Freud had warmly recommended Sachs as Boston's first permanent training analyst in 1933, although Ries suggests that Sachs still felt a lingering sense of hurt feelings after being rejected by Freud and his European colleagues (Ries, 1995). He points out that Sachs never listed the film among his works, and in his memoir of Freud (Sachs, 1944), Sachs wrote that he had incurred Freud's disapproval only once. He also acknowledged that "Freud did not find in me some of those qualities he valued most highly. In the bond between us, something was missing."

Jones's relentless attack on the film continued (Ries, 1995, pp. 780–783), rationalized by his fear that in England the film would discredit psychoanalysis and interfere with his efforts to obtain public acceptance of psychoanalysis as a medical science. He obtained a vote from the London Psychoanalytic Society on December 2 dissociating itself from the film, as yet unnamed and not yet released, and he published protests against it in the *Lancet* and the *British Medical Journal*. A second vote was taken by the Society on January 8, 1926, and Jones took the extraordinary step of writing the British Board of Film Censors, offering to bring a delegation of analysts to explain why this film should not be shown! The archives of the board were destroyed during the war, but a reply to Jones (January 13, 1926) has survived, asking for the title of the film. Jones had managed, in protesting the film, to omit all the names involved, including those of Freud, Abraham, Sachs, and G. W. Pabst. In his next *Rundbrief* (Paskauskas, 1993, pp. 583–586), Jones reported his "close agreement" with Freud's views on film.

When the film opened in London the following summer, it was well received, and instead of "torrents of abuse" that Jones had described, the *Times* (July 6, 1927) reported that "the picture has been described as 'sensational.' It is nothing of the kind, and that is its merit." A scene had been cut by the distributor (Chodorkoff & Baxter, 1974), possibly influenced by Jones, who was still writing to Freud in the Rundbriefe (June 20, 1927) about *The Secrets of a Soul* as "Sachs's film." His continued animosity to Sachs, and his need to absolve Abraham of all responsibility for the film, suggest some personal malice, beyond his self-appointed role as protector of the psychoanalytic movement. Glover followed Jones's path, even in his later introduction to the Freud-Abraham correspondence (Abraham & Freud, 1963, p. xiii), holding Sachs responsible and excusing Abraham because of his illness. Glover dismissed the film itself as "rather simple-minded" and "naïve to the verge of ridiculousness."

Bernfeld's objection to the film was more complicated, occurring at a time when he had just obtained Freud's approval for his great work, *Sisyphus or the Limits of Education*, and when he was about to move from Vienna to Berlin. Driven by a lifelong concern for preserving the purity of analytic theory, Bernfeld saw the film as a form of bowdlerization, as a superficial presentation of analysis as a method of curing neurotic symptoms, instead of its deeper significance as a means of "investigating the human condition." Bernfeld was also engaged in writing a film script of his own, partly autobiographical, that he never completed (Ries, 1995, pp. 780–783).

We are indebted to Ries once again, and through him to Dr. Ludger Hermanns of Berlin, for evidence that Freud's habitual sense of humor was not totally lost in confronting film. This is a newly discovered manuscript, apparently from the Ernst Simmel archives, undated but with a letter from Freud to Simmel (October 26, 1925). The manuscript includes a lecture by Simmel and an elaborate film script in three parts, with outrageous skits that parody psychoanalysis, crude jokes, erotic dances, and advertisements for getting analyzed at the Psycho-Analytic Institute and Polyclinic at Potsdammerstrasse 29! Freud read the manuscript and wrote to Simmel:

I was greatly amused. . . . The jokes are excellent and the seriousness behind them valuable enough. The film [script] is also very funny, but it of course suffers from the basic fault between film and psychoanalysis. For in my judgment analysis does not lend itself to any kind of cinematographic representation.

In short, though amused, Freud reiterated his skepticism about films in general, and, as far as we know, he never saw *Geheimnisse einer Seele*.

## THE FILM ITSELF

After all the complex controversies generated by this film, and Freud's negative reaction to it and to the very idea of making a film about psychoanalysis, the film itself will seem something of an anticlimax. It was released in March 1926 in Berlin and in the major movie houses of Europe. In Berlin, the opening-night audiences were provided with a 32–page pamphlet by Hanns Sachs, called *Psychoanalyse: Rätsel des Unbewussten*, or "Riddles of the Unconscious" (Sachs, 1926). This contained the cast of characters, brief nontechnical discussions of Freud's theory of dreams and methods of treatment, and the conclusion that "no single film can portray psychoanalysis, with its nearly endless possibilities." The film received generally favorable reviews, and in the only one written by an analyst, J. Harnik (1926) praised both Abraham and Sachs for their achievement in presenting visually the important elements of an analysis: the uses of the dream and the interpretation of parapraxes and compulsive thoughts. He acknowledged that at the high point of the film, the resolution of the neurotic conflict was represented as an abreaction, "giving the impression of a 'cathartic cure,'" as in Freud's "early American lectures" (pp. 580–581). Nevertheless, he concluded that in connecting the patient's symptoms to an early childhood trauma the film clearly illustrated a psychoanalytic process.

To summarize briefly, the film portrays a childless couple in which the husband, a young chemist, develops an acute phobia of knives, with compulsive thoughts about killing his wife. These symptoms are cured after a few months of psychoanalysis, along with his pre-existing impotence. There is a happy ending, with a flash forward to the happy couple with the child they had always wanted. To a present-day audience, this film has an innocent charm, appealing in its quaint period details, though some may find it naïve or even "simple-minded," as Glover did. Perhaps this simplicity was the aim of its original director, Hans Neumann, in his effort to convey some analytic concepts to a general audience. He had originally used a scene with an intruder, prompted by a case in Freud's *Introductory Lectures*, that was omitted from the final version. But the scene had convinced him that a psychoanalytic

film could be made. The theme of a knife phobia may have had special resonance for the final director, G.W. Pabst, who had an obsessive fascination
with knives, which play such important roles in his other films (Anne Freid-
berg, as quoted in Atwell & Rentschler, 1990, pp. 41–51).

The opening shot shows the husband's face in a shaving mirror as his
wife approaches with a straight-edge razor still in his hand. She playfully
attempts to kiss him, is put off by his shaving cream, and asks him to shave
the back of her neck. Suddenly a piercing scream from outside startles them
both, and he accidentally makes a small nick on her neck. On his way to work,
the young chemist passes an ambulance and he overhears his neighbors talking about a murder committed with a razor. At his lab, a woman and her
young daughter visit; he is effusive in giving the girl candy and she looks back
at him seductively as they depart. Returning home, he is disturbed by newspaper accounts of the nearby murder, and thrusts the papers into the fire. He
is also disturbed by his wife's excitement over the visit of her cousin, an
explorer from an exotic tropical country. He has sent them presents ahead: a
short samurai sword and the statuette of an Oriental fertility goddess. At bed-
time his wife is disappointed when her husband leaves her at the bedroom
door, and what follows is his elaborate nightmare.

The dream sequence (see Figure 6.2) alternates scenes of the husband
tossing in bed, fragments of the day's residue, a thunder storm with violent
winds and rain outside, and a verbal pun about "ein schweres Unwetter" (the
storm) and "der Vetter" (his wife's expected cousin). Within the dream scenes
a policeman with a rifle appears in a tree; he turns into his wife's cousin and
shoots at him. The husband flies off into space. An Italian campanile with an
external spiral staircase erects itself, the husband runs up the stairs and in the
belfry he sees in the tolling bells the faces of three women, one of whom is his
wife. He looks down from on high into a moat filled with water, where he sees
his wife and her cousin in a canoe, among lily pads. His wife pulls a large doll
from the water, which she and her cousin embrace.

The next day the husband develops various parapraxes: dropping his
razor, he decides to get shaved at his barber's. At work he drops a test tube
when his lab assistant announces the arrival of the cousin. At dinner with his
wife and the cousin, whom he had greeted effusively, he cannot touch his
knife, and asks his wife to cut up his meat. Abruptly he rises and says, "I cannot eat with you." He leaves for a neighborhood café, where he orders a drink,
pays, and forgets his key on the table. This is observed by a man nearby, who
follows him home and at his gate returns his door key, saying, "You must have
a reason for not wishing to go home."

The next day the husband moves into his mother's house and tells her of
his distress; she asks if he knows anyone who can help him. He recalls the man
who had returned his key, and how this stranger had explained his comment

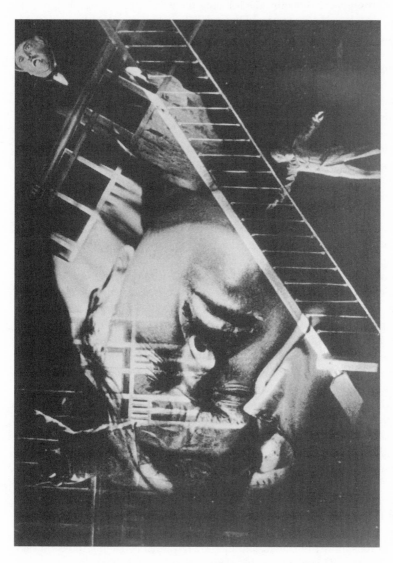

FIGURE 6.2. Dream sequence from *Secrets of a Soul* (UFA, 1926). Courtesy of the Museum of Modern Art/Film Stills Archive.

about forgetting his key by saying, "It's part of my work." The husband returns to his café and quickly learns that the man is Herr Dr. Orth, who lives in the neighborhood. He consults the doctor at once, and confides his knife phobia and his compulsive thoughts about killing the wife whom he deeply loves. "Is this not madness?" he asks, and Dr. Orth calmly replies, "We have a method, psychoanalysis, and when the unconscious is uncovered, you will be cured." The patient eagerly returns the next morning. Treatment begins with doctor and patient face-to-face over a coffee table, quite close and both very animated. Soon the husband, now the patient, takes to the couch, but often turns to face the analyst, who sits very near, sometimes patting the patient reassuringly on the shoulder. The process of analysis is presented by means of dreams, childhood scenes, early memories of his marriage, fantasies, and the analyst's interpretations. They are conveyed to the audience by visual images and subtitles, as if the spectator were "hearing" what the patient is telling his analyst. The campanile, for example, is in an Italian town where they had their honeymoon. In looking at a vacant apartment, the husband visualizes a baby's crib, which then vanishes. Dropping a test tube on hearing of the cousin's arrival is called "a typical parapraxis." The water in the moat is interpreted as amniotic fluid, "which means a baby is coming," and the analyst asks if the patient recalls anything similar. He then remembers (and visualizes) a children's party long ago, where his future wife gave a large doll to her cousin, not to the patient. He has fantasies of his wife in "compromising situations," represented by Near Eastern scenes in which his wife performs seductive dances and her cousin smokes a water pipe. The oedipal nature of his conflict is suggested by his mother's solicitude, cutting up his food, hiding the knives, and urging him to eat. The dénouement occurs when he is recalling the scene in his nightmare, where he is brandishing the cousin's samurai sword in front of the Oriental statuette, which has become life-size. To illustrate his actions, the patient leaps from the couch, seizes a letter opener from the analyst's desk, and brandishes it violently. And so, Dr. Orth points out, the patient is now to able to touch a knife and his phobia is cured!

This is the end of the analysis, with the interpretation that the knife phobia and his irrational impulses to kill his wife concealed an unconscious jealousy of her cousin, and his symptoms are resolved when the patient becomes conscious of these underlying impulses. In the process he is also cured of his pre-existing impotence, which had predisposed him to intense jealousy of her relationship with her cousin. Thus he is able to resume a loving relationship with his wife, and they are rewarded by having the child they had longed for. This happy ending is represented in an epilogue by a dramatic flash forward to a romantic summer cottage on a hill. The husband is fishing in a stream below, the sound track shifts from Schumann's "Kinderszenen" to Schubert's "Die Forelle," and the husband catches a trout. He races up the hill, where his wife and their young child are playing in an idyllic rural landscape, and he embraces them. FINIS.

A current critic (Anne Friedberg, as quoted in Atwell & Rentschler, 1990, pp. 41–51) comments on "the many images that remain unanalyzed and uninterpreted," but finds the total effect uncluttered and effective. The serene, happy ending is far removed from the violence and "sensationalism" that Jones had predicted the film would contain. Though not one of Pabst's greatest films, he deserves credit for avoiding the exploitation of psychoanalysis for violence and melodrama. The present-day spectator may find the finale overly sentimental, and question how accurate a picture it gives of psychoanalysis in the early 1920s. The exemplary cure within a few months is plausible, in an era when analyses could be very short. The theatrical cure by abreaction may be condoned as dramatic license, in making a commercial film attractive to a popular audience. Some British critics objected to the analyst's following his prospective patient home and returning his door key, and this sequence was omitted in some versions of the film. In retrospect, the major difference from present-day analytic practice lies in the intimacy and emotional expressiveness of both the patient and his analyst. The latter is a friendly, warm-hearted enthusiast, very different from the cool analytic neutrality that Freud was advocating in that same period, although we now know he could be informal and talkative with some of his analysands. We must also remind ourselves that this was a silent film, with all the conventions of that genre, with its exaggerated emotionality in making its affects unmistakably clear. Nevertheless, the film gives quite a convincing picture of psychoanalysis if we make due allowances for its didactic intent and its aim for a general public.

SUMMARY AND CONCLUSIONS

In this chapter, Freud's only known encounters with the movies have been described in some detail. To summarize briefly, the primitive early films he actually saw in 1907 and 1909 were enjoyable experiences, not very important but amusing period pieces, when Freud appears as an average, uncritical movie goer. In 1925, however, when an "educational film" about psychoanalysis was proposed by two of his oldest followers, Karl Abraham and Hanns Sachs, Freud's reaction was strongly negative. He proclaimed a priori that analytic concepts were unsuited to "plastic representation," without ever seeing the movie. In spite of his objections, the film, *The Secrets of a Soul,* was produced, directed by UFA's great G. W. Pabst, and received by the public with moderate success.

The controversy about the film continued, however, with Abraham and Sachs as its defenders and Freud, Ernest Jones, and Eitingon united against it.

Even after Abraham's untimely death in December 1925, Jones continued his attack on the film and on Sachs as its chief author. He mobilized the London Psychoanalytic Society against the film, and even sought to have it banned by the British Board of Film Censors.

The film itself proved to be an innocent portrayal of a childless couple in which the husband suddenly develops an inexplicable knife phobia. He is cured by a kindly analyst, who makes him aware of his unconscious jealousy of his wife's male cousin. He is also freed from a sexual inhibition and is now able to have a child. There is a happy ending, with a flash forward to the young couple and their child in an idyllic rural landscape.

The reader may ask whether the controversy generated by this film is an analytic tempest-in-a-teapot, scarcely deserving of so much detail. The battle among the analysts over *The Secrets of a Soul* was not trivial, however, and there were some serious personal consequences. The lifelong friendship between Abraham and Freud was irreparably damaged during an especially painful period in the last months of Abraham's life. His untimely death left Sachs as the sole object of Jones's continuing attacks. Besides Sachs's hurt feelings as a wounded loyalist, Jones's rancor may have influenced the secret "Committee" in dropping Sachs at their 1927 IPA meeting. Sachs's isolation from Freud and his former colleagues may in turn have influenced Sachs in accepting the invitation to Boston in 1933, to become the Boston Psychoanalytic Institute's first permanent training analyst.

The reader may also ask if Freud's attitude toward movies had any relation to a related topic, his disinterest in music and his aversion to avant-garde art. The age difference may have influenced Freud's reaction to films between his youth and his later years. We know he wrote enthusiastically about seeing Sarah Bernhardt and attending the opera, when he was writing from Paris to his prospective bride (E. Freud, 1960, pp. 165–206). And in 1907, he attended a performance of *Carmen* the night after his first movie, as we have described. Peter Gay (Gay, 1988, 168–173) has offered a lively discussion of this topic, contrasting Anna Freud's terse remark, "He never goes to concerts," with Freud's interest in opera. But as Gay points out, Freud's interest was in opera as spectacle, as a drama with its characters like Don Giovanni and their psychological conflicts, not in the music that gives opera so much of its emotional impact. Could Freud's indifference to music mean he was ill at ease with the direct expression of strong emotion? Would the melting, tear-drenched melancholy of Schubert's *Lieder* have offended his affinity for self-control and the voice of reason? What Freud's reactions to the tear jerkers of the 1920s might have been, in contrast to the slapstick comedies of 1907–1909, we cannot say, because there is no evidence that he ever saw any of these movies.

## NOTE

There is more than one print of *Secrets of a Soul,* with marked differences in quality and selection of scenes. Of the two versions I have used, from the Harvard Film Archive, there is an English version, of unknown date, with good visual quality, few subtitles, and a faded but engaging operatic sound track. The German version, a 1984 reprint by Norddeutscher Rundfunk, is very bad visually, bleached out and overexposed, but there are many more subtitles, more details, and even some scenes that are not in the English version.

For the correspondence between Freud and Abraham, any unannotated letters will be found in *The Letters of Sigmund Freud and Karl Abraham* (Abraham and Freud, 1963).

## REFERENCES

Abel, R. (1998). *The ciné goes to town: French cinema 1896–1914.* Berkeley: University of California Press.

Abraham, H., & Freud, E. (Eds.). (1963). *The letters of Sigmund Freud and Karl Abraham.* New York: Basic Books.

Atwell, L. (1977). *G. W. Pabst.* Boston: Twayne Publishers.

Atwell, L., & Rentschler, E. (Eds.). (1990). *The films of G. W. Pabst.* Newark, NJ: Rutgers University Press.

Breuer, J., & Freud, S. (1955). *Studies on hysteria.* In J. Strachey (Ed. & Trans.), *Standard edition of the complete psychological works of Sigmund Freud* (Vol. 2, pp. 1–335). London: Hogarth Press. (Original work published 1893–95)

Chodorkoff, B, & Baxter, S. (1974). *Secrets of a soul,* an early psychoanalytic film-venture. *American Imago, 31,* 319–334.

Eisner, L. (1973). *The haunted screen, expressionism in the German cinema.* Berkeley: University of California Press.

Eppensteiner, B., Fallend, K., & Reichmayr, J. (1987). Die psychoanalyse in film 1925/26 (Berlin/Wien). *Psyche, 44,* 129–139.

Fallend, K., & Reichmayr, J. (1992). Psychoanalyse, film und öffentlichkeit. In *Siegfried Bernfeld oder Die Grenzen der Psychoanalyse* (pp.132–152). Basel: Stroemfeld/Nexus.

Falzeder, E., & Brabant, E. (Eds.). (2000). *The correspondence of Sigmund Freud and Sandor Ferenczi 1920–1933* (Vol. 3). Cambridge, MA: Harvard University Press.

Freud, E. (Ed.). (1960). *Letters of Sigmund Freud.* E. Freud (Ed.). New York: Basic Books.

Freud, S. (1960). *Briefe 1873–1939*. Frankfurt-am-Main: Fischer-Verlag.

Freud, S. (1973). The uncanny. In J. Strachey (Ed. & Trans.), *Standard edition of the complete psychological works of Sigmund Freud* (Vol. 17, pp. 217–252). London: Hogarth Press. (Original work published 1919)

Friedberg, A. (1990). An *unheimlich* maneuver between psychoanalysis and the cinema: *Secrets of a soul* (1926). In E. Atwell & E. Rentschler (Eds.), *The films of G.W. Pabst* (pp. 41–51). Newark, NJ: Rutgers University Press.

Gay, P. (1988). *Freud: A life for our time*. New York: W. W. Norton.

Grosskurth, P. (1991). *The secret ring*. Reading, MA: Addison-Wesley.

Harnik, J. (1926). Psychoanalyischer film. *Int'l Zeitschrift Psychoanalyse, 12*, 580–581.

Jones, E. (1955). *The life and work of Sigmund Freud* (Vol. 3). New York: Basic Books.

Jones, E. (1957). *The Life and Work of Sigmund Freud*, Volume III. New York, NY: Basic Books.

Kracauer, S. (1947). *From Caligari to Hitler: A psychological history of the German film*. Princeton, NJ: Princeton University Press.

Lang, F. (Director), & Pornmer, E. (Producer). (1922). *Dr. Mabuse, the gambler* (Motion picture). Germany: Ullstein-UCO Film/UFA

Marcus, L. (2002). Dreaming and cinematographic consciousness. *Psychoanalysis and History, 3*, 51–68.

McPherson, K. (Director). (1930). *Borderline* [Motion picture].

Münsterberg, Hugo. (1916). *The Photoplay*. New York: Appleton.

Murnau, F. W. (Director), & Prana, Berlin (Producer). (1921). *Nosferatu* (Motion picture). Germany: Prana.

Pabst, G. W. (Director), & So-Far Film Production GmbH, Berlin (Producer). (1925). *Street without joy* (Motion picture). Germany: So-Far Film Production GmbH.

Pabst, G. W. (Director), & Neumann, H (Producer). (1926). *The secrets of a soul* (Motion picture). Germany: UFA.

Pabst, G. W. (Director), & Nero-Film AG, Berlin (Producer). (1929). *Pandora's box* (Motion picture). Germany: Nero-Film AG.

Pabst, G. W. (Director), & Tonbild-Syndikat AG, Berlin (Producer). (1931). *The threepenny opera* (Motion picture). Germany: Tonbild-Syndikat AG.

Paskauskas, R. (Ed.). (1993). *The complete correspondence of Sigmund Freud and Ernest Jones, 1908–1939*. Cambridge, MA: Harvard University Press.

Porter, E. (Director), & Edison (Producer) (1903). *The great train robbery* (Motion picture). United States: Edison.

Rank, O. (1971). *The double: A psychoanalytic study*. H. Tucker, Jr. (Trans.). Chapel Hill, NC: University of North Carolina Press. (Originally published 1914)

Ries, P. (1995). Popularize and/or be damned: Psychoanalysis and film at the crossroads in 1925. *International Journal of Psychoanalysis, 76*, 759–791.

Rye, S. (Director), & Deutsche Bioscop (Producer). (1913). *The student of Prague* (Motion picture). Germany: Deutsche Bioscop.

Sachs, H. (1926). *Psychoanalyse, rätsel des unbewussten.* Berlin: Lichtbildbühne.

Sachs, H. (1929). Zur psychologie des films. *Die Psychoanalytische Bewegung, 1,* 122–126.

Sachs, H. (1944). *Freud, master and friend.* Cambridge, MA: Harvard University Press.

Schur, M. (1972). *Freud: Living and dying.* New York: International Universities Press.

Wiene, R. (Director), & Pommer, E. (Producer). (1919). *The cabinet of Dr. Caligari* (Motion picture). Germany: Decla-Bioscop, Berlin.

Woolf, V. (1924). *Mr. Bennet and Mrs. Brown.* London: Hogarth Press. (One of three Hogarth pamphlets that included Roger Fry's *The Artist and Psychoanalysis*)

# 7

# Talk Therapy

## The Representation of Insight in the Cinema

### SHOSHANA RINGEL

#### THE MEANING OF INSIGHT:
#### FROM FREUD TO INTERSUBJECTIVITY

The process and meaning of insight starting from Freud's drive/conflict formulation has gradually evolved to current relational and intersubjective perspectives. According to Mitchell (1997), in classical psychoanalytic theory "psychopathology results from repression, or a blocking from awareness of disturbing impulses, memories, thoughts and feelings." Mitchell continues by stating that repression is "undone through insight, which helps link conscious awareness with unconscious impulses, memories, thoughts, and feelings" (p. 36). Accordingly, the analyst's therapeutic action was understood to be the correct and well-timed interpretation of the patient's intrapsychic conflicts, which generated insight leading to therapeutic change.

The analyst's interpretations in classical psychoanalysis focused on transference and resistance that reflected the patient's unconscious conflicts. According to the classical formulation therefore, "Interpretation leads to insight and insight changes psychic structures" (Mitchell, 1997, p. 36). Myerson (1965) further argues that there are two types of insight in classical psychoanalysis. The first is the awareness of "the instinctual forces activating the regression," and the second the "realistic appraisal of the relationship between the self and the milieu," which Myerson calls "reality oriented insight" (p. 771). Myerson notes that the two types of insight are interdependent insofar as reality-oriented insight generally develops after the insight into unconscious instinctual forces has been established, which leads to mastery and adaptation of the ego. Valenstein (1981) agrees with Myerson and states that according to Freud, if patients gain insight into their unconscious conflicts, which were hidden " behind their symptoms" (p. 313), the insight becomes curative. Similarly, Richfield (1954) notes that "it is only when insight concerns the unconscious dynamic forces thwarting these goals that it has been considered a factor of ultimate therapeutic significance" (p. 395). Thus, according to classical psychoanalysis the understanding and bringing into consciousness of the patient's unconscious psychic life is the primary cause for psychological cure.

Since Freud, several profound shifts have occurred that parallel concurrent new social and cultural developments. These changes reflect a general philosophical shift from modern to postmodern perspectives. In Freud's time, the prevalent scientific belief was in an objective reality in which one could stand outside phenomena and study them objectively. In our current culture, which is influenced by postmodern thinking, the prevailing belief is that "to study something is to interact with it" (Mitchell, 1997, p. 37). Therefore, the therapist's "theoretical framework becomes an organizing principle for the data, rather than a blueprint of the mind" (p. 37).

An additional significant difference between Freud's era and our own is that the understanding of the context of interpretation has shifted because of changing social and cultural structures. In Freud's fin de siècle Vienna the analyst had unquestionable authority, or what Freud called the unobjectionable positive transference that the patient invested in the analyst, which was instrumental in the patient's motivation to receive the interpretation. Today however, the prevailing mode is for a more egalitarian relationship and mutuality in the therapeutic dyad. The therapist is no longer apart from and above the therapeutic process, and the search for insight has moved from a purely internal quest to the interpersonal context of the analytic situation (Poland, 1988). Finally, clinical sources now question the assumption that interpretation by itself necessarily leads to insight, as there is anecdotal evidence that patients do not necessarily remember interpretations as a significant aspect of their treatment, but rather the nature of the therapeutic relationship and the therapist's personality and emotional impact (Mitchell, 1997). Even Chused (1996), a more classically oriented analyst, points out that the role of interpretations in the process of insight and therapeutic change has evolved and that interpretations and insight, in themselves, may not be as significant as once thought. Like Mitchell (1997) and Renik (1996), she states that the best interpretations concern current interactions between therapist and client in which the therapist is an active participant, rather than a remote and author-itative interpreter of the therapeutic process.

Mitchell (1997) points out that rather than hearing the analyst's inter-pretation as something new, which leads to a new insight, the patient may instead hear the interpretation as a repetition of something old and familiar, such as the father's authoritarian voice, for example. Consequently, the verbal content of the interpretation may be less important to the process of insight than the relational dynamics between client and therapist. Another key dif-ference between Freud's paradigm and ours, according to Mitchell, is the issue of time. Initially, Freud's analyses lasted only a few months, and it was assumed that for curative insight to occur the analyst needed only to arrive at a correct interpretation. Subsequently however, it became clear that it took much more time and many transference-countertransference repetitions for patients to be able to utilize interpretations.

In current relational and intersubjective theories (Aron, 1996; Bromberg, 1994; Mitchell, 1997; Stolorow, Atwood, & Brandchaft, 1997), therapeutic action, that is, the process of gaining insight and achieving thera-peutic change, is located in the mutual engagement between therapist and client through the transference-countertransference matrix that brings about a more lasting structural and interpersonal change. This process entails change and transformation of the patient's old relational patterns in the transference, as well as the therapist's transformation of relational patterns in the counter-transference (Hoffman, 1998). Thus, real change occurs through change in the emotional relationship between the therapist and client. Interpretations by themselves, as previously discussed, may fail because they can be experienced as an aspect of old patterns, rather than as new phenomena. The therapist therefore has to participate in the therapeutic interaction through bringing the therapist's own personal experiences, which interact with the patient's experi-ences. In this relational paradigm, the working through of mistakes and mis-understandings may be an important aspect of helping the patient develop new interactive patterns, and is part of the authenticity and honesty of the therapeutic process itself.

This notion of transference-countertransference enactments also con-veys the relational view of therapeutic action. Several authors (Aron, 1996; Davies, 1994; Davies & Frawley, 1994; Mitchell, 1997; Renik, 1996) empha-size enactments, or the transference-countertransference engagement between client and therapist that the therapist inevitably gets drawn into, as an important opportunity for both therapist and client to gain insight into maladaptive relational patterns. Rather than merely making interpretations, the therapist is actively involved in the process of acquiring new insight. As Mitchell argues, "the analyst is envisioned not as outside that stair system pointing to the problems and illuminating the way through interpretations.

The analyst and the patient are on the stairs together" (1997, p. 60). Insight is always embedded in the relational context, and knowledge and meaning are constantly cocreated between therapist and client (Hoffman, 1998).

Finally, an interesting postmodern perspective on insight is presented by Wilson (1998), who elaborates on the dialectical process of insight in the following words: "The analysand experiences profound oscillations between the opening of psychic space and the closing in on compelling insight, between doubting and certainty, between a sense of difference and a sense of identity" (p. 56). Wilson suggests that our field favors similarity and coherence to confusion, otherness, and ambiguity. He elaborates that the experience of insight can lend itself to verbal narration, or can be experienced as a nonverbal bodily sensation or confusion. In summary, the path from insight to therapeutic change is currently viewed as a complex, multifactorial process that is unique to each therapeutic encounter. The impact of insight on the therapeutic process, on "deep structure" (Gentile, 1998) and on interpersonal change, and its heuristic meanings have become much more multilayered, unpredictable, and ambiguous.


## INSIGHT THROUGH DREAM ANALYSIS


Dreams as a representation of insight are a central theme in two of the three movies that will be discussed in this chapter. Dream analysis was a prevalent method to bring about insight from the beginning of the psychoanalytic movement. Freud and his followers considered dreams to be a primary tool of self-analysis, as well an important aspect of the treatment, and Freud viewed dreams as the "royal road to the unconscious" (Freud, 1900/1973; Lippman, 2000). As will be discussed in relation to *The Dark Past* (Mate, 1948), dream analysis at that time was influenced by Freud's drive/conflict theory and was designed to uncover the latent content of the patient's repressed infantile sexuality and unconscious oedipal desires. Freud recommended that the analyst's own unconscious should be turned, like a "receptive organ," towards the patient's unconscious, as a telephone to the receiver (Freud, 1912/1973). Therefore an intuitive appproach to dream analysis was preferable to a logical, scientific approach, according to Freud (French & Fromm, 1964). Freud viewed dreams in terms of a chain of associations and wish-fulfilling unconscious fantasies; they possessed a latent content, consisting primarily of primary process material, which was, in turn, hidden behind the manifest content—the dream as remembered—and subject to secondary process elaboration.

French and Fromm (1964) developed a different approach to dream interpretation. They suggested checking the manifest content of the dream first, to see how it is related to the patient's actual life. While they agreed with Freud that analysts should use their intuitive abilities in order to associate to the manifest level of the dream, they suggested that analysts also act like detectives, searching for clues to uncover the mystery. They proposed a process of critical reasoning based on detailed evidence to support intuitive insights and interpretations, which they termed an "objective critical judgment." They also argued that dream content involved a process of empathic thinking, rather than verbal thinking, and viewed dreams and their associative phenomena as a "gestalt," illuminating particular concrete problems or focal conflicts of the analysand that needed to be solved. They argued that the dream's playful fantasy leads to an "earnest purpose" that needs to be uncovered.

In more current times, a number of self psychologists have further elaborated on the significance and meaning of dreams (Fiss, 1993; Fosshage, 2000). In self-psychology, dreams are seen to represent one's sense of self, and to have an important role in integrating fragmented and disconnected self-states. Dreams can be a metaphor for the patient's inner life, relational experiences, and the transference-countertransference interplay between patient and therapist. From a self-psychological perspective a dream can contribute to the development of the dreamer's psychological organization through the consolidation of a new solution. The dream can be seen as an effort at "conflict resolution" (Fosshage, 2000, p.105) and can also function as a vehicle for restoring a cohesive sense of self, and for regulation of affect (Kramer, 1993). Dreams can promote greater insight and self-awareness and may consequently lead to facilitating psychic structures and contribute to self-consolidation and integration (Fiss, 1993). "Self-state" dreams, similar to Clarice's dream in *The Silence of the Lambs* (Demme, 1990) and Tony's dream in *The Sopranos* (Chase, 1999), are dreams that metaphorically represent the dreamer's state of self (Hartmann, 1996).

Fosshage (2000) believes that dreams reveal the dreamer's immediate concerns through affects, metaphors, and themes. Rather than concealing internal reality as Freud suggested, dream images can be used directly for their evocative power in considering relevant issues and gaining insight. Fosshage offers guidelines for working with dreams, which emphasize the dreamer's experience, affective reactions, and associations. He also notes that dreams may not invariably have a transferential meaning, unless the analyst is clearly in the dream, or is represented in the patient's dream. Unlike classical analysis, in Fosshage's view the dreamer needs to be encouraged to rely on the dreamer's own dream experience and associations, rather than on the analyst's interpretative translations, in order to facilitate an "empowered sense of self" and to gain insight. Unlike Fosshage, Ellman (2000) argues that dreams usually have important transference-countertransference implications. This view is also shared by Ogden (1997), who interpreted his patient's dream as directly reflecting the analytic situation.

Dreams often reveal the meaning of current patient-therapist interactions according to Levenson (2000). He believes that it is important to understand not only the patient's associations to the dream but also the therapist's, and notes that the first reported dream "often seems to be the most powerful augur of future [therapeutic] themes" (p. 121). Therefore in his relational-interpersonal view, the dream becomes an interactive process in which both client's and therapist's associations contribute to a fuller explication of the dream's meaning for the therapeutic relationship, leading to the eventual acquisition of insight.

## THERAPEUTIC ACTION AND THE THERAPIST'S SUBJECTIVITY

If one adopts a relational point of view, it becomes necessary to address the therapist's role as an agent of therapeutic change, since this is a significant component of the process of therapeutic insight. Such a role differs markedly from the classical view of the abstinent and neutral analyst who served as a projection screen, to a more subjective and personally engaged analyst/subject. In the relational view, the therapist's subjectivity is unavoidable, the therapist's influence, personal experiences and personal opinions are an integral part of the treatment, and therefore the therapist's personal characteristics have a direct bearing on the process of insight and therapeutic change. The very possibility of therapeutic neutrality and abstinence has been challenged in the relational literature (Aron, 1996; Mitchell, 1997; Renik, 1996). Increasingly, the therapist's subjectivity is emphasized as part of the therapeutic matrix through personal influence and self disclosures. Aron (1991) suggests that the client-therapist relationship is continually constructed through mutual influences of subject upon subject. The therapist as a person, and the client's associations to the therapist, become important aspects in the process of insight. Renik (1996) argues that the therapist's neutrality is a myth, and that the therapist's actions and interpretations by themselves point to the therapist's personal influence and unique perspective (actually, in *The Sopranos* the therapist admits several times that she cannot be completely objective, although she does not directly critique Tony's illicit "line of work"). Therefore, in the relational literature there is an explicit acknowledgement of the therapist as a real, multidimensional figure in the treatment.

This relational view of the therapeutic process, according to some, originated with Ferenczi's "mutual analysis" (Aron & Harris, 1998). Ferenczi came to believe that the only way his fragile and difficult patients could be cured was through a mutual analysis and the analyst's self-disclosure, whereby he agreed to participate openly in the analytic process and answer his patients' questions, thus avoiding the possibility of retraumatizing them. This process of "mutual analysis" is clearly at work in *The Silence of the Lambs*, when, as will be discussed later, Dr. Lecter and Clarice agree to share self-disclosures with each other.

The representations of insight in the movies discussed in the following sections suggest a progression from a classical approach in *The Dark Past* to a gradually more relational process starting from *The Silence of the Lambs* and culminating in *The Sopranos*. There is an evolutionary process that begins with the more or less formulaic portrayal of a one-person therapeutic process to the far more spontaneous two-person relational model. Moreover, we witness the representation of insight as a single powerful event, which becomes the ultimate cure, to a more nuanced and gradual process built on incremental moments in the treatment. Lastly, the view of the therapist in these movies also evolves from that of a neutral interpreter of the patient's pathology, to one who is personally involved, contributes subjectivity to the therapeutic process in a variety of ways and who is deeply influenced by (as well as influencing) the patient.

## THE DARK PAST (1949)

*The Dark Past* is a remake of the movie *Blind Alley*, a 1939 production directed by King Vidor. According to Gabbard and Gabbard (2000), this cinematic era was characterized by a portrayal of the therapist as "oracular . . . and godlike" (p. 44). In the movie, organized as a story within a story, the psychiatrist is represented as a scholar (professor) and a therapist, a traditional family man and a proponent of (at the time) cutting-edge psychoanalytic theory, a man who traverses two worlds. It opens with the psychiatrist, Dr. Collins (Lee Cobb) telling a colleague about his special interest in and empathy for criminals, and his desire to help them through psychoanalysis. He then narrates the story of the time both he and his family were taken hostage by a gangster and his gang. During the incident, Dr. Collins discovers that the gangster, Al Walker (William Holden), suffers from hand paralysis and a recurring nightmare, and he becomes deeply interested in him. An unconventional therapist-patient relationship develops and Dr. Collins eventually helps Walker to "recover" by gaining insight into an early childhood traumatic memory, which becomes the key to his current pathology (see Figure 7.1).

*The Dark Past* presents a classical view of the treatment process. Dr. Collins is portrayed as a Freud-like figure who smokes a pipe and who is seen as wise, insightful, and altruistic. He uses a more or less classical dream analysis to uncover the inner workings of Walker's mind and to interpret his intrapsychic conflicts. Dr. Collins wants to help the violent gangster, despite the fact that he took the family hostage and threatened to kill them. Initially,

FIGURE 7.1. Dr. Collins (Lee J. Cobb), an academician and psychiatrist, offers gangster Al Walker (William Holden) highly condensed psychoanalytic insights as the gangster's moll (Nina Foch) looks on in this scene from *The Dark Past* (Coumbia Tri-Star, 1949). Courtesy of the Wisconsin Center for Film and Theater Research.

Walker is resistant to being analyzed, but ultimately he agrees to try and then proceeds to recall key memories of his past through associations to his recurrent nightmares. Walker's early history includes strong oedipal motifs, such as his conflictual love towards his mother and his powerful desire to get rid of his abusive father so he can have Mom all to himself. Unconscious guilt and wishes to acquire his father's power are strong elements in his subsequent actions. In a typically classical fashion, Dr. Collins is seen as an objective neutral figure who doesn't get upset even when his own son's life is at stake, and who discloses nothing of his own personal feelings. The underlying assumption of the movie is that insight will follow interpretation and will subsequently result in cure. In this case, Walker will no longer be able to kill once he realizes that all his victims are representations of his own father. In their interactions, the detective-like psychiatrist carefully follows all of his patient's clues. He investigates Walker's repetitive nightmare, which will give him the key to the gangster's pathology. The nightmare is as follows: Walker is alone, with sheets of rain falling all around him that he can't get away from. Suddenly an umbrella appears above his head, but it has a hole and some drops come through (a metaphor for the breast, or mother, who cannot protect him?). Scared, he raises his hand to stop the raindrops from coming through. He feels pain in his hand, and although he wants to run away he cannot. As the rain is transformed into solid columns (evocative of a phallic image), he feels as though he is trapped behind bars.

Dr. Collins proceeds to analyze the dream despite Walker's stubborn resistance, and explains to him that his nightmare is composed of "symbols in the unconscious mind." Walker describes his childhood as a triangle with a hated, abusive father and a beloved mom, who "fussed all over me, kissing and stroking me" except during the father's presence, when she would forget all about him. To help Walker uncover the early event that led to his repetitive nightmare, Dr. Collins asks him to free-associate. Walker finally recalls the events symbolized in the dream, and arrives at the terrible insight that he had caused his hated father's death in a classic oedipal fashion, so that he could have Mom all to himself. Dr. Collins interprets that Walker literally has his father's blood on his hands (which is why his hand is paralyzed), and that he suffers from an unconscious guilt. He suggests that Walker is driven to take back his father's gun (penis?) or power, and views everyone who opposes him as his father, whom he has to repeatedly kill off. Following this critical interpretation and Walker's newly acquired insight, the hysterical conversion that has paralyzed Walker's hand resolves spontaneously, and with it his ability to kill.

*The Dark Past* presents a classical one-person view of the psychoanalytic process. The analyst remains distant and authoritative, and we find out very little about his own inner life. Although there seems to be a powerful pull between analyst and gangster, the therapeutic process is somewhat formulaic, a cookie-cutter approach to dream analysis that is predicated on a hierarchical relationship between client and therapist. The analyst is portrayed as the all-knowing expert on his patient's pathology, whose role is to uncover the latter's unconscious motivations and thereby help him gain insight into his internal conflicts. At the end of the movie we are left to wonder whether Walker's insight has actually led to his final demise, as he is shown unable to shoot at the policemen who have come to capture him.

## THE SILENCE OF THE LAMBS (1990)

The plot of *The Silence of the Lambs* concerns Clarice Starling, a young FBI agent in training who is given the assignment to study and observe Dr. Hannibal Lecter, a psychiatrist who is imprisoned for literally eating his patients. By studying Dr. Lecter Agent Starling hopes to get some clues as to the identity and whereabouts of another mass murderer who is still at large, and to rescue a young woman whom he has abducted before it is too late. The story's most poignant theme is the relationship that develops between Agent Starling and Dr. Lecter.

*The Silence of the Lambs* presents another unconventional perspective on the therapeutic relationship and the process of insight in the cinema. Although Dr. Lecter is identified as the psychiatrist he is also a serial murderer, and Agent Starling, ostensibly the inexperienced novice who comes to benefit from his insights and advice, represents rationality and law and order. The movie's premise is that Agent Starling and Dr. Lecter are engaged in a relationship struggle that is based on both a powerful mutual attraction and mutual manipulation (see Figure 7.2). Agent Starling tries to figure out how Lecter's mind works and what he thinks in order to understand the serial killer's mind. Dr. Lecter, it appears, is genuinely curious about Agent Starling, and wants to find out who she is and what makes her tick. Both agree to answer each other's questions, reminiscent of Ferenczi's notion of "mutual analysis" where both patient and therapist analyzed each other.

In the first scene in which they are shown together Lecter (Anthony Hopkins) is seen standing in his cell towering over Agent Starling (Jody Foster). He appears enigmatic, powerful, and frightening. He is also portrayed as fiendishly brilliant, perceptive, and intuitive, and he immediately takes charge of their relationship, knowing that Agent Starling needs him badly. Dr. Lecter is always shown alone in his cage, which is perhaps an allusion to the therapist alone in his office, without friends or a visible personal life. Lecter's therapist is both a sad and dangerous figure, a predator who feeds off his patients for his own sense of aliveness, connection, and sustenance, and who needs literally, to

FIGURE 7.2. Agent Clarice Starling (Jodie Foster) and serial murderer Dr. Hannibal Lecter (Anthony Hopkins) engage in a variant of what Sandor Ferenczi might have termed "mutual analysis" in this scene from *The Silence of the Lambs* (Orion Pictures, 1991). Courtesy of the Museum of Modern Art/Film Stills Archive.

fill himself up with their life's blood. His preference for the human liver, considered in a medieval context to be the center of life, suggests that Dr. Lecter craves to ingest and internalize his patients' humanity, something that he, apparently, lacks. Dr. Lecter represents the therapist as a lonely voyeur, getting vicarious thrills through his patients. He seems to want to literally ingest Agent Starling as well. He asks her intimate and embarrassing questions, sniffs her, and draws a suggestive portrait of her for a keepsake. Although his personal life and his motivations remain largely mysterious, he is no longer the neutral psychiatrist-detective figure of *The Dark Past*. He is dominated by primitive drives and irrational forces, and is dangerously unpredictable.

Though Lecter confronts Agent Starling on her dishonesty with him and humiliates her by interpreting her desire to cover up her "white trash" origins, he refuses to look at his own dark motivations. We can only speculate about his past experience and the dark demons that control his inner life. At times, Lecter seems to be a two-dimensional caricature rather than a real person. Only his intense loneliness and genuine interest in Agent Starling humanize him. In order to find out more about her life, Lecter demands a reciprocal arrangement between the two of them, "I tell you things, you tell me things, quid pro quo, yes or no." Agent Starling then tells him of her childhood, her beloved father's death, and her subsequent move to her uncle's sheep ranch in Montana. As Dr. Lecter continues to probe, she remembers waking up one night hearing the "spring lambs screaming." Horrified, she opens the barn door, but none of the lambs leave, and finally she runs away, trying to carry one of the lambs with her to freedom. She can't save him, however, and this lamb is killed like all the others. Clearly, this memory remains extremely traumatic for Agent Starling, and Lecter accurately interprets that even now, Agent Starling still wakes up to hear the "screaming of the lambs." He helps her arrive at the important insight that this traumatic experience has become a prime motivation in her life, her reason for becoming an FBI agent and saving the innocent.

Agent Starling then realizes that she is capable of discovering her own truth and finding her way to justice and inner freedom. By the end of the movie she finds the inner resources necessary to become a mature adult and competent professional. Dr. Lecter hands her the key, but it is up to her to learn how to use it in order to unlock the mystery and solve the crime. This is beautifully represented at the end of the movie after Clarice is shown shooting the killer in the dark. As he collapses through a door, fatally wounded, light fills the room and everything is suddenly illuminated. By the end of the movie Agent Starling becomes self-assured and confident; she is no longer the inexperienced novice. Dr. Lecter has left her with a final gift: the key to understanding others is through one's own self-understanding. He tells her, "look deep within yourself."

## *THE SOPRANOS* (1999)

*The Sopranos* is a made-for-TV movie series on HBO that has had a tremendous cultural impact, with its star, Tony Soprano (James Gandolfini), becoming a familiar household name. Because of its cultural significance and due to its being available on video, it seemed important to include it in this chapter, although only the show's initial season will be discussed.

The therapeutic relationship in *The Sopranos* is arguably the most relational and complex depiction on screen thus far, and raises some important clinical and ethical dilemmas. The Sopranos are an Italian American family living in New Jersey. Tony Soprano (James Gandolfini), the head of the family, is in the Mob, or "waste management," as he himself calls it. Due to a recent series of panic attacks, Tony has been advised by his doctor to see a psychiatrist, and therefore begins a relationship with Dr. Melfi (Lorraine Bracco), a female psychiatrist and an Italian American like Tony.

*The Sopranos* follows a long cinematic tradition in its focus on the Mafia culture and the mobster as a central character. The best-known films on the subject of the Mob include *The Godfather* (Coppolla, 1972) and *Goodfellas* (Scorcese, 1990), which are continually referred to by the mobsters in *The Sopranos*. Outlaws and gangster figures such as Billy the Kid, Bonnie and Clyde, Bugsy Siegel, and the Godfather have held an iconic cultural status for a long time, possibly because of their uninhibited violence, sexual charisma, and a lifestyle free of ordinary legal and ethical constraints. This American love affair with the gangster, therefore, may stem from a collective longing for the apparent freedom, challenge, and excitement that often seem missing from our ordinary lives. *The Sopranos* is one of the first movies in this genre to present the mobster as an everyday man, a traditional father and husband who can be sensitive and vulnerable as well as a tough criminal, and who is grappling with internal doubts, conflicts, and insecurities.

Tony raises the dilemma of this new and more "politically correct" gangster figure when he states disdainfully, "Where are those cool, collected Gary Cooper types? Now the masculine ideal is the sensitive, emotional, and vulnerable man who expresses his feelings and cries openly." In an interesting twist, the violent and ruthless mobster who ostensibly seeks out therapy for his panic attacks ends up attempting to figure out his inner life and resolve his internal conflicts. Tony is presented as intensely loyal to his Mafia "family," sometimes to his own detriment, and will do anything to protect their business interests. In addition, he is a loyal family man although, as befits his mobster status, he also has girlfriends. Tony starts therapy following several significant crises in his personal and professional life. His father has recently died, his mother is headed for a nursing home, and there are troubles on the

horizon both within his Mafia family and from the "Feds." These circumstances form the backdrop for Tony's treatment.

The therapeutic process includes insights derived from dreams and verbal interpretations between client (Tony) and therapist (Dr. Melfi). The story
line suggests a Shakespearean plot as the core conflict, that is, a Hamlet-like
triangle of suffering hero, betraying mother, and untrustworthy uncle rather
than the typical oedipal triangle. Tony is seen living a double life. He is both
a traditional family man living in a middle-class New Jersey suburb with a
churchgoing wife and two average teen-age kids, and a Mafia boss whose
daily "professional" endeavors involve violence, murder, and extramarital sex,
all of which is supposedly a secret from his family. The details of this part of
his life also have to be kept a secret from his therapist, who informs Tony during their first meeting that "ethically" and "technically" she is obligated to
report any information about Tony presenting "a danger of harming someone." In other words, she seems to suggest that Tony should leave the messy
stuff outside her office, so that she won't have to face her own ethical
dilemma. As the therapeutic relationship develops, however, Tony's life of violence, impulsivity, and unbridled instinctual gratification gradually permeates
the treatment situation and Dr. Melfi's personal life as well. Consequently, her
ethical dilemma becomes unavoidable. Should she treat a criminal, possibly a
murderer, and help him "get better" so he can continue with his violent
endeavors? Dr. Melfi's ex-husband articulates her dilemma well: "You are
going to have to get beyond the cheesy moral relativism of good and evil and
he (Tony) is evil."

One of the first themes to emerge in Tony's story is the theme of loss.
The initial loss involves his father's earlier absence from Tony's life for a long
period of time (when he was incarcerated), and then his recent death. Another
is the gradual loss of his mother as Tony realizes she can no longer live independently and that he will have to put her in a nursing home against her will.
Related to this is the loss inherent in his eventual realization that she had
betrayed him by trying to have him killed. The final loss is Tony's decrease in
status and security in his own Mob community. This theme recurs in Tony's
fantasies and dreams as well, in the image of ducks that leave him for the win-
ter, and in the dream of the duck that flies away with his penis in his beak.
Tony appears conflicted and trapped in his life, and disconnected from his
feelings. There seems to be a split between his personal and professional
selves, an ongoing tension that he does not seem interested in resolving. He
enters treatment as his carefully compartmentalized world begins to disinte-
grate around him.

Tony's presenting problem is a series of recent panic attacks for which
there is no physical explanation. During his first session, he narrates the story
of a group of wild ducks that landed in his pool. This duck family, with a

mother and several young ducklings, had stayed near his house all summer long playing in the pool. However, in the autumn the ducks flew away and Tony's first panic attack occurred soon thereafter. In the second session, Tony touches on his conflicted feelings towards his mother. He describes his father, who became a "squeaking little turtle before he died" due to his mother's controlling and demeaning behavior. His mother begins to take on almost mythical proportions. Here for the first time, Tony also admits to some qualms about his work, and shares an insightful view of his inner life: "I find I have to be the sad clown—happy on the outside, crying on the inside." He reports his first dream to Dr. Melfi during their third session.

*The Dream*

Tony dreams that his belly button is screwed onto his belly. He unscrews it and his penis falls off. Tony picks it up and holds it, looking for a "guy to put it back on." Suddenly, a bird swoops down, takes his penis, and flies off with it. "Was the bird a duck?" asks Dr. Melfi. "What is it about ducks that means so much?" Tony begins, "These wild creatures and their babies that came to the pool"—and then starts to cry. Dr. Melfi interprets, "When ducks give birth to babies, they become a family." Tony then realizes that he is afraid of losing his family, just as he lost the duck family. He admits, "This is what I am full of dread about." There are, of course, other possible meanings. The dream may represent castration fears, or, via its allusion to the umbilical tie between mother and son, the powerful hold that Tony's mother exerts over him. However, Tony is not yet ready to deal with her directly. The dream may also signify Tony's fear of the therapeutic process, of losing his power to his female therapist and of becoming vulnerable (Dr. Mike Comer, personal communication, 2001). Interestingly, in his dream he is looking for a "guy" to put his penis back on, rather than a woman, suggesting a certain fear or mistrust of women. Dr. Melfi, however, prefers to pursue the safer interpretation at this point and to go along with Tony's association to his family. The dream also signals a subtle shift in the treatment process as Tony slowly becomes more willing to allow Dr. Melfi access into his internal world.

*Tony's Insights*

Tony's relationship with his mother becomes the central focus of the treatment. Despite Dr. Melfi's efforts to probe into the conflictual feelings that Tony clearly experiences towards his mother, including anger, he maintains his "good son" persona, refusing to explore any negative feelings towards her, expressing instead an intense guilt as he is placing her in a nursing home. Ultimately Tony's unconscious rage towards his mother is evoked as an aspect of the maternal transference to Dr. Melfi and he storms out of the office enraged at her suggestion that he may be angry with his mother. In a second dream, the negative coloration of his maternal transference becomes apparent as he sees Dr. Melfi wearing his mother's face. Eventually Tony's life of violence and crime starts to permeate the consulting room and Dr. Melfi's personal life. He instructs a crooked detective to follow and investigate her, and consequently the boundary between the treatment situation and his violent and chaotic life begins to break down, contaminating Dr. Melfi's social life as well as her psyche.

The unusual relationship that develops between Tony and Dr. Melfi makes it difficult for her to maintain a traditional treatment frame in terms of time, place, and confidentiality. She seems to be obsessed with Tony, as she starts to discuss him with her family and with her own therapist, and to dream of him. Her character as the therapist is represented as multidimensional and fallible and she is shown making mistakes, being confrontational, and enacting boundary violations, as well as being frightened and angry. She is certainly no longer a neutral figure. Dr. Melfi's own personal life is also far from perfect. She is portrayed as a divorced woman who has conflicts with her ex-husband and who lacks a stable primary relationship. She has become actively involved in the therapeutic dyad, a subject as much as an object, disclosing her fears and anxieties, asking Tony for his advice, and at times expressing her fear and anger. She is even shown breaking the treatment frame and conducting a session with Tony in her car during an emergency situation. Her apparent boundary violations and unconventional treatment methods may be questionable, but they also make the therapeutic process in *The Sopranos* spontaneous, exciting, and alive, and serve to draw in and to intrigue the viewer. After all, this is a TV series. Dr. Melfi, however, never actually succumbs to her erotic transference and is able to draw the line, unlike several therapists in previous movies, such as *Spellbound* (Hitchcock, 1945) and *The Prince of Tides* (Streisand, 1991).

Tony's erotic transference in the *The Sopranos* is one way through which insight is represented. Although many writers focus on the pathological aspects of the erotic transference, Eigen (1994) argues that it has a healing aspect, and can be viewed as an attachment to an ideal self. Benjamin (1994) further suggests that the desire for the therapist is fueled by the boundaries in the treatment and the therapist's self-control (p. 151). In *The Sopranos*, however, the treatment boundaries seem quite permeable, and the erotic transference is portrayed as more or less mutual. As is typical in *The Sopranos*, Tony's expression of erotic transference is dramatic. He not only expresses his attraction for Dr. Melfi verbally but also goes over and actually kisses her passionately. Dr. Melfi, for her part, wears tight, revealing skirts and crosses her legs seductively. She does not hide her growing interest and fascination with Tony, as he becomes the focal figure in her own therapy and her dreams. As he kisses her, she does not lose her cool, however, is able to hold the line between them, and suggests to Tony, in a somewhat stereotypical fashion, that his feelings for her are not real love, but a projection of something that is missing in his own life. One wonders how truly honest she is both with herself and with Tony here, and whether self-disclosure would have contributed to a deeper insight process for Tony (see Davies, 1994). In a rather unconvincing manner, we then see Tony internalizing this insight and applying it to his own life, as he expresses uncharacteristic tenderness towards his wife Carmela.

Another representation of insight in *The Sopranos* is through the trans-ference-countertransference matrix in which Dr. Melfi and Tony process his difficult relationship with his mother. This occurs both through a dream metaphor (when Tony dreams that Dr. Melfi has transformed into his mother) and when, after Dr. Melfi suggests that his mother has borderline personality disorder, Tony becomes so angry that he almost chokes her. Dr. Melfi is seen during this scene as overly confrontational, despite Tony's repeated warnings to her not to "go there." Her efforts to break through Tony's denial of his mother's betrayal cause a serious empathic rupture between them. Ultimately, however, Tony gains insight into his mother's resentment and her betrayal of him, as well as his repressed rage, and Dr. Melfi remains a steady, reliable object who would never leave.

This writer continues to hope that in the process of therapy, Tony will gain the ability to contain his violent impulses, learn to embrace the alienated parts of himself that he considers weak and unmanly, and realize that the pursuit of power, sex, and money will not, finally, make him happy. These wishes, however, may not be realistic in light of the intentionally irreconcilable conflicts within Tony's life and personality, and more importantly, because of the broader TV audience's great interest in Tony's violence and Mafia exploits. In small ways Tony does seem to undergo a process of some growth and maturation, as he becomes a more articulate, certainly a far more psychologically minded, patient. He becomes more introspective and is able to examine his psychological processes to some extent. His view of women, for example, changes somewhat as he starts to appreciate Dr. Melfi's subdued, gentle, and professional style, so unlike that of the sexualized, objectified women in his own environment.

As he starts to gain insight into the depth of his mother's betrayal of him, Tony finally allows his conflicted feelings toward her to surface. He becomes aware of the deep anger, betrayal, and hatred underneath the traditional Italian family values that he has maintained since childhood. His depression finally lifts and in the episode finale he is shown screaming at his mother at the top of his lungs. One is left wondering, however, whether these insights will affect Tony's criminal activities; will he continue to kill others, or order killings, without a sense of remorse? Will therapy only help him to

become better and more confident at what he does for a living? These questions contribute to Dr. Melfi's ethical dilemma in *The Sopranos*. While her
surpervisor encourages her to terminate the treatment, and while another
therapist refuses to treat Tony, Dr. Melfi, although highly conflicted, does not
seem able or willing to end the treatment. One has to keep in mind, of course,
that the series would lose much of its complexity and intrigue were Tony's
therapy to end.

The process of self-examination in *The Sopranos* also includes the viewer
and the therapist. As viewers, we are granted full access to Tony's analytic life,
as well as to his life outside of the treatment, with both his family and the Mob.
We witness his violence and flagrant disregard for human life, his cruelty and
crudeness, his pursuit of power, money, and sex. Yet we are asked to accept Tony
as a sensitive and likable person who is struggling with internal conflicts, guilt,
and loss as we all do. This situation sets up an ethical dilemma both for us and
for Tony, a dialectic between Tony the mobster and Tony the family man as a
conflicted human being. Like him, we as viewers can maintain this dialectical
tension by keeping both as far apart as possible. Tony's insistence on preserving
this split may stem from conflicted loyalties between his biological family and
his mafia "family." In fact, as we grow to understand that Tony seems to be
trapped in this paradox, we may experience more empathy and appreciation for
his predicament. Will the therapeutic process eventually help Tony to integrate
those two divergent worlds, which are in constant tension with each other, and
enable him finally to develop a sense of compassion and remorse?

Dr. Melfi also has to encounter this same ethical dilemma. Should she
treat a man who kills others and disregards the law and human life? Should
she help someone who possibly murders, certainly cheats, steals, and manipulates people? Initially, she seems to believe that she can keep Tony's mob life
and his psychological problems discrete. She tells him, in so many words, not
to disclose his criminal acts to her, as she will then have to "inform the authorities." However, she soon finds out that she is not able to keep herself completely outside the mayhem. The violence and crime become part of the treatment process and infiltrate her own personal life as well. In treating Tony, Dr.
Melfi becomes an active participant in his life, and engages in transference-
countertransference dynamics that occur both in and out of the consulting
room. She is no longer able to serve as a blank screen for Tony. Dr. Melfi is
portrayed as an active participant in the therapeutic encounter with her own
flaws, unique personal experiences, and the full complexity of her feelings. As
their relationship develops, we have the distinct impression that she continues
to treat Tony not only for professional motives but also because she finds the
danger and intrigue in his life tremendously fascinating and exciting, thereby
intensifying her ethical dilemma. Tony's milieu has become, in effect, her drug
of choice, essential for her own psyche.

## CONCLUSION

The three movies discussed in this chapter demonstrate a cultural shift starting from an initial view of insight as located within the patient's intrapsychic structure. In *The Dark Past,* the patient's intrapsychic conflict is excavated through the expert interpretation made by the therapist that leads to final resolution. This view contrasts with the portrayal of insight in *The Sopranos,* where insight emerges as a collaborative endeavor between patient and therapist and is located in the interpersonal arena rather than only in the patient's unconscious, with *The Silence of the Lambs* playing a transitional role between these two perspectives. From this relational view, insight evolves through transference-countertransference engagement between the client and the therapist throughout the treatment process, and is viewed as a dynamic, evolving process based on incremental moments rather than on a single event.

While the acquisition of insight seems to have a somewhat formulaic nature in *The Dark Past,* there is more ambiguity, spontaneity, and unpredictability in *The Silence of the Lambs* and *The Sopranos.* The therapist is no longer a neutral, objective figure who remains an outside observer/interpreter of the client's pathology. The therapist has become a full participant in the therapeutic process, and can be seen as a complex, imperfect human being who may grow and change alongside the client, particularly in *The Sopranos.* In this relational dyad, the hierarchical structure of the treatment has become more flexible (sometimes dangerously so, but never quite over the line) in a uniquely unconventional treatment context. In addition to the client's and the therapist's personal as well as interactive process of insight, the audience's participation in the plot has evolved as well. Although in *The Dark Past* we are expected to take on a more dispassionate detective-like role in order to solve the mystery that unfolds on screen, by contrast in *The Sopranos* we are asked to struggle with ethical and moral questions, closely identifying with the characters and becoming more engaged participants. Can we accept Tony as both a sadistic mobster and as a sensitive, conflicted individual? How can we justify liking and identifying with a character who murders without mercy in front of our eyes?

*The Sopranos* raises philosophical questions about the role of psychotherapy itself in our social and cultural milieu. We are left wondering whether it is appropriate for therapists to cure the symptom, in this case Tony's panic attacks, but to leave the personality structure and the criminal behavior intact. Or, is the role of therapy to foster the self-examination and insight that might eventually lead to moral, compassionate, and ethical conduct? In our current national climate, where horrific sufferings have been inflicted as a result of violent terrorist acts, one cannot help but wonder whether therapists need to start grappling with questions of justice and ethical responsibility more actively. In a vastly exaggerated manner, *The Sopranos* raises the dilemma of many men who are frequently trapped in a role that emphasizes a macho persona based on power, money, and physical prowess. This role typically does not permit these men to express and articulate the gentler, more vulnerable facets of their personality, an issue that therapists may need to address. Finally, despite its having thus far a rather questionable therapeutic outcome, Tony's relationship with Dr. Melfi may be his only hope for redemption.

## REFERENCES

Aron, L. (1991). The patient's experience of the analyst's subjectivity. *Psychoanalytic Dialogues, 1*(1), 29–51.

Aron, L. (1992). Interpretation as expression of the analyst's subjectivity. *Psychoanalytic Dialogues, 2*(4), 475–507.

Aron, L. (1996). A meeting of minds. Hillsdale, NJ: Analytic Press.

Aron, L., & Harris, A. (1998). The legacy of Sandor Ferenczi. Hillsdale, NJ: Analytic Press.

Benjamin, J. (1994). What angels would hear me? The erotics of transference. In *Like subjects love objects*, pp. 143–174. New Haven, CT: Yale University Press.

Bromberg, P. (1994). Speak that I may see you: Some reflections on dissociation, reality and psychoanalytic listening. *Psychoanalytic Dialogues, 4*, 517–547.

Chase, D. (Producer/writer/director). (1999). *The Sopranos* [Television series]. United States: HBO.

Chused, J. (1996). The therapeutic action of psychoanalysis: Abstinence and informative experiences. *Journal of the American Psychoanalytic Association, 44*(4), 1047–1071.

Coppola, F. (Director), & Ruddy, A. (Producer). (1972). *The godfather* [Motion picture]. United States: Paramount Pictures.

Davies, J. M. (1994). Love in the afternoon: a relational reconsideration of desire and dread in the countertransference. *Psychoanalytic Dialogues, 4*, 153–170.

Davies, J. M., & Frawley, M. G. (1994). Dissociative processes and transference-countertransference paradigms in the psychoanalytically oriented treatment of adult survivors of sexual abuse. *Psychoanalytic Dialogues, 2*(1), 5–37.

Demme, J. (Director), & Bozman, R., Saxon, E., Utt, K. (Producers). (1990). *The silence of the lambs* [Motion picture]. United States: Orion Pictures.

Eigen, M. (1994) From attraction to meditation. *Contemporary Psychotherapy Revue, 9*, 28–41.

Ellman, S. (2000). Dreams: commentary on paper by Hazel Ipp. *Psychoanalytic Dialogues, 10*(1), 143–157.

Fiss, H. (1993). The royal road to the unconscious. In A. Moffitt, M. Kramer, & R. Hoffman (Eds.). *The functions of dreaming*, pp. 400–409. Albany: State University of New York Press.

Fosshage, J. (2000). The organizing functions of dreaming—A contemporary psychoanalytic model: Commentary on paper by Hazel Ipp. *Psychoanalytic Dialogues, 10*(1), 103–117.

French, T., & Fromm, E. (1964). *Dream interpretation: A new approach.* New York: Basic Books.

Freud, S. (1973). *The interpretation of dreams.* In J. Strachey (Ed. & Trans.), *Standard edition of the complete psychological works of Sigmund Freud* (Vol. 5, pp. 509–621). London: Hogarth Press. (Original work published 1900)

Freud, S. (1973). *Recommendations to physicians practicing psychoanalysis.* In J. Strachey (Trans.), *Standard edition of the complete psychological works of Sigmund Freud* (Vol. 12, pp. 111–120). London: Hogarth Press. (Original work published 1912)

Gabbard, G., & Gabbard, K. (2000). *Psychiatry and the cinema* (2nd ed.). Washington, DC: American Psychiatric Press.

Gentile, J. (1998). Listening for deep structure: Between the a priori and the intersubjective. *Contemporary Psychoanalysis, 34,* 67–89.

Hartmann, E. (1995). Making connections in a safe place: Is dreaming psychotherapy? *Dreaming, 5*(4), 213–228.

Hartmann, E. (1996). Outline for a theory on the nature and functions of dreaming. *Dreaming, 6*(2), 147–170.

Hitchcock, A. (Director), & Selznick, D. (Producer). (1945). *Spellbound* [Motion picture]. United States: Selznick Studios.

Hoffman, I. (1998). *Ritual and spontaneity in the psychoanalytic process.* Hillsdale, NJ: Analytic Press

Kramer, M. (1993). The selective mood regulatory function of dreaming: An update and revision. In *The functions of dreaming*, A. Moffit, M. Kramer, & R. Hoffman (Eds.). Albany: State University of New York Press, pp. 139–195.

Levenson, E. (2000). An interpersonal perspective on dreams: Commentary on paper by Hazel Ipp. *Psychoanalytic Dialogues, 10*(1), 119–125.

Lippman, P. (2000). *Nocturnes: On Listening to dreams.* Hillsdale, NJ: Analytic Press.

Mate, R. (Director), & Adler, B. (Producer). (1948). *The dark past* [Motion picture]. United States: Columbia Pictures.

Miller, J. M. (2000). Knowing and not knowing: Some thoughts about insight. *Psychoanalytic Study of the Child, 55,* 220–237.

Mitchell, S. (1997). *Influence and autonomy in psychoanalysis.* Hillsdale, NJ: Analytic Press.

Mitchell, S. (2001). No search or getting down to business? *Psychoanalytic Quarterly,* *70,* 183–199.

Myerson, P. G. (1965). Modes of insight. *Journal of the American Psychoanalytic Association, 13*(4), 771–793.

Ogden, T. (1997). *Reverie and interpretation: Sensing something human.* Northvale, NJ: Aronson.

Poland, W. (1988). Insight and the analytic dyad. *Psychoanalytic Quarterly, 57,* 341–369.

Renik, O. (1996). The perils of neutrality. *Psychoanalytic Quarterly, 65,* 495–517.

Richfield, J. (1954). An analysis of the concept of insight. *Psychoanalytic Quarterly, 23,* 390–408.

Scorcese, M. (Director), & Winkler, I. (Producer). (1990). *Goodfellas* [Motion picture]. United States: Warner Brothers.

Stolorow, R., Atwood, G., & Brandchaft, B. (1997). *The intersubjective perspective.* Northvale, NJ: Jason Aronson.

Streisand, B. (Director/Co-producer), & Karsch, A. (Co-producer). (1991). *The prince of tides* [Motion picture]. United States: Columbia Productions.

Valenstein, A. (1981). Insight as an embedded concept in the early historical phase of psychoanalysis. *Psychoanalytic Study of the Child, 36,* 307–318.

Vidor, C. (Director). (1939). *Blind alley* [Motion picture]. United States: Columbia.

Wilson, M. (1998). Otherness within: Aspects of insight in psychoanalysis. *Psychoanalytic Quarterly, 67,* 54–77.

# 8

# Imagining Desire and Imaging the Real

## A Love Story

### BARBARA J. SOCOR

The unconscious is . . . a universal and involuntary fetishism.
—William Kerrigan, *Interpreting Lacan*

## INTRODUCTION

Film is a fabrication. And psychoanalysis is in the construction business. For both are interpretive, textual undertakings[1] seeking to craft a story that coheres for the viewer or the patient. While the project of the one is borne by depiction, and that of the other by declamation, both endeavor to evoke feeling and provoke discussion. And both evaluate their efforts by the successful narrative rendering of conflict, catharsis, and cure (or a "happy ending").

Munsterberg's (1916) early observation that film "tells us the human story by overcoming . . . space, time, and causality, and by adjusting the events to the forms of the inner world, namely . . . memory, imagination, and emotion" (as cited by Schneider, in Gabbard & Gabbard, 1999, pp. xv–xvi) speaks to the longstanding affinity and common interests that film and psychoanalysis share.[2] Both trade in fantasy, and both, as Bergstrom (1999) observes, "are drawn to the darkness in their quest for logics of meaning" (p. 1).

The appellation "talking cure" suggests that psychoanalysis aims to achieve a remedy for psychic complaints by having complainants speak their minds, whereas the moviegoer is summoned to look. Of course looking plays a role in psychoanalysis as well. Indeed, in recounting the scenes of one's life Freud (1913/1958) encourages his patients to "act as though . . . you were a traveller sitting next to the window of a railway carriage and describing to someone inside the carriage the changing views which you see outside" (p. 135). Still, "psychoanalytic looking" is not a trip to the movies, nor is it designed to entertain, although that may be a kind of "secondary gain" of the process, much as a successful movie is a tonic of sorts. Yet, as narrative undertakings the two projects approach their raw material in similar fashion: as unruly, even rambling texts in search of thematic coherence and emotional significance.

The rendering of significance, as distinct from discovering it, is a social constructionist[3] position that aptly characterizes both projects. As Donald Spence (1987) has observed, "truth is everywhere and nowhere" (p. 104), and so cannot be determined with any finality. Despite the inconclusive nature of the veridical, Spence continues, events whose origins and very existence are cloudy nonetheless possess a "psychical reality and what might be called narrative truth" (p. 106). Similarly, Kaplan (1990), in her work *Psychoanalysis and Cinema*, observes that psychoanalysis is a discourse in which "analyst and . . . analysand are seen to construct 'fictions' in the course of their interaction" (pp. 12–13).

In this view, "truth" is a matter of fabricating a satisfying parable, one that effectively evinces the essence of the patient's (or moviegoer's) abstract, and otherwise unrepresentable, psychological life. Truth in the narrative sense is about bringing significance to serendipity. Much earlier, Lacan (1953/1977) also made the point that, in effect, a patient's history is what the patient says it is: "In psychoanalytic anamnesis, it is not a question of reality . . . because the effect of full speech is to *reorder past contingencies by conferring on them the sense of necessities to come*" (p. 48, italics added).

As well, the relationship between film and psychoanalysis is a specific instance of the more abstract affiliation that links the image to the word. Lacan (Lacan & Granoff, 1956) implies such an association when he discusses the fetish as a surrogate for the "truncated relationship of the unconscious to the Symbolic" (Kerrigan, 1983, p. xii). That is, because unconscious meaning does not fully enter into language, it is "spoken" through the fetishized object instead, becoming a visible, tangible, and often reassuringly commonplace *thing* that replaces and silences the meaning of the unconscious. And that muted meaning is the absent maternal phallus. In this connection Lacan and Granoff (1956) introduced three distinct registers of the mind as they characterize the psyche's response to its own knowledge: the Real, the Imaginary, and the Symbolic. Each domain describes the mind's relationship to the knowledge of the absent phallus specifically, and to absence as the human condition, generally. Thus, the Real is an unmediated and frightful void, the Imaginary a visualized fantasy of completeness, and the Symbolic a rendering into language of the real absence, thus permitting it to be experienced as true. If the Real cannot be registered in the Symbolic it will resort to the Imaginary, that is, to the fetish.

Kaplan (1990) has commented that "it is interesting that many critics theorizing about the relationship between . . . film and psychoanalysis do not go on to apply their theories to the task of criticism itself" (p. 15). This discussion proposes to undertake that task by applying selected concepts from Lacan's work to two filmed depictions of the "love" transference: *The Prince of Tides* (Streisand, 1991) and *Final Analysis* (Joanou, 1992). Each serves to illustrate an instance of the "truncated relationship of the unconscious to the Symbolic." As well, the very different relationships depicted in these films highlight the illusory function and fetishistic character of the transference.

Aspects of Lacan's views of the transference and of desire will be explored in an effort to elucidate the "preferred fictions" that both psychoanalysis and film create. Of course repairing to Lacan's work when examining the meaning of film is by no means an untested enterprise.[4] Thus, rather than understanding them simply as celluloid distortions of psychoanalytic veridicality, the assertion is made that the transferences are themselves enactments of surrogate relationships that deny and replace unconscious truth—that is, that they are fetishes.

The stipulation is made that what is granted the status of truth is a collaboration between the analyst and analysand (or the director and the moviegoer) to produce a harmonious and satisfying interpretation of events such that in the successful analysis, as in the successful film, what is spoken and what is seen are resonant representations of "other" states of mind, that is, a good story. As well, that love cures will not be challenged, or affirmed, here. Rather, it will be maintained that the transference portrayals seen on the screen are externalized portraits of the psyche playing at fulfillment. *The Prince of Tides* and *Final Analysis* demonstrate this claim. But before going to the movies, the theoretical stage must be set.

## Transference Views

Of the many elements that constitute and define the transference relationship (for example, intensity, ambivalence, tenacity), the most characteristic is probably its inappropriateness (see, for example, Greenson, 1967, p. 162). Indeed, the very presence of the transference is confirmed by the inordinately intense, persistent, and even capricious affective claims of the analysand upon the analyst. Furthermore, the reactions and emotions expressed are not well suited to the context in which they are given voice. Rather, their assertion seems more properly to belong to a time and place long in the past. And as such, these affects are understood to be transferred from that past and repeated in the analytic situation. Thus, the classic transference is conceived essentially as "an anachronism, an error in time" (Greenson, p. 152) in which feelings more properly associated with earlier circumstances are reenacted in the present. This distortion was understood by Freud to be a defensive resistance (1912/1958, 1913/1958), a repetition (1914/1958), and somewhat later (1920/1955), a manifestation of the death instinct. To put it directly if a bit simply, the traditional transference permits the patient to love in the present so as to be cured of the past. So, the aim of the transference in this conceptualization may be understood as an unconscious effort to forestall, if not to prevent, the symbolic restoration of the past by returning what was to what is, by declaring that what had been lost now is found.

The transference has always been a staged affair. A seduction for two, it is not simply the analysand's monologue, but rather a conversation in which the patient parries interpretation with wish and the analyst counterthrusts with the analyst's own vision. In this way patient and analyst together enact a singular version of their now joined unconscious script. That is to say, together patient and analyst stage another narrative, in which other selves live through alternate roles, fashioned by the unconscious. Or, as Goffman (1959) has observed, "The self . . . is a dramatic effect arising diffusely from a scene that is presented" (pp. 252–253).

Indeed, as I have suggested elsewhere (Socor, 1997), the self is allusive in nature, containing references to—making allusion to—what it is not, to what is absent from it. In this way, the fullest sense of self is always being suggested but is always not present. Thus, enactment in the transference, what Currin (2000) defines as "a behavior, attitude, or happening in which both patient and analyst find themselves functioning outside of the analytic frame" (p. 75), presents an opportunity to become the self that one alludes to. Behaving as if one were living another life, the self becomes a part in a scene written by the unconscious. This may or may not be a desired therapeutic strategy,[5] but it is a very successful approach—and perhaps the only viable one—for film, where the viewer can easily, and without psychic penalty, enter an alternative and allusive self. Conversely, enactment, familiarly recognized as "acting out," can also veer an analysis wildly off course. Indeed, Maroda (1998) has characterized enactment as "an inevitable mutual event . . . culminating in a . . . certain sense of being emotionally out of control" (from the abstract, p. 517).

Lacan (1964) also takes issue with the traditional view of the transference. Here, instead of representing it, the transference is the antagonist of the unconscious, and works to still it. Rather than a reenactment, the transference is an unyielding battlement to the emergence of the unconscious, a weapon in the contest to silence other voices. The transference thus offers (the illusion of) certainty, confirming the subject's sense, even if imaginary, that the subject speaks in one voice, with nothing missing. And if successful, the transference will "[persuade] the other [e.g., the analyst] that he has that which may complement us," so "[assuring] ourselves of being able to continue to misunderstand precisely what we lack" (Lacan, 1964 p. 133).

A Lacanian approach encourages the patient to hear and heed the voice of the unconscious by breaching the transference barriers, for the transference is an elaborate hoax, a "smoke screen" that veils unconscious knowledge, and separates subjects from their desire. This transference attests to the view that the human subject is, by definition, "broken" (see Carveth, 1997), whereas the classical transference lends support to the fiction of "oneness." This, says Lacan, not only fortifies the breach, but also lacks sense, is *ab sens*.

Lacan (1949/1977) theorizes that the origin of the psychic distortion of completeness rests in the infant's identification with the mirror image. Thus, born of the mirror and borne by the imagination, the subject submits to illusion. This is what Lacan (1949) refers to as the "Ideal-I," and it is a fetish, a specular fantasy in denial of the Real, whereas the classical transference represents the analysand's best narrative effort to sustain the fiction of the undivided self. And if the tale is sufficiently compelling, if the analyst is charmed, captivated, or complicit in the patient's love story, the seduction is complete. And this collusion is palliative, serving to ease the patient's suspicion that the insufficiency is existential. But this regularly repeated transference parable is profoundly self-alienating. For no subject can be congruent with the ideal that the mirror reflects, yet the objectifying semblance is fiercely adhered to, for even as it renders reification it confers certainty.

## THE LOOK OF LOVE

Desire is committed to permanent revolution.
—Eugene Goodheart, *Desire and Its Discontents*

Human desire cannot be slaked, and satisfaction is inimical to it, so when Lacan speaks of desire he does not speak of love. To understand what he is intending it is well to note what desire is not: it is not need, and it is not wish. Rather, desire is a perpetual straining toward transcendence.

Need is a state of internal tension and can be satisfied by securing the object that will alleviate it. Thus, "Need is directed towards a specific object"

(Laplanche & Pontalis, 1973, p. 483). Here is the infant seeking the breast, the hunter gaining his prey, the lovers appeasing their passion. This is "doing what comes naturally," and it is precisely life in this "state of nature" that must be surpassed if human being is to emerge. For the simple fulfillment of need is not in itself adequate to establish the awareness of self that signifies the human. As Kojeve (1947) has remarked, "If animal Desire is the necessary condition of Self-Consciousness, it is not the sufficient condition. By itself, this Desire constitutes only the Sentiment of self" (p. 4). Natural desire simply allows one to feel alive insofar as one feels the tension of an unmet need. It is a disposition, not an awareness.

Nor is desire a wish. For wishes are tied to memories of satisfaction, and as such are "fulfilled through the hallucinatory reproduction of the perceptions which have become the signs of this satisfaction" (Laplanche & Pontalis, 1973, p. 482). Memories are bundles of coded sense perceptions, pockets of significance, often visual in character, which have become intimately associated with earlier satisfactions. The wish can only be fulfilled when some or all of the associated signs are successfully organized and evoked.

Thus, need is of the natural world, and wishes are of the imaginary world, but desire is not of this world at all. Rather, "Desire is a 'spiritual' energy; it 'represents' the indefinable in human life" (Goodheart, 1991, p. 3). So, whereas need and wish regularly achieve satisfaction, this is not the end of desiring. Indeed, it is the essence of human being to experience an ontological sense of lack that sustains a persistent state of desiring. To be human means to be incomplete, and it means desiring fulfillment (that is, completion), as it may be granted in the recognition, the look, of another desiring human. But to achieve permanent fulfillment is not (humanly) possible. Human desire forecloses its satisfaction because wanting, not having, is the authentic human condition. Thus,

> The gap between desire and its object is insurmountable. Indeed, it is the very gap that nourishes and sustains desire, because its satisfaction would be its extinction.... Desire is committed to permanent revolution, to an enduring disappointment as a way of guaranteeing its survival. (Goodheart, 1991, p. 3)

What is of interest, then, in revisiting *The Prince of Tides* and *Final Analysis* is not so much that these films may misrepresent the practice of psychoanalysis, or misconstrue the role of the analyst, for it can hardly be otherwise. Indeed, "We can scarcely expect the medium to provide balanced insights into the multifaceted, constantly evolving questions of psychotherapy: any serious attempt at such an undertaking would probably bore audiences silly" (Gabbard & Gabbard, 1999, p. xxii). The more interesting question is why such misconstructions are capable of providing a satisfying viewing experience. Keeping in mind some of Lacan's observations on the obstructionist nature of the transference, and the deceptive character of the Imaginary, this discussion will venture a theoretical reply to the question posed.

## THE PRINCE OF TIDES

My wound is geography. It is also my anchorage, my port of call.
—Pat Conroy, *The Prince of Tides*

*The Prince of Tides* is the story of the Wingo family as told by Tom Wingo (Nick Nolte), principally to the psychiatrist Susan Lowenstein (Barbra Streisand). Tom, whose marriage is strained by his emotional distance and seeming inability to connect, agrees to go to New York City to speak with Dr. Lowenstein following another suicide attempt by his troubled twin sister, Savannah (Melinda Dillon). The story is of a nearly unbearable trauma buried within the lives of the family members and made emblematic by Savannah. As the film unfolds we come to understand that though Tom goes to New York on his sister's behalf, this is his story.

The film opens with a scenic overview of the landscape of Tom's childhood, the "tides and marshes" of South Carolina. It is established from this beginning that the landscape of his youth is also the lineament of his inner life. Where Tom grew up, and how he did, including the variety of mores and the pace of daily existence characteristic of small-town living, are contrasted to the cacophony and chaos that is New York City. Indeed, the simplicity and innocence of the country is placed familiarly in opposition to its boisterous and seductive city sister, though the movie clearly shows that evil also occurs in the country, and goodness can flourish in the city.

While, like all films, *The Prince of Tides* depends upon the image to show its story, from time to time it also tells its tale with words. Thus, in a series of interspersed voice overs, Tom speaks selected segments of the story, and so is both immersed in the action that the viewing audience sees, and is also at a remove from it, as the narrator. In the latter role, he is talking to the listener in the darkened theater, placing the audience behind the couch, as it were. In this way, the moviegoer too is immersed and at a remove, a participant and an observer.

The trauma which has guided and stifled the Wingo lives is the sudden and violent rape of Savannah, Tom's mother Lila (Kate Nelligan), and Tom himself by escaped convicts. The subsequent secrecy and outright denial of this horrific event that Lila Wingo insists upon becomes as damaging to the children, and the adults they become, as the event itself. When Tom arrives in New York he has practiced this silent disavowal for many years.

Tom comes to the city reluctantly, and is dubious about the psychological enterprise. Indeed, in the book version of *The Prince of Tides* Tom's cre-
ator, Pat Conroy, has him say of the entire undertaking, " Why did I have to
be born in the century of Sigmund Freud? I despise his mumbo jumbo" (p.
381). Rancor of this intensity is not given a screening, but it is certainly clear
that Tom is skeptical, and very wary of delving too deeply into his well-
guarded past.

The relationship between Tom and the psychiatrist is introduced as a
professional one in which Dr. Lowenstein hopes to enlist her patient's brother
in the search to understand Savannah. From the first the relationship is an
ambiguous one. Near the end of an early talk with Tom she observes, in timeless doctor to patient language that "time's up," and at another point refers to
one of their talks as a "session." Tom quickly finds that his "information" is
being responded to as treatment material. Thus, when he recounts a childhood
event in which his mother tells him that he is her favorite, and later learns
from his siblings that she has told each of them the same thing, the following
exchange ensues:

> LOWENSTEIN: Why did you tell me that story?
>
> TOM: Doesn't it show why Savannah could never trust anyone?
>
> LOWENSTEIN: You mean why *you* could never trust anyone.

Now this is clearly an interpretation. Tom says to Lowenstein, "It's not your
job to listen to my problems." And of course, he is quite correct. But if the
movie were to adhere to the accurate, where would this relationship, and this
story, go?

In this exchange and others Dr. Lowenstein shifts the terms of their
meetings. For in the actual consulting room Tom's comments would be accepted
as information, and interpretive insights would remain unspoken. So from the
point of view of standard practice Dr. Lowenstein violates the terms she set.
From the point of view of the film, however, this portrayal allows the audience
to see both a bit of Tom's inner life and a glimpse of the doctor's concern for
him. Indeed, it might be said that seeing Dr. Lowenstein as a person who cares
about another without being paid to is depicting any analysand's generic wish.
Nevertheless, the fiction that Tom is not a patient must be sustained.

This is a foil. By making Tom an informant the "forbidden" nature of
the relationship is clouded. Indeed, the film seems to suggest that a sexual
relationship with a patient's relative is not a source of ethical concern. In psychotherapeutic venues, however, such behavior would likely raise questions
and eyebrows.

Thus, in matters of love conventional ethical practices still appear sacro-
sanct: analysts should not yield to their infatuations. On the other hand, "fol-

lowing one's heart," surrendering to natural sentiments, is seen as the way to happiness (and "cure"). These two conventions are, so to speak, uneasy bedfellows. Each is considered a good in itself, but being good and feeling good are not always compatible, except perhaps at the movies, where you can, for a time, have it all.

So as he settles into a kind of routine in New York, entering an alternate life, the relationship between Tom Wingo and Dr. Susan Lowenstein rapidly becomes one between "Tom" and "Lowenstein." It is interesting to consider that Tom never seriously refers to her as either *Dr.* Lowenstein or *Susan.* That is, he does not fully recognize her as either a professional or an intimate, but rather as something in between. Perhaps something, someone, imaginary. Further evidence that the psychiatrist is being portrayed as a fantasy is garnered in the scene following Tom's telling of the night he and his family were raped: Dr. Lowenstein holds Tom in her arms and comforts him. Now this is surely a human response on the doctor's part, and what any vulnerable patient might fantasize about, but it is not what can be expected to actually transpire. Yet as this maternal moment is made real for Tom, the viewer too can picture it as a wish come true.

Dr. Lowenstein is portrayed as an openly caring psychiatrist who, by her willingness to be a real person, and not just a psychiatrist, is able to help Tom. And the viewer has the conviction and the convention reaffirmed that love, not "mumbo jumbo," cures. It is simplicity, and reliance upon feeling that is trusted, not the dispassionate, even corrupting, effects of reason.

Now, it is not simply a matter of Tom considering in voice-over that "her questions are making me as dizzy as her perfume." For this is not only about managing the transference. Instead, Dr. Lowenstein also becomes entangled in a web of feelings for Tom. Within the analytic configuration this would readily be recognized as a countertransference situation, and Dr. Lowenstein might be expected to consult with a colleague, or her own psychiatrist, as Tony Soprano's Dr. Jennifer Melfi regularly does, but she does not.

Instead, she allows herself to yield to her feelings. And the viewer is invited to understand that Tom, through his love, will in turn cure Lowenstein (see Figure 8.1). And, as we see, Dr. Lowenstein is an unhappy woman—and unhappy, as female analysts on the screen often are, in matters of love and domestic tranquility, the heart and hearth of the stereotypical woman's being. We also witness Dr. Lowenstein's unhappy son, Bernard (Jason Gould), and learn of her brilliant and cultured but also arrogant husband Herbert (Jereon Krabbe), who is unfaithful to her and unforgiving in his aspirations for his son.

Because Tom persists as an "informant" we are invited to dispense with any dissonance that may arise when Dr. Lowenstein asks for his help. Bernard wants to play football, that is, wants to be a "real man," but is blocked by his

FIGURE 8.1. Tom Wingo (Nick Nolte) and his psychiatrist Susan Lowenstein (Barbra Streisand) enact powerful mutual attractions in a scene from *The Prince of Tides* (Columbia Pictures, 1991). Courtesy of the Museum of Modern Art/Film Stills Archive.

father's refusal to put his (effete) violin playing at risk. Now coach Wingo—he is indeed a high school football coach at home—undertakes this assignment, and in due time makes Bernard a passing good football player, and a much happier young man. Bernard, in turn, allows Tom to rediscover and to value the man he is.

So, the film seems to imagine, not only does love cure, but the love of a good and uncomplicated man, not adept at words but excellent at discerning the simple pleasures of life, can cure what ails a woman analyst and her son. And she *is* cured, or at least happy, for as she tells Tom, "I can't stop smiling. I smile all the time."

Inevitably, Tom and Lowenstein's pastoral cannot avert the reemergence of "real life." After a time they are called upon to relinquish the uncomplicated pleasures of Elysium, as all who would become grown-ups must. Aptly, they are summoned from their reverie when Tom's wife, Sallie (Blythe Danner), telephones, calling him to his other life. Dr. Lowenstein sees, and so knows, this immediately upon exiting her office building. For there is Tom, anxiously awaiting her, now himself the herald of realities the analyst might more usually relate to the patient.

Significantly, Tom and Lowenstein do not struggle against this imposition, but they do mourn their personal paradise lost. Lowenstein in particular seems to know that "her work is done here." She jokingly remarks that she has "got to find a nice Jewish boy. You guys [goys?] are killing me." Tom, on the other hand, says, "Just hold me, please, I feel like I'm dying."

And indeed, he is dying: to the imaginary and to the idyllic. He is forgoing fantasy for the symbolic and thus necessarily incomplete world of the full human being. In leaving Lowenstein, Tom reclaims the larger world, returning to the geography that wounded him and that made him the man he is now able to be. In the Lacanian sense, Tom has experienced the seductive perfection that is the Imaginary, and has stepped back through the looking glass, wherein he is enjoined to "lose the life you have, for greater life (Wolfe, 1940/1968, p. 680).

Tom and Lowenstein spend a last night together at the Rainbow Room. The location of this evening is significant, for it is also the site of Tom's dream of Lowenstein, in which they are alone, dancing in that room. Now, for a brief while, it too is a dream come true. During this evening, Lowenstein is plagued by intrusions from reality and so cannot be fully complicit in this last fantasy. She wants, from time to time, to know why they cannot continue as a couple. Tom, in exasperation, finally asks, "Lowenstein, why are you making it so hard?"

Now if this scene were anything but imaginary, if Lowenstein were Susan, or even Dr. Lowenstein for him, Tom would know how difficult this was for her. He might understand that while he was leaving for "greater life," she was remaining, to become a memory. What Tom is actually asking is why she is so "out of character." For Lowenstein had offered him a perfect world. Now that he was ready to leave, why was she insisting on marring the fantasy? Or was she? Perhaps if we look at the latent implications of this movie we shall find that she was actually helping to advance a particular conclusion to a shared fable. Indeed, *The Prince of Tides* possesses a number of features associated with the universally recognized "journey of the hero" described by Joseph Campbell (1949).

> The hero adventures out of the land we know into darkness; there he accomplishes his adventure . . . and his return is described as a coming back out of that yonder zone. Nevertheless . . . the two kingdoms are actually one. The realm of the gods is a forgotten dimension of the world we know. And the exploration of that dimension, either willingly or unwillingly, is the whole sense of the deed of the hero. The values and distinctions [of] normal life . . . disappear with the terrifying assimilation of the self into what formerly was . . . otherness. (1949, p. 217)

This is reminiscent of Lacan's (1964) conception of the unconscious, which is not a foreign psychic realm, but simply an unexplored one. The unconscious is the "otherness" of one's being. Lacan too asserts that the human subject undertakes a journey: into the interior regions of the self, there to confront one's desire and speak it, returning to conscious life no longer bound to the Imaginary, but master of it.

The structure of Tom's undertaking, like that of an analysis, bears the markings of this journey: Tom is first introduced as a man alienated from himself. He sets out upon a voyage fraught with danger (that is, he travels to an unknown city, where he is challenged to confront his deepest fears). And he too is transformed. Tom acknowledges the nature of the journey he is on when he asks Dr. Lowenstein, "Is this what people pay you to do? Turn them into someone else?" Once his conversion is complete, he also leaves the "yonder zone" to resume his place in the "greater world."

Tom's metaphorical pilgrimage was heroic precisely because it was transformative. In Lacanian language, it was an "assumption of his desire," a passage from the idealized presence of the Imaginary to the spoken absence of the Symbolic. *The Prince of Tides* depicts that journey, and in so doing speaks to the ubiquitous psychological longing that is human desire.

For it will be recalled that the region of the Imaginary is that of fantasy. And it was there, in the deceptive embrace of "perfect understanding" that Tom at last began to feel the tug of his other life. This is the restless tug of dissatisfaction that arises from within the plentitude of imagined fulfillment. Tom's relationship with Lowenstein was an idealization and suffered the discontent of all such deceptions, for desire cannot be fulfilled. Indeed, the chimera of fulfillment is characteristic of the Imaginary. The appropriation of desire can only transpire in a metaphorical fashion. That is to say, it requires that Tom leave Lowenstein.

Tom returns to his family a changed man, one able to reflect on his journey and say of himself at its end, "I am a teacher, a coach, and a well-loved man. And it is more than enough." He can now take up a life in which he recognizes that human being is by its nature incomplete, that it has suffered a wound that cannot heal. Knowing this confirms that Tom has entered the Symbolic, wherein he will speak this lack, and acknowledge the psychic emptiness at the center of the richest life. He will mourn the loss of illusion that for a time allowed him to believe in the achievement of wholeness through another. Of that loss he will say: "[I]t is the mystery of life that sustains me now, and I look to the north, and I wish again that there were two lives apportioned to every man and every woman."

And so Tom summons what is not, and lends voice to longing. He speaks his desiring condition, and so performs the distinctly human act of restoring in word what was lost in deed, rendering present what is also absent. In acknowledging the split, in wishing that there were "two lives apportioned," Tom preserves, rather than fulfills, his desire, thus penetrating the very mystery that sustains him. He tells us, in a final voice-over, that for him Lowenstein is no longer an actual lover, nor an imaginary perfection. Rather, she has become an eternal internal presence, called upon for sustenance. This is the Symbolic, and this is how Tom says it:

> At the end of every day I drive through the city of Charleston, and as I cross the bridge that will take me home I feel the words building inside me. I can't stop them or tell you why I say them, but as I reach the top of the bridge these words come to me in a whisper. I say them as a prayer, as regret, as praise. I say: "Lowenstein, Lowenstein."

The Real completes the Lacanian trinity (1956) of psychic states, each of which describes the relationship of the individual to the voice of the unconscious, and the truth it bears (see Hurst, 2000). And that truth is borne by the same instantiating event: the intrusion into the mother-child dyad of the first other, the father. All two-sided relationships suffer this trespass, creating a psychic space between the original members of the doublet. This subject(ive) space, and the knowledge introduced therein, is either sustained by the Imaginary or the Symbolic, or it is bankrupt in the Real.

The Imaginary is dominated by idealized images of self and other. This neurotic structure is supported by the mechanism of repression, which initiates a forgetting of the knowledge of lack that the father carries with him. Repression also obscures the dyadic relationship, and the child's privileged position as sole object of desire. Accordingly, the other is idealized, and the subject is now at the psychological mercy of this other's inclination to grant recognition. The neurotic's aim is to win back what was seized by the father: the mother's exclusive gaze. This is the look of love.

And this is the Imaginary realm in which Tom Wingo began his journey. So, while Dr. Lowenstein may be said to have fractured the analytic frame, she reinforced the Imaginary structure by serving as the idealized figure that Tom desired. Dr. Lowenstein is an analog for the psychic mirror, in which we all remain the flawless and singular object of desire.

The psyche may also resort to the mechanism of *foreclosure* in response to the disquieting paternal imposition. Doing so inaugurates the Real. Here, the psychic space established by the actual intrusion implodes, leaving no space for the symbolic father. And since what is missing is neither translated into language nor fetishistically imagined, it cannot be borne internally. Instead, the arrival of the Other is experienced as authentically violent. Unlike the position in the Imaginary, in which the subject lives *for* the Other, in the Real the subject "exists only *within* the Other" (Hurst, 2000, p. 95, italics added). This is so because the paternal infringement has not been repressed; it has been expelled. In consequence, the violation is experienced as unconditionally outside the person, returning to haunt in the form of delusions and hallucinations, as intrusions from the Real.[6] And it is in the Real that unspeakable nightmares are lived, day by day.

### FINAL ANALYSIS

> The symptom no longer signifies but is lived.
> —John Muller, "Language, Psychosis,
> and the Subject," in *Interpreting Lacan*

The Real is not subject to representation. It is unimaginable and unspeakable, and that is precisely what constitutes its realness. So imaging the Real is a paradoxical undertaking, approaching its likeness in portrayals of the psychotic experience. For in psychosis too there is no mediation, nothing to soften the blow. Here, knowledge is mutilating, and words wound. Whether fully symbolic or merely substitutive, the act of conferring meaning upon an object cloaks its utter strangeness in language. When, as in the Real, objects are stripped of this raiment, they become fearsome and dreadful in their naked truth: there really is nothing there. In portraying the missteps of a psychiatrist blinded by passion, *Final Analysis* tells such a tale.

The film depicts events in the life of Dr. Isaac Barr (Richard Gere) when his patient, Diana Baylor (Uma Thurman) encourages him to consult with her sister, Heather Evans (Kim Basinger). Two aspects of this film in particular illustrate the deadly seduction of the Lacanian Real: first, the portrayal of the psychiatrist as he becomes entangled in the transference web that has been woven for him, and second, the identity merger that challenges the idea of self.

As the film opens, the viewer encounters Dr. Barr in his consulting room, listening to Diana recount a recurrent dream, speaking to him in an unambiguously provocative manner. But the erstwhile psychiatrist repeatedly brings his patient back to her dream. He is plainly to be seen as a man of professional rectitude. Diana is intent upon getting Dr. Barr to speak with her sister, an offer he shows no inclination to accept. Indeed, when Diana suggests that he really *"should"* speak with Heather because "she knows some things," he replies, "Maybe those are the things that we'd do best to uncover in our work here, Diana."

The film establishes Dr. Barr's professional credentials and his dedication to his patients at the expense of his personal life. Thus we learn that Dr. Barr is an expert witness, who frequently testifies at criminal trials, that he is head of forensic psychiatry at Oakland State Hospital, and is responsible for the evaluation and treatment of the criminally insane. And of just such a patient he declares that rather than remand him to the "human warehouse" that is the state hospital, he would "be happy to take on the treatment . . . free of charge."

When his friend Mike (Paul Guilfoyle) encourages him to "get out of [the] office sometime [and] meet people," Dr. Barr offers a response that is also a foreshadowing: "I look at people's thoughts, try to figure out what they really mean. You do that enough, after a while people, they stop surprising you. I just want to be surprised, Mike." Here we are reminded that Isaac is a "meaning maker," one who reads signs and interprets symbols for a living. And because he understands this world so well, it no longer captivates him. He wants to encounter someone he cannot understand, and to whom he cannot assign a meaning, someone who will surprise. Dr. Barr, we see, is looking for something else.

Heather's advent is worthy of note. She looms in the threshold of the doctor's office bathed in shadow, an unexpected presence prefiguring the serendipitous arrival of the Real. She stands for a moment in the dark, looking in at Dr. Barr who is working late in his dimly lit office.

HEATHER: Hi, I'm Heather Evans, Diana's sister. She did say I was coming by? I *hope*.

ISAAC: Yeah . . . yeah she did mention . . .

Dr. Barr seems to have forgotten about Heather, and clearly was not told to expect her. She appeared unbidden, from the dark. Once settled in the office they have the following exchange:

HEATHER: How often does this happen?

ISAAC: What?

HEATHER: A patient's sister coming by and talking to you?

ISAAC: Not very often . . . actually, *never.*

HEATHER: Never.

So Heather is Isaac's "surprise," and she is "something else."

Heather reveals that Diana was raped by their father. Similarly, Tom's sister was also raped, and he too was in the psychiatrist's office as a family member, to fill in gaps in the patient's history. However, the very different circumstances of their presence is instructive: Tom was summoned and expected, while Heather simply appeared and startled, much as a wish is invoked and the Real intrudes.

After disclosing Diana's story, Heather asks Dr. Barr in a whisper, "Do you think you can help us?" "*Us?*" Is Heather in need of help too? Does she share more with Diana than it might appear? Or intend more? Not reading these possibilities, somehow losing his professional facility, Dr. Barr responds, also in a whisper, "Yes, I think I can."

There is a second meeting between Heather and Dr. Barr, and this time it is at the doctor's request. Diana has told Dr. Barr that she has a gun, given to her for "protection" by Heather. This troubles the doctor, and he asks that Heather contact him. Heather waits for Dr. Barr outside his home and surprises him (as is her wont, and his desire), as she speaks from the shadows: "Diana said you wanted to see me?" And then, by way of explanation for her startling presence she adds, "I didn't want to bother you at your office" (but presumably did want to "bother" him at home).

HEATHER: Did you really think I'd give Diana a gun?

ISAAC: No.

HEATHER: But you wanted to see me anyway.

ISAAC: Yes, I did.

They go for coffee. It is a conventional-appearing date in which we witness Dr. Barr, somewhat unconventionally, sharing the secrets of being "a shrink" with his patient's sister (see Figure 8.2). In turn, Heather tells Dr. Barr that she is married, and that her husband, Jimmy (Eric Roberts), is a gangster. At the conclusion of the evening they prepare to say good night. The attraction between them is unmistakable. When there is nothing left to say, when words have been exhausted, Isaac and Heather seem ready to part:

HEATHER: So, this is it, we're finished?

ISAAC: To be honest, I don't know if I really want it to be. You're a patient's sister, it doesn't feel right.

FIGURE 8.2. Psychiatrist Isaac Barr (Richard Gere) dines with Heather Evans (Kim Basinger), the sister of his patient, in a scene from *Final Analysis* (Warner Brothers, 1992). Courtesy of the Museum of Modern Art/Film Stills Archive.

Having given the nod to professional principles, the scene cuts to the two in bed, passion trumping professionalism (at the movies, just about every time). The morning after we see Isaac in conversation with his colleague, Alan Lowenthal (Robert Harper), to whom he is recounting his meeting with Heather, and his attraction to her. Alan turns to him and asks, in dismay and astonishment, "You didn't *sleep* with her?" Confessing that he did, Isaac goes on to assure Alan, and himself, that he is "safe," for he "went through the AMA's principles of ethics. Even the special annotations for psychiatry didn't say any anything about sleeping with a patient's sister." While Isaac seems to take professional cover in the special annotations, Alan remains appalled by the news of Isaac's indiscretion, and attempts to remind his comrade of some fundamental principles:

> ALAN: Isaac, you know as well as I do romantic love is a projection, you're not seeing this woman . . .
>
> ISAAC: Get 'outta here . . .

Isaac is dismissive, even mocking. Nonetheless, his erstwhile colleague plods on:

> ALAN: You're not seeing this woman . . . it's a vision of her . . . you're in a delusional state.
>
> ISAAC: I'm not delusional.
>
> ALAN: Yes it is, it's delusional. There is no human being . . . no woman is so . . . special that all of your normal thought patterns get . . .

Here Heather enters the office.

> ALAN: Oh . . . can I help you?

Isaac introduces Alan, who is now solicitous, inviting her to sit down:

> HEATHER: No, I didn't mean to interrupt you guys.
>
> ALAN: Oh . . . *no problem.*

Here, of course, Alan is also seen to be succumbing to Heather's allure. His professional homily is reduced to a homely mass of psychobabble by her "impossible" presence. His words, any words, lose their meaning in her presence. The highly complex symbol structure that is their profession yields to the force of Heather's unbidden "hereness."

The insertion of Heather into this scene at the moment that Dr. Lowenthal is arguing for the necessity of adhering to the ideas that render their work meaningful, suggests that we are witnessing the disruption of the

Symbolic by the Real. In fact, like the Real, Heather simply bursts upon the scene, occasioning its collapse. Shortly after her arrival Isaac asks Alan if he doesn't have "someplace else to be." Any opportunity for Isaac to consider the wisdom of his colleague's advice, the meaning of his words, is now past. Reason goes out the door, indeed is sent out the door, with Dr. Lowenthal.

Some consideration of Diana Baylor and her relationship with Heather is in order. All the scenes of Diana's therapy with Dr. Barr include her obsessive recounting of the same dream. Thus, in a flattened tone, she begins:

> DIANA: I had the dream again . . . I'm arranging flowers on a table. . . . I decorate the flowerpot with fancy paper . . . feels like velvet. There are three different kinds of flowers. There are lilies, and there are . . .

And then she breaks off, switching topics and affect. The dream, which unfolds in the course of a number of sessions, is a matter for Dr. Barr's interpretation, and does not appear to have any significance outside his patient. Later, Dr. Barr attends a talk by a colleague that includes a reference to a classic dream told to Freud by one of his patients, which involves the arranging of three different kinds of flowers, and can be found, the speaker advises, in *The Interpretation of Dreams*. This is an epiphany for Isaac. He is seen rushing to the library, where he finds the Freudian text, that is, where he returns to the word, and literally begins to read meaning into the events he has been inarticulately experiencing.

This dream, with some minor variations, actually does appear in *The Interpretation of Dreams*, and is presented by Freud (1900/1953) as illustrative of the "naïve dreams of healthy people" (p. 374). Diana, who is neither naïve nor healthy, provides someone else's dream—indeed, a classic example of the symbolic dream. Presenting such a dream, replete with referred meaning, is Diana's protective, and purloined, identity.

Of Diana we also know that she feels herself to be overshadowed by Heather. Compared to her she feels "like a caterpillar, creepy and crawly."

> ISAAC: A caterpillar turns into a butterfly.
> DIANA: Heather's the butterfly.

It soon becomes clear that Heather had coolly planned the murder of her husband and intended to frame Isaac for it should he discover the truth. Indeed, Heather had earlier obtained his fingerprints on an item identical to the one used to murder Jimmy. The murder weapon is a dumbbell, and what better evocation of the Real than a "dumb," that is, inarticulate, instrument? When Isaac confronts Heather with the truth she plans to have him charged as the murderer, and asks Diana to get the evidence. Diana balks at this, but does something else. She trades identities with her sister. Diana remains at the hospital as Heather, and Heather leaves to obtain the dumbbell.

The film's climactic scene involves Heather and Isaac in a frenzied life and death chase to the top of the rickety lighthouse, the setting of their earlier tryst. Here they engage in an elemental clash, from which only one can emerge. For this is a battle not merely for the dumbbell. It is more primal and, paradoxically, more symbolic. Indeed, the darkness, the driving rain, and the roiling sea are a furious evocation of this struggle for meaning, and for the salvaging of the human subject. Should Heather prevail, then the unmediated and unreasoned force of the senseless also prevails. Her triumph promises the horror that is revealed when the scrim of metaphor is stripped away and words become dumb "things." Heather is the unrepressed and unrestrained terror of the Real. For "in the psychotic state, there is no distance or perspective on experience, there is . . . no repression, and therefore no true . . . relationship" (Muller, 1983, p. 29). And Isaac, a man of the symbol, has been seduced by this whirlwind, drawn through a fissure in his own psychic fortification, where his life, literally and metaphorically, is imperiled. Not unlike his biblical namesake, Isaac is in danger of being sacrificed.

### HIC ET NUNC

> Love is most nearly itself
> When here and now cease to matter
> —T. S.Eliot, "East Coker"

Heather does not prevail; she dies, but not before Dr. Barr, now returned to reliance upon the word, makes a last attempt, a *final analysis,* to bring her into the Symbolic. She is holding a gun toward him and he is holding out words to her. Isaac tells her that he knows it was she who killed her father, she who was raped. There is a reason for her actions. They, and she, are not inexplicable, and so can be retrieved from the brink of Real disaster. He is seeking, by his words, to create a symbolic space between Heather and the immediacy of the gun. For, by "transforming what is physically at hand . . . into what is symbolically present" (Muller, 1983, p. 29) Isaac endeavors to transform their experience, redeeming it from the immediacy of the Real, wherein nothing need be remembered because everything is present. This insupportable amplitude is all that has failed to be symbolized. As Lacan and Granoff (1956) observe, "What experience in analysis proves . . . is precisely that, instead of giving reality to the symbol, the patient attempts to constitute *hic et nunc,* in the experience of the treatment, that . . . point of reference which we call bringing the analyst into his game" (270). The here and now is both an ecstasy and a "horror" (Muller, 1983). The Real is an unrelenting rapture that in its vigor and sheer endurance becomes dreadful. In the final moments atop the lighthouse, where murder, passion, and blinding rage are all fully present, so too is the terror of the Real.

Isaac's last attempt to situate Heather in the Symbolic fails. Although he tells her that what happened to her is over, and in the past, Heather cannot cross that bridge. She says, "It's *not* over. You think you can shrink me like one of your fuckin' patients? You think that makes me feel better? I don't give a shit about you or my father. I don't give a shit about anything." Heather is lost. Words have failed to separate her from her fury. There will be no modulation, for there is no mediation. She is truly unspeakable. She is what remains forever outside the symbolic, forever unrepresentable, and as such is an everlasting threat to human subjectivity. Heather must be rejected if Isaac is to be reclaimed. In their final struggle the faulty railing gives way and Isaac falls, seemingly to his death. But he has grabbed hold of the ledge, and also of Heather's ankle. She falls, indeed is pulled, backward toward the void by the force of his grasp, into the maw of the indifferent sea. The weapon is rendered harmless as the senseless is transformed into the meaningful. In Lacanian terms, Isaac managed to support the psychic space and to sustain the subject. For true human desire is always deferred, it is never here, never now. Realization, this film suggests, can be deadly.

The Real is the frontier beyond which the psyche cannot go without encountering its own insupportable strangeness. Heather took Isaac on such a journey, through obsessive passion, murder, merged identities, and death. When these materialize it is madness, and it temporarily captures Isaac. But Isaac had to bar Heather from (human) existence. For,

> to be finitely human means to live as decentered subjects, split . . . from unconscious desire, forced to channel our wants through the narrow defiles of the signifier, which offers a limited satisfaction by affording us symbolic presences. The alternative is either death or psychosis. (Muller, 1983, p. 31)

The film does not end with Heather's death. Instead, in a paradoxical epilogue attesting to the adage that the "past *is* prologue," we see Heather's sister Diana, in the closing scene of the movie, at dinner:

DINNER COMPANION: I want to know everything about you, *Heather*.

DIANA: Well, the first thing you should know about me . . . I'm an only child.

Shedding her former psychological skin, Diana emerges from the cocoon that had been her "creepy, crawly identity," to become the "butterfly." For the essence of Heather—the Real—was not forfeited at the lighthouse, only its particular incarnation. It is the remainder that cannot be symbolized, only embodied. This residue is always just beyond the frontier of the Symbolic, and this is entirely consonant with the Real: it is "the domain outside symbolization" (Wilden, 1968, p. 281), the border transgressed at the price of subjectivity and sanity. Diana is not like Heather; she *is* Heather.

## METAPHORICAL TRANSFERENCE

> Who could know what resonance the film might have for one of
> the spectators watching it?
> —Alain de Mijolla, "The Psychoanalytic
> Situation on Screen," in *Endless Night*

This discussion has considered some of the ways in which the analyst becomes entangled in the vicissitudes of the transference relationship, and described the implications of Lacan's psychic trinity as it elucidates the significance of this relationship in *The Prince of Tides* and *Final Analysis*.

As has been suggested, the Imaginary and the Real are not the regions of the human subject, nor is the transference the voice of the unconscious. Rather, the transference relationship is the patient's attempt to bring the analyst into "his game," drawing the analyst into an actual liaison that serves to rebuff the unconscious knowledge of lack. Thus, in the Imaginary the transference functions as a fetish, establishing a surrogate relationship to stand in place of what is missing. This is a fantasy, and it sustains desire while also obscuring its failure to be realized. That is to say, "Fantasy, in its very staging of desire, defends against desire, manages against the abyss of the desire of the Other" (Heath, 1999, p. 48). But in the Real, where objects are stripped of any interceding veil of significance, all desires threaten to enact the violence and disfigurement that are its inheritance. And these are "the desire[s] with regard to which we must not 'give way' . . . not the desire[s] supported by fantasy but the desire of the Other beyond fantasy . . . a radical renunciation of all the richness of desires based upon fantasy-scenarios" (Zizek, as cited in Heath, p. 48).

Both manifestations, insofar as they aim to thwart the unconscious, are necessarily the adversaries of the Symbolic. These films offer a screen upon which to view the wishes and seductive horrors behind the blanketing symbol, for they are allegories of desire, showing us who we fear we are, who wish we were, and who we may become. "Seeing a film is indeed to be individually involved in *different positions*" (Heath, 1999, p. 38, italics added), to image the pleasures and dangers of unspeakable desire only to reenter the Symbolic, there to allude to, and so also, and necessarily, to relinquish, the imagined delights of the self fulfilled.

## NOTES

1. See, for example, Schwaber, 1981; Culler, 1982; Spence, 1982, 1987; Kaplan, 1990.

2. See also, Bergstrom, 1999; Villela, 1999; Schneider, 1985; Chodorkoff & Baxter, 1974; Wolfenstein & Leites, 1950.

3. See, for example, Gergen, 1985, 1990; Sampson, 1988.

4. See, for example, Metz, 1982; Copjec, 1995; Carveth, 1997; Zizek, 1993, 2000.

5. Recent literature (see, for example, Bateman, 1998; Plakun, 1998; Davies, 1999; Currin, 2000; Steiner, 2000; Wegner, 2000; and Ralph, 2001) has considered the idea of enactment from a variety of viewpoints, ranging from the more traditional notion that it is a problem arising in the countertransference (for example, Bateman, 1998), to the provocative notion that enactment, though admittedly outside the traditionally conceived analytic frame, can be employed, as Plakun (1998) suggests, to "advance the treatment."

6. See, for example, Lacan & Granoff, 1956; Kerrigan, 1983; Hurst, 2000.

## REFERENCES

Bateman, A. (1998). Thick- and thin-skinned organizations and enactment in borderline and narcissistic disorders. *International Journal of Psycho-Analysis, 79*(1), 13–25.

Bergstrom, J. (Ed.) (1999). *Endless night*. Berkeley: University of California Press.

Campbell, J. (1949). *The hero with A thousand faces* (2nd ed.). Princeton, NJ: Princeton University Press.

Carveth, D. (1997). The borderline dilemma in Paris, Texas: Psychoanalytic approaches to Sam Shepard. A Hyperlink Journal for Psychological Study of the Arts. Retrieved August 19, 2001 from <http://www.clas.ufl.edu/ipsa/journal/articles/psyart>1997/carvet01.htm ISSN: 1088–5870. Article number 971002.

Chodorkoff, B., & Baxter, S. (1974). Secrets of a soul: An early psychoanalytic fihn venture. *American Imago, 31,* 319–334.

Conroy, P. (1986). *The prince of tides*. Boston: Houghton Mifflin.

Copjec, S. (1995). *Read my desire: Lacan against the historicists*. Cambridge, MA: MIT Press.

Culler, J. (1982). *On deconstruction*. Ithaca, NY: Cornell University Press.

Currin, J. (2000). What are the essential characteristics of the analytic attitude? Insight, the use of enactments, and relationship. *Journal of Clinical Psychoanalysis, 9*(1), 75–91.

Davies, J. (1999). Getting cold feet, defining "safe enough" borders: Dissociation, multiplicity, and integration in the analyst's experience. *Psychoanalytic Quarterly, 68*(2), 184–208.

Freud, S. (1953). The interpretation of dreams. In J. Strachey (Ed. & Trans.), *Standard edition of the complete psychological works of Sigmund Freud* (Vol. 5). London: Hogarth Press. (Original work published 1900)

Freud, S. (1958). The dynamics of transference. In J. Strachey (Ed. & Trans.), *Standard edition of the complete psychological works of Sigmund Freud* (Vol. 12, pp. 97–108). London: Hogarth Press. (Original work published 1912)

Freud, S. (1958). On beginning treatment. In J. Strachey (Ed. & Trans.), *Standard edition of the complete psychological works of Sigmund Freud* (Vol. 12, pp. 121–144). London: Hogarth Press. (Original work published 1913)

Freud, S. (1958). Remembering, repeating and working-through. In J. Strachey (Ed. & Trans.), *Standard edition of the complete psychological works of Sigmund Freud* (Vol. 12, pp. 145–156). London: Hogarth Press. (Original work published 1914)

Freud, S. (1955). Beyond the pleasure principle. In J. Strachey (Ed. & Trans.), *Standard edition of the complete psychological works of Sigmund Freud* (Vol. 18, pp. 3–18). London: Hogarth Press. (Original work published 1920)

Freud, S. (1959). Inhibitions, symptoms and anxiety. In J. Strachey (Ed. & Trans.), *Standard edition of the complete psychological works of Sigmund Freud* (Vol. 20, pp. 77–178). London: Hogarth Press. (Original work published 1926)

Gabbard, G. (1997). The psychoanalyst at the movies. *International Journal of Psycho-Analysis, 78,* 429–434.

Gabbard, G., & Gabbard, K. (1999). *Psychiatry and the Cinema* (2nd ed.). Washington, DC: American Psychiatric Press.

Gergen, K. (1985). The social constructionist movement in modem psychology. *American Psychologist, 40,* 266–275.

Gergen, K. (1990). Toward a postmodem psychology. *Humanist Psychologist, 18,* 23–34.

Goffman, E. (1959). *The presentation of self in everyday life.* Garden City, NY: Doubleday Anchor Books.

Goodheart, E. (1991). *Desire and its discontents.* New York: Columbia University Press.

Greenson, R. (1967). *The technique and practice of psychoanalysis* (Vol. 1). Madison, CT: International Universities Press.

Heath, S. (1999). Cinema and psychoanalysis: Parallel histories. In J. Bergstrom, Ed., *Endless night.* Berkeley: University of California Press.

Hurst, W. (2000). What about Lacan? *Modem Psychoanalysis, 25*(1), 91–108.

Joanou, P. (Director), & Roven, C., Thomas, T., Witt, P. Junger (Producers). (1992). *Final Analysis* [Motion picture]. United States: Warner/Roven-Cavallo.

Kaplan, E. A. (1990). From Plato's cave to Freud's screen. Introduction to E. Ann Kaplan (Ed.), *Psychoanalysis and Cinema,* pp. 1–23. New York: Routledge.

Kerrigan, W. (1983). Introduction to J. Smith & W. Kerrigan (Eds.), *Interpreting Lacan*, pp. ix–xxvii. New Haven: Yale University Press.

Kojeve, A. (1947). *Introduction to the reading of Hegel* (J. H. Nichols, Jr., Trans., A. Bloom, Ed.). Ithaca, New York: Cornell University Press.

Lacan, J. (1964). *The four fundamental concepts of psycho-analysis* (J. A. Miller, Ed., A. Sheridan, Trans.). New York: W. W. Norton.

Lacan, J. (1977). The mirror stage as formative of the function of the I as revealed in psychoanalytic experience. In *Écrits: A selection* (Alan Sheridan, Trans.), pp. 1–7. New York: W. W. Norton. (Original work published 1949)

Lacan, J. (1977). The function and field of speech and language in psychoanalysis. In *Écrits: A selection* (Alan Sheridan, Trans.), pp.30–113. New York: W. W. Norton. (Original work published 1953)

Lacan, J., & Granoff, W. (1956). Fetishism: The symbolic, the imaginary and the real. In S. Lorand, Ed., and M. Balint, Assoc. Ed., *Fetishism: Psychodynamics and therapy*, pp. 265–276. New York: Gramercy Books.

Laplanche, J., & Pontalis, J.-B. (1973). *The language of psycho-analysis* (D. Nicholson-Smith, Trans.). New York: W. W. Norton.

Maroda, K. (1998). As the emphasis on analytic treatment as a relationship continues to grow, all aspects of mutuality are being examined. Although much has been said regarding the analyst's emotional responses to the patient, enactment has been seen as a recreation of some past event in the patient's life. Perhaps because of the threatening nature of the concept, analysts have not paid attention to the potential for recreating their pasts. Sometimes in symmetry with the patient, at other times as an act of countertransference dominance that disrupts the treatment and may traumatize the patient. This article focuses on enactment as an inevitable mutual event beginning with mutual projective identification, followed by mutual, unplanned behavior, and culminating in a mutual sense of puzzlement and a certain sense of being emotionally out of control. The dangers of enactment are discussed, as well as its therapeutic uses [Abstract]. *Psychoanalytic Psychology, 15*(4), 517–535. Journal URL: <http://www.apa.org/journals/pap.html>

Metz, C. (1982). *The imaginary signifier: Psychoanalysis and the cinema* (C. Britton et al., Trans.). Bloomington: Indiana University Press.

Mijolla, A. de (1999). The psychoanalytic situation on screen. In J. Bergstrom, Ed., *Endless night*. Berkeley: University of California Press.

Muller, J. (1983). Language, psychosis, and the subject. In J. Smith and W. Kerrigan, Eds., *Interpreting Lacan*. New Haven: Yale University Press.

Plakun, E. (1998). Enactment and the treatment of abuse survivors. *Harvard Review of Psychiatry, 5*(6), 318–325.

Ralph, I. (2001). Countertransference, enactment and sexual abuse. *Journal of Child Psychotherapy, 27*(3), 285–301.

Sampson, E. (1988). The decentralization of identity. *American Psychologist, 40,* 1203–1211.

Schneider, I. (1985). The psychiatrist at the movies: The first fifty years. In J. Reppen and M. Charney, Eds., *Psychoanalytic Study of Literature, 53–67.* Hillsdale, NJ: Analytic Press.

Schneider, I. (1999). Foreword in G. Gabbard & K. Gabbard, *Psychiatry and the Cinema* (2nd ed.). Washington, DC: American Psychiatric Press.

Schwaber, E. (1981). Empathy: A mode of analytic listening. *Psychoanalytic Inquiry, 1,* 357–392.

Socor, B. (1997). *Conceiving the self: Presence and absence in psychoanalytic theory.* Madison, CT: International Universities Press.

Spence, D. (1982). *Narrative truth and historical truth.* New York: W. W. Norton.

Spence, D. (1987). *The Freudian metaphor.* New York: W. W. Norton.

Steiner, J. (2000). Containment, enactment and communication. *International Journal of Psychoanalysis, 81*(2), 245–255.

Streisand, B. (Director/Co-producer) & Karsh, A. (Co-producer). (1991). *Prince of tides* [Motion picture]. United States: Barwood/Columbia/Longfellow.

Villela, L. (1999). From film as a case study to film as myth: Psychoanalytic perspectives on the analysis of cinema and culture. *Annual of Psychoanalysis, 26/27,* 315–330.

Wegner, P. (2000). Passion, countertransference enactment, and breakdown in the psychoanalysis of a young woman. *Journal of the American Psychoanalytic Association, 48*(3), 811–838.

Wilden, A. (1968). Translator's introduction in J. Lacan, *The Language of the Self.* Baltimore: Johns Hopkins Press.

Wolfe, T. (1968). *You can't go home again.* London: Penguin Books. (Original work published 1940)

Wolfenstein, M., & Leites, N. (1950). Cyberspace, or the unbearable closure of being. In J. Bergstrom, Ed., *Endless Night.* Berkeley: University of California Press.

Zizek, S. (Ed.) (1993). *Everything you always wanted to know about Lacan (But were afraid to ask Hitchcock).* New York: Verso.

Zizek, S. (Ed.) (2000). *Enjoy your symptom!: Jacques Lacan in Hollywood and out* (2nd ed.). New York: Routledge, 2001.

# 9

## Translating Psychotherapy Narratives from Literature onto Film

### An Interview with Theodore Isaac Rubin

JERROLD R. BRANDELL

### INTRODUCTION

Theodore Isaac Rubin, a practicing psychiatrist and psychoanalyst who resides in New York City, is the author of some thirty fiction and non-fiction works, among them *David and Lisa* (Rubin, 1961). *David and Lisa* is a sensitive portrayal of the relationship that develops between two disturbed adolescents who meet in a residential treatment facility. David, obsessional and perfectionistic, lives in dread of being "touched," and Lisa, maternally deprived and waif-like, is able to communicate with others only in rhyme. At the time of the book's original release, some reviewers characterized it as a "classic love story," although *David and Lisa* is also a narrative of the process of psychotherapy, and of the power of the therapeutic milieu in promoting recovery. Two cinematic renderings of this story have been released, a distinction that appears to place *David and Lisa*, with its thematic focus on the treatment process, in a category by itself. The first film version of this story, produced in 1962, was directed by Frank Perry, and starred Keir Dullea as David, Janet Margolin as Lisa, and Howard da Silva as the psychiatrist, Dr. Swinford. A second version of the story, produced by Oprah Winfrey in 1998, was directed by Lloyd Kramer, and starred Lukas Haas as David, Brittany Murphy as Lisa, and Sidney Poitier in the role of the psychiatrist, Dr. White.

Dr. Rubin graciously consented to this interview, which was conducted on September 21, 2001 by Jerrold R. Brandell.

INTERVIEW

JERROLD R. BRANDELL: It's obvious to anyone familiar with your work, your leadership role in American psychiatry and psychoanalysis, that you've drawn upon a wealth of clinical experience in writing *David and Lisa* (Rubin, 1961), not to mention a number of other works, such as *Jordi* (Rubin, 1962), and *Little Ralphie and the Creature* (Rubin, 1998). Can you tell me a little about the experiences that may have contributed to the writing of *David and Lisa?*

THEODORE ISAAC RUBIN: Well, I have seen a number of patients during the years, of course. Just to give you some general background, as a matter of fact I saw several people who were very much like Lisa and also like David. However, this was not during the time that I was in psychiatric practice, but rather, many years ago, when I worked in the emergency room of the Santa Monica Hospital. And I did see several people who had very similar manifestations that eventually I portrayed in Lisa. And as for David, I saw more clinical material that he would validate or that would validate him over the years in psychiatric practice, as well as, again, in the emergency room. In clinical practice, there is of course, no shortage ever of obsessive compulsive people. So, that largely led to this particular story. And I might also mention that my wife at one time was a principal of the League School for schizophrenic children, and she did work with several people, one in particular, who inspired *Jordi. David and Lisa* was almost a natural follow-up to *Jordi*, the way I view it.

JRB:            Was the book commercially successful prior to the 1962 film production?

DR. RUBIN:   It was fairly successful, but nothing like the kind of success it had after the film was shown.

JRB:            Yes, well, the film won several awards as I recall.

DR. RUBIN:   Yes, it won the Venice Film Award and Frank Perry was nominated for an Academy Award for his directorship, and it won a number of other awards that I can't even recall, but I remember those, which were principal awards.

JRB: Yes, can you tell me something about how *David and Lisa* came to be produced in the first place? Did you ever think of *David and Lisa* cinematically prior to being contacted by the production people or whoever first approached you?

DR. RUBIN: No, not at all, I had never even imagined it, did not have that in mind at all. What happened was that a young woman named Anne Breyer, whom I didn't know, read the book, and then brought it to her to her parents, Eleanor and Frank Perry. They liked the book very much and Frank was looking for a movie project for his first production, so that was how it started. They contacted me and eventually it became a movie—a very low budget movie, I might add.

JRB: My understanding is that it cost about $180,000 to produce, which even by 1962 standards must have been considered a small sum.

DR. RUBIN: Yes, that's true. It was less than $200,000. Well, of course, it was many years ago, and it was different then than it is now, but nevertheless, it was impressive. Maybe it contributed in some way to the quality of the movie. They didn't have enough money to spoil it with any kind of fancy photography or what have you; it was very simply stated.

JRB: What was the nature of your involvement in the original production?

DR. RUBIN: I had a number of meetings with them. I also told them what hospitals and other treatment facilities to go to where they were likely to get the kind of ambiance they needed, and to meet with some patients who might help them to understand what's it's really like for people like this. And so they went to Bellevue, and several other places, where they hospitalize adolescents. But other than that, they really did it from the book.

JRB: In the 1998 Harpo Films production, you're listed as a coauthor of the screenplay [with Eleanor Perry and Lloyd Kramer].

DR. RUBIN: Yes, I was. We wrote it together actually, but since it was taken in large part from the first screenplay and from the book itself, that wasn't terribly difficult to do.

JRB: So you felt that you had some degree of artistic control in both productions or perhaps more so in the latter production?

DR. RUBIN:   More so in the latter certainly. A little in the first version, but I might tell you that in the first, when we saw the screen tests, I was against using Janet Margolin. She later turned out to be excellent—but I thought she looked too healthy and was a little older than I had pictured Lisa to be. However, she certainly turned out to be wonderful.

JRB:         At the time of the original film version, what had been your feeling about popular film's portrayal of psychoanalysts or psychotherapists?

DR. RUBIN:   It was terrible [laughter]. And it still is for the most part, almost invariably. I've seen a number of shows where there's a psychiatrist or a psychoanalyst who is portrayed as a complete lunatic, or as an incredible eccentric, going around the hospital playing a guitar or something like that. They're made to appear almost clownish, and years ago, it was even worse. There was really a bias and there still is. I think people are afraid of the whole subject and the psychiatrist becomes the messenger. Perhaps I shouldn't say it was the first film because I think *The Snake Pit* (Litvack, 1948) also portrayed the psychiatrist in a favorable light, and at least with some degree of realism.

JRB:         Yes, yes. Of course there are other examples. I believe that right around the same period *Pressure Point* (Cornfield, 1962) was produced with Sidney Poitier. . . .

DR. RUBIN:   Yes, a few were okay, but there were some that were dreadful. And others, they were terrible in that the therapists were idealized. Many of these films were extremely simplistic, even though they may, in other respects, have been good films. I think of the one that Ingrid Bergman starred in.

JRB:         Oh, *Spellbound* (Hitchcock, 1945)?

DR. RUBIN:   Yeah, *Spellbound*. That was a good film, it was good entertainment but it doesn't happen that way [laughter]. You know, at least the psychiatrist wasn't made to look like a complete dunce. Well, even that, in part, revealed a certain bias, but in *David and Lisa*, the actors were really very good and the part of the psychiatrist, by Howard da Silva, was superb.

JRB:         Well, it's interesting, since many therapists describe da Silva's portrayal as one of the more realistic portrayals [see Figure 9.1].

DR. RUBIN:   Yes, well, I certainly agree. And incidentally, that was one of the first films that da Silva acted in after he was on the [McCarthy

FIGURE 9.1. Dr. Alan Swinford (Howard da Silva) gradually gains the trust of his disturbed adolescent patient, David (Keir Dullea) in *David and Lisa* (Continental Pictures, 1962). Courtesy of the Wisconsin Center for Film and Theater Research.

era] blacklist, so that was a good break for him. It started his career again.

JRB: Yes. Well, do you feel that the story was successfully adapted for the original movie version?

DR. RUBIN: I think it was, of course. It's a conceit on my part because they literally followed it line by line. The dialogue, et cetera . . . came right out of the book. The only objection I have to the story was a part that I had nothing to do with—again, a conceit on my part. The parents do not appear in the book and I wouldn't have objected to the parents; however, the implication was that these kinds of parents produce these kinds of results—in other words, David. And I found this to be a vast oversimplification and sort of glossed over, and not what the book was about. The book was about two people who were sick and meet each other, and as a consequence, help each other, but it's not about the dynamics or possible origins of schizophrenia or any of the other mental diseases. But they felt they had to put that in, and from my point of view, clinically, it did not fit. Maybe I'm being a little too technical about this; but it's from a professional point of view, and not from the moviegoer's point of view, I guess. I didn't [at the time] hear anybody object to it so perhaps they were right. I don't know.

JRB: In balance, as you compare the two film versions, which do you prefer?

DR. RUBIN: The first.

JRB: The first one?

DR. RUBIN: Yes. I think the first. The second was okay, but I don't think it was as good as the first, largely because of the original cast who were just incredible. Keir Dullea, I think, was exceptional. I think something else that made the first version very effective was that it was filmed in black and white.

JRB: I was going to ask about that because I noticed that, of course, they made the 1998 version in color.

DR. RUBIN: Yes.

JRB: I wonder if you have thoughts about this subject matter in terms of black and white versus color?

DR. RUBIN: I think that the subject matter is really better-suited to black and white film. I think that while the color photography was actually quite beautiful in the second version, I think it takes something away from the story, from the drama and from the people. It's especially important with this kind of subject matter. I think black and white gives it the right kind of ambience, the right kind of feeling; it's simpler and sharper, and it also, without too much effort, gives you somewhat of a feel of what's going on inside of people who are that disturbed. There's an eerie quality [to reality] that people who are not mentally ill would not ordinarily appreciate. And I think that black and white photography lends itself to that kind of feel.

JRB: Speaking of black and white, I found it interesting that the earlier film version has these veiled references to racism on the part of David's mother, although that particular element was not included at all in the later film version.

DR. RUBIN: Yes, well, it wasn't in the book either, but they put it in. Maybe that was good. I think they wanted to demonstrate as much as they could that David's mother was that kind of a person, rather constricted and biased. This was in order to account for David's pathology. For me, it didn't come off. I would not have included that because I don't think it really had anything to do with his pathology. And I might say that in those days this kind of illness, whatever we may call it diagnostically—and diagnosis is not something I'm terribly interested in—I think it detracts from the person himself. When they say "schizophrenic" I begin to think that there's not only a prejudice against such patients, but one doesn't see beyond the schizophrenic manifestations, and these are different in each individual. But in those days, psychodynamics was *it;* there were hundreds and hundreds of books written by psychiatrists about schizophrenia, schizophrenogenic parents, and so on. Now we're discovering what some people felt was true in those years, that it's largely a physiological illness and that most of these illnesses have a physiological basis, that there is actual brain pathology involved. And I can't tell you the number of articles about schizophrenogenic parents, which, by the way, had the effect of making parents of schizophrenic children very, very guilty. They felt terribly guilty, awful that they hadn't done enough.

JRB:        Well, I suppose in spite of all their other contributions, many of which were much more enduring and useful, Bruno Bettelheim and Frieda Fromm-Reichmann bore some responsibility for that.

DR. RUBIN:    Yes, yes.

JRB:        I noticed in the 1998 version of the film, right off the bat there's a statement about the "parent blaming" thing being something of the past. Sidney Poitier makes this remark to David's mother, I think, as he's being admitted to Border School. Along the lines of what you were suggesting, that seems to be a significant sort of change.

DR. RUBIN:    Yes. That is. And had I known much more about it than I did at that time, I would have indicated that it is, in large part, a neurological manifestation.

JRB:        That actually leads me to another question. If you were to rewrite this story in light of more recent clinical experience, or current theories of how the therapeutic process operates with adolescents and so on, are there elements that you would be inclined to change?

DR. RUBIN:    It's interesting that you asked that, because when I gave this
book to my then-editor, Val Webb, he told me that we had a
very big offer from the Book of the Month Club, if I were to
extend the story, if it had at least another 50 pages. And I was
very bullheaded about it. I said absolutely not, and it ended
there. Now, years later, I thought, you know something? I should
have at least given it a shot. The Book of the Month Club? That
wouldn't have been bad. But would I change it now? I don't
know. I almost think I would rather write an entirely new story
than to do that. And of course, I don't have a hell of a lot of
experience with medications. I've used certain medications with
patients, but am far less experienced than my three children, all
of whom are psychiatrists. They understand the chemistry
much, much better than I do. And I don't have an enormous
interest in it, either. So I don't know. *Little Ralphie* [first published in 1998] also had almost nothing to do with medication,
so I don't know that I would do it differently.

JRB:          Just as an observation, there's really much more actual therapeutic interaction in *David and Lisa*—certainly in the original story,
and in the first film version—than you ever expect to see in the
popular cinema. And that I think is one of the great attractions
that this film has had. It revealed aspects of the process of therapy that you never saw in the movies.

DR. RUBIN:    Well you know, I don't mean to mislead you on the way I feel. I
believe that therapy is crucial for all people. I would put everybody into therapy and not for my own selfish reasons; I feel that
they really need it. We all need it, and I think that there's certain
progress that cannot be made without therapy. One of the issues
is that if you have people who have been isolated for a long time
due to their illness—and there's always a certain amount of isolation—they really don't know what it is to be a person. And I
think one of the roles of a therapist is not just to reveal patients'
problems and solve them and so forth, but really to teach them
what being a human being is all about. Teach them about limitations and assets, and how you make use of your time and
energy in your life, which many of these people don't know. They
also don't know the degree of constriction they've had. So [the
real progress occurs] when you begin to open this up. Medication
doesn't do this, of course—it relieves symptoms and that's terribly important, but it can't offer what's possible through the therapeutic relationship. Of course, there's a place for both.

JRB:    Yes, of course. Let me ask you in more kind of a specific way, what prompted the decision to insert the scene—I think it's in both film versions, and more or less the same—in which David injures Lisa by yelling at her when she interrupts his friend's impromptu piano recital? This friend is a young boy in the first version, a girl in the second. Was this, in your estimation, an effort to heighten the drama, to build up to the dénouement and so forth?

DR. RUBIN:    I think so. I think it was to create drama and to make their eventual feelings for each other more poignant. Especially from David's point of view. But it's also characteristic of somebody with a personality like David's, that he would not take well to being interrupted.

JRB:    So, it does fit the character?

DR. RUBIN:    It fits, yes.

JRB:    You think it was necessary for the story?

DR. RUBIN:    No.

JRB:    Okay [laughter]. Now in the original story, my guess based upon the dialogue and description is that David is supposed to be Jewish, though I may be mistaken about that.

DR. RUBIN:    No, no. I haven't read the story in some time but I don't recall that being my intent.

JRB:    I'm thinking of his comments to the psychiatrist about not being Talmudic and so on.

DR. RUBIN:    Oh yes. Well, on the other hand, that's [a reference] used by a lot by people, especially in New York—where everybody's Jewish [laughter].

JRB:    What about the anecdotal content that pertains to New York City life? Was the setting supposed to be New York City in the earlier film version?

DR. RUBIN:    No, the earlier film version was shot in Philadelphia [which was also the location of the residential school].

JRB:    Philadelphia? Okay, I see. Then in the 1998 version, it's a West Coast setting?

DR. RUBIN:    Right. The later version was set in California, I suppose because it was more convenient for them to shoot it there.

JRB:            Let me ask you something a bit different. In terms of the inte-
                riority of David's emotional life, or for that matter, any literary
                character's, whether you feel that this can be captured in the
                medium of popular film?

DR. RUBIN:      This is extremely difficult. I've asked myself that before. Inter-
                estingly there's a man now in touch with me who is interested in
                [filming] *Little Ralphie and the Creature.* I don't know whether
                this will go anywhere, but nevertheless, my big question is how
                he's going to represent this [emotional interior]. There are ways,
                I guess, but it's very difficult. I did a book—it's rather hard to
                get, been out of print for years—it was called *Cat.* It's about a
                man, and the whole story takes place inside the man's head
                while he is in a catatonic stupor. What would you do? Act out
                whatever happens in the stupor? I guess it's possible. But I see it
                as very difficult, very challenging to get a real feel for it. Besides,
                my guess is that current audiences are just not going to work
                very hard at getting the point.

JRB:            As a follow-up let me ask you how you felt about the way in
                which the dreams of the "execution clock" were handled?

DR. RUBIN:      I thought it was handled really well, especially considering they
                had only $180,000. It was the way I had pictured it, more or less,
                and it was good.

JRB:            Well, it was interesting, in the 1962 version, that David appears
                to be horrified not only by his role in the dreams as the execu-
                tioner but also that he appears to take some sadistic pleasure in
                decapitating the victims which, of course, adds to the horror.
                And, of course, in the earlier version, really, the dream sequence
                is more vivid, the violence more graphic.

DR. RUBIN:      Yes, I was thinking really of the earlier version, and this hap-
                pens to be something that's true at one and the same time. Peo-
                ple (just to give you an example) are horrified by a parent's
                death. And at the same time, what they won't admit is that they
                are gratified by it, too. These [reactions] are more or less diluted
                in most of us, though there may be a sense of freedom involved
                [in the death of a parent]. But these reactions are the hardest
                things to get to. Nevertheless, this kind of ambivalence runs
                through all of us in almost everything, and especially with a
                [character such as] David. This is a person who is extremely
                detached and afraid of any kind of affiliation with anybody,
                afraid to make any kind of an emotional investment. Therefore,

if an emotional investment should take place, he may, on the one hand, like this fact. But, on the other hand, he may feel exceedingly enraged that anyone could get him to *feel* to this extent. He wants to feel [relatedness to people], yet at the same time he wants to do away with them. And the horror he has is not just the horror of his own feelings, but involves both his hostile feelings and his more constructive feelings. He's in conflict constantly over this, and the way somebody like David handles the conflict is through seclusion, so that the stimulation of these feelings doesn't take place.

JRB: Let me pose this question as a kind of follow-up to some of what you've said about the whole idea of interiority, and the effort to represent that on film. Do you think that film, when it's well done, can capture what we regard as the incremental process of structural change in dynamic psychotherapy, the kind of enduring change that people think of when they think about psychoanalytic treatment or intensive psychoanalytic therapy?

DR. RUBIN: I think it can but it requires a relatively sophisticated audience. If the film were shown at the Angelica [an "art house"] or on the West Side, it might do very well, but in the ordinary places, no. People are simply not tuned into any of this. I wrote a paper for the *American Journal of Psychoanalysis* describing what I call a *transitional personality*, this is an [evolving] personality that changes from minute to minute, is always in transition. People who are always in transition don't want to hear about what happened before, or what will happen. It's the immediate. Time is reduced to fragments, and there's no sense of continuity. As a consequence, history is demeaned, and anything intellectual [that] requires the postponement of gratification is also demeaned. When I was much younger, they used to talk about one-year or two-year business cycles—now they talk about three months, [or even] a week. So if you do very serious films such as you're really suggesting, I think it would be okay, but for a very limited audience.

JRB: In your story, David experiences a gradual awakening or reawakening of his capacity to feel, to love, the true test which appears to reside in this deepening relationship with Lisa. At the same time the Alan/Jack character, the psychiatrist, is a very compassionate healer, whose benevolence and therapeutic flexibility seem to exert a very powerful effect on his patient. The original story, which I gather, you wrote in the late fifties, '59?—

DR. RUBIN:   I don't even remember, but something like that.

JRB:         But it's written at a time where there was really no such thing as relational psychoanalysis, and there was certainly no psychology of the self.

DR. RUBIN:   No, but there was. Of course, we already had Freud and Karen Horney and from my point of view, Karen Horney really was a genius. Horney understood character structure like nobody else did. And so the people who were trained by her in the institute that she founded really were doing that kind of therapy a long time ago. As a matter of fact, these self psychologists—Kohut and others—they have never matched her and much of their thinking comes right out of her writings.

JRB:         That is, of course, a criticism that has been leveled at self psychology from various quarters in recent years.

DR. RUBIN:   Yes, yes, but of course, Horney herself and other people had said that if you sit on the shoulder of a giant, you'd be taller than he was. She had started out as a Freudian, and then there was the first big split in the psychoanalytic movement; when she left, a number of people left with her and started another institute.

JRB:         Well it certainly seems that this psychiatrist was anything but classical in the way in which he—

DR. RUBIN:   Well, they tried to really make the character look like me right down to the aquarium in the office, and I am *certainly* not classical. I went with the Horney School. I couldn't stand what I consider to be the rigidity [of classical psychoanalysis]. I just couldn't get religious about it. The New York Psychoanalytic still maintains its orthodoxy today to a large extent.

JRB:         Are there particular attributes or personal qualities that you were most interested in portraying in the Dr. Swinford/Dr. White character for the original story?

DR. RUBIN:   Let me tell you first, that I would never have called him Swinford [laughter]. That was Eleanor Perry's idea. "Swinford" sounds so pretentious. But I think that the doctor has to be available. I do not believe in this business with the blank screen. I'll sum it up [for you] this way and you'll understand in a second what I mean. I was very depressed some years ago, but I went on seeing patients. I accomplished more during that time than at any other time in my practicing and the patients *knew* I was depressed. The point is that we have much more in common than we have apart, and I feel that's okay. I do not hold with those who feel [so strongly about] the purity of the transference. I just don't hold with it at all. As a matter of fact, my own feeling is that there has to be plenty of give and take; it has to be a human experience. I don't see much result from many people who have been [classically analyzed] on the couch, in a number of cases over a period of years. At the beginning of the whole analytic movement here in the United States, you often found [that it attracted] very detached people, people more like David, very reserved. These were the people that the institutes, the analytic institutes chose. These days, you find people who are more outgoing and to use Horney's terms, somewhat *expansive*, who will reach out to people, who aren't withdrawn, and [will] just listen. I think that has changed considerably, but I must also say that psychiatry is really doing very poorly in this country. There are fewer and fewer patients, and as a specialty, there are few people going into it. For the first time, residencies are empty.

JRB:    Let me ask you in a more specific way, about the transference, which in David's treatment and in the psychiatric progress summary at the end of the story, is characterized as "positive." What core transference experience did you intend readers to extrapolate from this positively-valanced relationship?

DR. RUBIN:    Well, I really feel that the transference is everything, the relationship is everything. If people are going to get well they have to have a really strong positive transference, since otherwise it's not going to happen. They got sick in terms of relating—even though there may be a physiological base, though I don't know how much of a physiological base there is in people who are ordinarily neurotic, which constitutes most of us. It's through a relationship that they can get well. They have to get different messages entirely. The way they look at themselves, the world, their self-esteem, all of this comes through the transference. If it's not a positive transference, not a hell of a lot is going to happen and if the patient is incapable of relating, I mean *really* incapable, such as sociopaths that I've had some experience with, it's a hopeless job. Nothing is going to happen. So, the transference is very important. We talk about analyzing the transference, and "transference" itself is a very much overused [term]. How does this patient relate to me? What seems to hurt them? What seems to make them feel better, how does it work?

What is he trying to do with me? How manipulative is he, and so forth? We can go into the past with that, but I don't feel that it's terribly helpful. I used going into the past a great deal, but the patient won't talk at all about what he really feels. So it's a way of breaking through. But otherwise, what's happening *now* is extremely important, though I'm not suggesting that the patient give you a diary of his day. But what he feels and how he's relating to people in general, and how he's relating to me is exceedingly important.

JRB: Although you've said that you didn't intend to emphasize the relationship with the parents the way the movies attempted to, would you say that the uncritical acceptance that David begins to experience in this treatment serves as a kind of corrective to the relationship with his mother, who's depicted as being so rigid, so inflexible, so scornful?

DR. RUBIN: Yes, acceptance is really where it's at. I have written about these things in three books: *Compassion and Self Hate* (Rubin, 1975), *One to One* (Rubin, 1983), and *Reconciliations* (Rubin, 1980), which by the way, has nothing to do with divorce reconciliation.

JRB: I appreciate the recommendations. I actually had another question about the relationship with David's father, though I'll amend it somewhat, in light of what you've already said: that of course, his father really plays no role in the original story. Is there, incidentally, any reference at all to the father?

DR. RUBIN: In the original story? [pause] No. Not at all.

JRB: But the character assumes some importance in the [1962] film version.

DR. RUBIN: Yes. Well they tried to show that the father was not really present and that he [the father] was bullied by the mother and so on. By the way, this is one of the theories that has prevailed for years: that if you have a father who was that way—either passive, out of the picture, subservient—and an aggressive mother, this becomes the basis for homosexuality. I didn't believe it then and I don't believe it now. But, nevertheless, this was a prevailing theory, and many people also felt that this [sort of family dynamic] was a basis for neurotic developments, but that's a cultural bias and I don't believe it.

JRB: In the 1998 version, I believe that the father has already died before the action takes place.

DR. RUBIN:   Yes, they wanted to get rid of him [laughter]. You have to understand something about me. I am very lazy. That's why *David and Lisa* should have been a longer book, and the movie should have been longer. I don't know how I developed that kind of writing but there's a great economy of words. I probably would have been better off—so far as a writing career is concerned—to have been less lazy.

JRB:             Well, it does have interesting implications and there are, in effect, three very different treatments of the father theme. There is the one we've just mentioned, where he dies before the story begins. Of course, in the original story, the father plays no part, for reasons you've already commented on. Then, in the Perry production, he's dominated and dismissively treated by the mother and so on, unable to relate emotionally to his son. I'm thinking, in particular, of that very painful scene in the son's bedroom.

DR. RUBIN:   Yes, they used this a lot for dramatic effect.

JRB:             I thought the way in which they used the flashback [in the Lloyd Kramer remake] of the father taking his son with him to get his shoes shined, I thought that was interesting. It's a whole different dynamic to have lost a father who was so proud of you. This is a very different kind of feeling.

DR. RUBIN:   Oh yeah, sure. But listen, we are all the victims of victims and *every* family is disturbed.

JRB:             Well, I wonder if you have any other thoughts. I've asked a number of questions, and there may have been things that I haven't asked you that would like to say a few words about, before we end.

DR. RUBIN:   I don't know. You've pretty well covered it, actually. Well, when the film came out it was very exciting. What I do remember very vividly is that I invited all my friends to the first screening. Most of them were psychiatrists and psychologists, people in the field, and they came out saying, "Well it was interesting but of course it will never go anywhere." What *was* interesting was that after that, it *did* go somewhere. When it played at the Plaza Theatre where it opened here in New York, there were lines around the block and that continued for quite a while; as a matter of fact it broke every record in every theatre that it played in. Then they said, "Oh boy, you know, it was terrific!" [laughter] But that's exactly what happened.

JRB:        Did you invite the same friends to the second screening in 1998?

DR. RUBIN:  No, [laughter] no, I did not. It was quite an experience, you know. I had, at first, no idea there'd be a film, and then when it came out and was so successful it was really a total surprise to me. I certainly had no idea that it would really do that well. It did particularly well with people in their early twenties, and teens and adolescents.

JRB:        Well, evidently Oprah Winfrey was sufficently impressed to want to bring this story "to a new generation of viewers," but I have to confess that like you, I preferred the first version.

DR. RUBIN:  Yes. Yes.

JRB:        It's more powerful, and eloquently handled.

DR. RUBIN:  I thought so. I thought that Frank Perry did a wonderful job and had some very good people working with him. You know this was his first job as a director so he had an assistant director who really told him how to do it, but they did a good job. I had no real complaints at all.

JRB:        Yes. Well I really do want to thank you for your kindness.

DR. RUBIN:  You're very welcome. I wish you the best.


## REFERENCES

Cornfield, H. (Director), & Kramer, S. (Producer). (1962). *Pressure point* [Motion picture]. United States: UAALarcas/Stanley Kramer.

Hitchcock, A. (Director), & Selznick, D. (Producer). (1945). *Spellbound* [Motion picture]. United States: Selznick Studios.

Kramer, L. (Director), & Winfrey, 0. (Producer). (1998). *David and Lisa* [Motion picture]. United States: Oprah/ABC.

Litvak, A. (Director/Co-producer), & Bassler, R. (Co-producer). (1948). *The snake pit* [Motion picture]. United States: TCF.

Perry, F. (Director), & Heller, P. (Producer). (1962). *David and Lisa* [Motion picture]. United States: Continental Pictures.

Rubin, T. (1962). *Jordi.* New York: Ballantine Books.

Rubin, T. (1961). *David and Lisa.* New York: Macmillan.

Rubin, T. (1975). *Compassion and self hate: An alternative to despair.* New York: David McKay Co.

Rubin, T. (1980). *Reconciliations: Inner peace in an age of anxiety*. New York: Viking.

Rubin, T. (1983). *One to one: Understanding personal relationships*. New York: Forge.

Rubin, T. (1998). *Little Ralphie and the creature*. New York: Forge.

# CONTRIBUTORS

**Jerrold R. Brandell** is professor and Distinguished Faculty Fellow, Wayne State University School of Social Work (Detroit) and editor-in-chief of *Psychoanalytic Social Work*. He is the author of *Of Mice and Metaphors: Therapeutic Storytelling with Children* (Basic Books, 2000) and editor of four other books, including *Countertransference in Psychotherapy with Children and Adolescents* (Jason Aronson, 1992). He has also written a number of papers and book chapters. A doctoral graduate of the University of Chicago, he completed his psychoanalytic training at Michigan Psychoanalytic Council, and maintains a part-time practice in psychotherapy and psychoanalysis in Ann Arbor, Michigan.

**Marilyn Charles** is a psychologist and psychoanalyst in practice in East Lansing, Michigan. A Training and Supervising Analyst with the Michigan Psychoanalytic Council and adjunct professor of clinical psychology at Michigan State University, she is the author of *Patterns: Building Blocks of Experience* (Analytic Press, 2002). Dr. Charles is also the author of numerous articles in such publications as the *American Journal of Psychoanalysis* and *Journal of the American Academy of Psychoanalysis*. She has recently completed work on a second book, currently under review, tentatively titled, *Constructing Realities: Transformations through Myth and Metaphor*.

**Alain J.-J. Cohen** is professor of comparative literature at the University of California, San Diego, where he has spent his entire career. He has published approximately eighty research articles and presented more than two hundred papers at invited talks and conferences around the world on the subjects of cinema, psychoanalysis, or semiotics. He has also made television programs on Godard, Kubrick, Woody Allen, and the role of painting in cinema.

**Sanford Gifford**, M.D., is clinical associate professor of psychiatry at Harvard Medical School and Director of Archives at the Boston Psychoanalytic Society/Institute. He was on the staff of Brigham & Women's Hospital, Boston, from 1948 to 1993. He completed his psychoanalytic training at the Boston Psychoanalytic Institute in 1954, where he taught seminars on Freudian theory and the history of psychoanalysis. He has published papers on the history of psychoanalysis and one book, *The Emmanuel Movement: The Origins of Group Treatment and the Assault on Lay Psychotherapy* (Harvard University Press, 1997). He is chairman of the History and Archives Committee of the American Psychoanalytic Association.

**Shoshana Ringel** received her Ph.D. from the Smith College School of Social Work. She is currently on the clinical faculty of the University of Maryland, Baltimore School of Social Work. Dr. Ringel has published papers in such journals as *Clinical Social Work, Psychoanalytic Social Work,* and *Smith College Studies in Social Work.* She is book review editor of *Psychoanalytic Social Work,* and also serves as a member of the Editorial Board of *Clinical Social Work Journal.*

**Andrea Slane** holds a Ph.D. in comparative literature and is completing a J.D. at the University of Toronto. She is the author of *A Not So Foreign Affair: Fascism, Sexuality and the Cultural Rhetoric of American Democracy* (Duke University Press, 2001).

**Barbara J. Socor**, Ph.D., is associate professor of social work and director of the Division of Social Sciences at Dominican College in Orangeburg, New York. She has written a number of papers and reviews in the fields of social work and psychoanalytic theory, and is author of the book, *Conceiving the Self: Presence and Absence in Psychoanalytic Theory* (International Universities Press, 1996). Dr. Socor received her training at Columbia University School of Social Work and New York University School of Social Work. She lives in Suffern, New York.

**Janet Walker** is professor of film studies at the University of California, Santa Barbara, where she is also an affiliated faculty member in Women's Studies. She is the author of *Couching Resistance: Women, Film, and Psychoanalytic Psychiatry* (University of Minnesota Press, 1993), coeditor of *Feminism and Documentary* (University of Minnesota, 1999), and editor of *Westerns: Films through History* (Routledge, 2001). Dr. Walker is currently writing a book examining the film and video representation of catastrophic past events in light of contemporary psychological theories of traumatic memory.

# INDEX